HOMEMADE BREAD

Other cookbooks by *Farm Journal*

FARM JOURNAL'S COUNTRY COOKBOOK
FARM JOURNAL'S TIMESAVING COUNTRY COOKBOOK
FREEZING & CANNING COOKBOOK
FARM JOURNAL'S COMPLETE PIE COOKBOOK
LET'S START TO COOK
COOKING FOR COMPANY

By the *Food Editors of* FARM JOURNAL

Homemade Bread

Edited by NELL B. NICHOLS

FARM JOURNAL *Field Food Editor*

•

Photography supervised by

AL J. REAGAN

ART DIRECTOR OF *The Farmer's Wife*

DOUBLEDAY & COMPANY, INC. GARDEN CITY, NEW YORK

CONTENTS

COLOR ILLUSTRATIONS

ALL ABOUT BREADS

If you like to settle down to read cookbooks, we invite you to this fascinating story of bread. Plump loaves, shiny-brown rolls and luscious coffee breads will pop out of the pages. You'll sniff in imagination the most enchanting of all fragrances, that of yeast bread leaving the oven. You'll remember the crunch of the knife as it cuts through the golden crust, and you'll almost taste the wheaty goodness of bread slices spread with butter.

You will marvel at the wonderful, faster-to-make breads that have been emerging from test kitchens—and country kitchens—as some of you recall Grandmother's friendly kitchen and the irresistible smell of her beautiful breads. Our new simplified versions retain the old flavors, good looks and aroma.

Food fragrances, psychologists say, linger in memory more strongly than tastes. This may explain why, when we asked many men and women for their most cherished childhood food memories, they mentioned warm homemade bread more times than all other kinds of foods put together. They talked of oven-fresh bread spread with butter and homemade berry jam . . . bowls of steaming vegetable-beef scented soup along with hot corn bread for supper on evenings when rain splashed against windowpanes . . . warm sugary-cinnamon rolls brought over by a neighbor to say: "Merry Christmas to your house from ours." Country hostesses know there's nothing like the aroma of yeast bread to sharpen appetites and build anticipation for the meal that is about ready.

For good measure we include in this cookbook, along with yeast-leavened breads, some of the great quick breads that so successfully dress up meals with so little effort—biscuits, muffins, popovers, pancakes, waffles, nut and fruit breads and gingerbread, for instance. Excellent packaged mixes for these breads line supermarket shelves. You use them, too, but there are occasions when you want to stir up "from scratch" quick breads like those in this book. They, too, are easier than ever to make.

Bread in History

The story of bread is the story of wheat. When a Kansas farmer described the best memory of his chilhood home, he said: "I picture level, emerald wheat fields in spring which, at harvest time, ripple gold in the wind. Our fields stretched from back of the barn as far as you could see." Breadmaking started about 10,000 years ago, so far as we know. The place was the Fertile Crescent, the part of the Middle East that follows an imaginary line drawn from Egypt through Palestine and Syria and south along the Euphrates and Tigris rivers to the Persian Gulf. There wheat first was a grass.

No one knows who made the first loaf of bread during the dawn of civilization, but we believe it was unleavened bread baked by the sun. During the excavation of the location where Ur, an ancient city near the Persian Gulf, once flourished, archaeologists discovered—and lighted—ovens used for bread baking that had been idle 3,900 years. These are thought to be the oldest ovens in the world. The Egyptians usually get credit for inventing the oven and discovering leavening. Bread baking improved greatly with their use. Bakers vied with one another to produce fancy loaves for offerings to pagan gods. You can see drawings of some of these breads in the Pharaohs' tombs in the Valley of the Kings. Bread frequently was money. Egyptians paid the slaves who built their historic pyramids with three loaves of bread and two jugs of beer a day for each worker.

The Greeks refined the milling of flour and also baking methods; the Romans learned from them and carried their skills to what now is Europe. The Romans also improved the cultivation of wheat and developed new varieties.

When the Christian era began, bread continued as the staff of life. Jesus, teaching his followers to pray, said: "Give us this day our daily bread." Early Christians, instead of baking bread for pagan gods, fashioned fancy loaves for feasting on church holidays, such as Christmas and Easter, and to give thanks at the end of the harvest season, much the way we celebrate on Thanksgiving Day. Food traditions live long and die slowly. We have turkey, cranberries and pumpkin pie for our November holiday, while people in Europe still feature their traditional breads on special days. You will find many recipes for Americanized versions of these lovely, delicious breads in this cookbook. When you bake them and serve them on holidays and special occasions, you'll find that old customs reflect a luster on today's breads.

Immigrants to what today is the United States brought their prized bread recipes to their new homes. No wonder our heritage is so rich. We have adopted and taken to our tables the great breads of the world. French bread no longer belongs only to France, or Stollen to Germany.

Original American Breads

During the early colonial years, corn was more plentiful than wheat, so corn bread was more common than wheat bread. Friendly Indians showed colonists how to grow corn and how to prepare it for food. Pioneer women improved on the cooking techniques. When people traveled, they went on foot or horseback, sleeping and eating in the forests. They carried corn bread for sustenance. That's why it was called journeycake. When roads and taverns were built and stagecoaches carried passengers, journeycake somehow became johnnycake, a name many easterners still use for corn breads. The kinds of breads made with cornmeal were—and still are—almost without limit. Every region has its specialties.

From the start southerners showed a preference for white cornmeal, northerners for yellow. Spoon breads, light and tasty, graced Southern tables. And on the frontier, pioneers, when they ran out of starter or yeast, made salt-rising bread. They stirred together water, a little water-ground cornmeal (ground between stones by water power), potatoes and salt; they set the mixture, uncovered, in a warm place, exposing it to the air until bacteria fell into it and formed gas or caused fermentation. Then they removed the potatoes and used the liquid as leavening for the one-time famous bread, made with white flour.

Another native yeast-leavened corn bread is Anadama Batter Bread (see Index). A Massachusetts fisherman, tired of the cornmeal mush his wife, Anna, spooned up for his meals, added molasses and yeast to it and baked the first loaf of this bread while muttering: "Anna-dam'er, Anna-dam'er" (or so the legend goes). This batter bread, toasted, still has a loyal following in New England.

Southern Beaten Biscuits

No discussion of our original breads is complete without a salute to beaten biscuits, perhaps the South's greatest contribution. These light brown, crusty biscuits differ from other kinds in that you serve them cold. Southern hostesses often pull them apart (they divide in half easily) and tuck in thin slices of cooked country ham for superlative sandwiches.

The tiny, thin biscuits start out as a stiff dough. The trick is to beat the dough, placed on a wooden block, with mallet, rolling pin, hammer or some other device until it blisters and becomes smooth. No one today has time to beat the dough 100 strokes for everyday meals (200 strokes for company) so you no longer hear the thump, thump, thump in kitchens.

While most beaten biscuits now are commercially made, a poultryman on

Maryland's Eastern Shore says they come daily from the kitchen in his home and other kitchens in the neighborhood. A machine takes over the work of beating, however. You put the dough through rollers, something like old-fashioned clothes wringers, to blister and smooth it.

The dough, rolled less than a half inch thick, is cut with small cutters, some of which used to have stickers in them to prick biscuit tops. Women now prick each biscuit with a fork. They bake them in a moderate oven until they're a pale gold (see Index for Beaten Biscuits).

Sour Dough

Sour dough breads of the Old West also have their champions today. Occasionally they are older men, many of whom once spent considerable time in cattle and sheep camps, where a crock of sour dough starter was a staple item. The starter, part of which was saved from one baking to the next, usually leavened sour dough biscuits and pancakes and gave them the characteristic tangy flavor.

The starters for some sour dough breads made today have their beginning in milk, according to a California rancher's wife. You pour the milk into a stone crock or glass container (never metal) and let it stand, uncovered, in a warm place (about 80°) 24 hours or until it bubbles or ferments.

If bubbling occurs, add 1 c. flour to the milk and let the mixture stand in a warm place (80°) 2 to 4 days, depending on how long it takes the entire surface of the mixture to bubble and give off a sour aroma. You can't expect to be successful every time you try to make this starter, for it often takes repeated attempts. That is why few women now make it and why ranchers and miners, in pioneer days, rode or walked miles to get a starter from a relative or friend. But once

you get your starter, you save back some of it at each baking, add equal parts of water and flour and leave it, uncovered, at room temperature until it bubbles. Then you cover and store it in the refrigerator. Usually it will keep up to two weeks, but for best results, use it once a week.

You cannot expect to duplicate in a home kitchen San Francisco's famed sour dough French breads, which visitors to the city frequently buy at the airport and carry for gifts to many parts of the country, especially to Hawaii. These marvelous commercial breads are made with hard wheat flour and with special starters, some of them many years old and guarded by bakers like pots of gold. The commercial bakeries also have special humidity-controlled ovens.

We give you in this cookbook FARM JOURNAL's modified and easier method of making sour dough starters and recipes for biscuits and griddlecakes which they leaven. Dehydrated commercial sour dough starter in packages may be found in some health food stores and specialty shops. Once you make your starter with it from directions that come with the dehydrated product, handle it the same way as homemade starters.

Boston Brown Bread

Another historic bread that deserves a mention is steamed Boston Brown Bread, a quick bread especially enjoyed in New England as a companion to a pot of baked beans. The custom of having this team of foods for supper on Saturday nights is a Puritan tradition that time has not erased. We steam our Boston Brown Bread (see Index) in tin fruit cans from the supermarket; these loaves make the right size slices.

Flour for "the Staff of Life"

The basic ingredients for yeast breads are wheat flour, yeast, liquid—usually water or milk—salt, sugar and fat—lard, butter, margarine, salad oil or shortening. More flour is used than any other ingredient. The magic in flour is gluten, a protein. When you mix flour with liquid and manipulate the mixture by beating, stirring and kneading, the gluten develops in long elastic strands that stretch and trap the bubbles of carbon dioxide gas which yeast gives off as it grows. It's these bubbles that cause dough to rise and bread to become light. Gluten thus forms the "framework" of bread, enabling the loaf to hold its shape when baked.

Hard wheats contain more gluten than soft wheats. Some supermarkets carry bags of flour labeled "high protein" and "for breadmaking," but most flour marketed today is all-purpose, a blend of hard and soft wheats. It contains enough gluten for breadmaking and not too much for cakemaking. As its name implies, it's a flour for all cooking and baking purposes.

Most flours today are enriched to provide good nutrition. The millers add vitamins and minerals to equal the natural supply in whole wheat grains. Because rye and whole wheat flours contain less gluten than all-purpose flour, you combine white flour with them when baking yeast breads.

Flour has the ability to absorb moisture from the air during humid or rainy weather. Then it cannot absorb as much liquid in the mixing bowl as when the air is dry. That's why flour measurements for yeast breads have to be approximate, within a certain range. The general rule, unless the recipe specifies otherwise, is to add flour until you have dough as soft as you can handle.

Yeast Makes Dough Rise

Yeast consists of living plants, which feed upon sugar and flour as they multiply. They give off carbon dioxide gas, which, as we have mentioned, makes dough rise. Women haven't always had it so good with yeast as they do today. Bread bakers in the ancient world used "barm," the thick scum on top of fermenting wine, for leavening. Sometime along history's path, women began to make their own yeast from hops. Unfortunately, the strength of this homemade product varied. In our grandmothers' day, cakes of dry yeast, containing a few slow-growing yeast plants, were used. To give the yeast time to grow, bread bakers set a sponge of water, flour and the crumbled yeast cake, and let it stand overnight in a warm place. By morning the yeast plants had multiplied enough that the ingredients for bread could be mixed. The other type of yeast then available was moist compressed yeast that was perishable.

During World War II, research workers discovered how to remove water from moist yeast. Active dry yeast was the result. Its first purpose was to give our military forces, regardless of where in the world they were stationed, fresh-baked yeast bread. This active dry yeast had remarkable keeping qualities, providing it was stored in airtight packages. Soon this yeast came to kitchen cupboards and was on hand ready for use. All a woman had to do (or has to do today) was look on the label for the expiration date stamped on it (usually about a year after yeast is packaged). Since yeast is a living plant, even though dehydrated, it cannot live forever.

Changes were recently made in this active dry yeast. It now comes in finer particles, which eliminates the necessity of dissolving it in water before you add it with other ingredients to the mixing bowl. Look at the new breadmaking methods in this cookbook—Instant Blend, Short-Cut Mixer, CoolRise and Rapidmix—to see how this improvement in yeast simplifies breadmaking (see Index for each of these methods). Try them to find out how easy they are and what fine bread they make.

Compressed yeast is still available in some communities. As mentioned, this moist yeast is perishable, but you can keep it in the refrigerator up to two weeks. Many country women keep compressed yeast up to six months in their freezers. Once you thaw it, however, use it immediately. One package of active dry yeast works the same as a ⅗ oz. cake of compressed yeast. You follow the recipes in the section "Conventional Method" when you bake with this yeast, crumbling and dissolving it in lukewarm liquid.

Ways to Make Bread

Women have baked satisfying breads for thousands of years, but never did homemade bread taste better than it does today. And never did breadmakers have it so easy. This is due primarily to the application of science and management to this branch of cookery, which simplifies and speeds up the process. The electric mixer whirls away and takes over a major share of the work on mixing the dough. Your oven's automatic heat control provides the right baking temperature. Electric knives slice bread, even when warm, to perfection. And you use very warm tap water right from your hot water faucet for the liquid in some of the methods. Kneading continues to be important in most methods and gives you the feel of the springy, pliable dough that you can work with as the artist works with clay. And as you knead, trouble and frustrations disappear and thoughts of the something good you are creating replace them. For those of you who do not enjoy or have the time for kneading, this cookbook also gives recipes for the batter breads, where beating substitutes for

kneading—also the newer Easy Mixer Method with the beating plus only about 1 minute of kneading.

Rising traditionally follows the kneading or beating, but in the Cool-Rise and Short-Cut Mixer Methods, the dough (covered) has a 20-minute rest on the board before you shape it into loaves. You have to use especially designed recipes whenever you give dough this rest period instead of the traditional first rising . . . we give you several of them. Temperature is important in encouraging dough to rise—85° is about right. The dough needs to be in a place free from drafts, which could cause the temperature to fluctuate.

Recipes You'll Find in This Cookbook

There's a fabulous collection of conventional yeast bread recipes in this cookbook. They are outstanding selections from farm and ranch kitchens across the country. We hand-picked them and then tested the recipes to get acquainted with them—to be sure directions were clear, and to know how to describe their virtues to you. You can follow these conventional recipes exactly, or you can alter some of the steps in making the dough the newer and quicker ways, as we explain in another section (see Index for Newer Ways to Bake Bread). Do try the new ways on your own treasured bread recipes, too.

To name the best recipes in this cookbook is impossible. We believe all of them are good. First of all, we nominate for honors the several versions of just plain white, whole

wheat and rye breads. Try them all and then you can settle on your favorites. The whole wheat breads have different, interesting flavors; some contain honey, others molasses. And there's one with a surprisingly good, faint lemon taste. There are all kinds of rye breads, those flavored with caraway seeds, grated orange peel or anise seeds. And there's one with the dill-caraway combination of flavors that's a natural for cheese sandwiches.

The bread specialties are a delight. Orange-Nut-Glazed Raisin Bread, flavored with a hint of ginger and orange peel, is distinctive and tasty. We're proud of the Cracked Wheat Bread a Minnesota farm woman bakes for her family and for her church bake sales, where it's a best seller. Finnish Coffee Bread, with its subtle cardamom taste, can't be surpassed. Braid strands of the dough, bake them in loaf pans, spread confectioners sugar frosting on top and you have superior coffee bread. Bake the unbraided dough in loaf pans, omit the frosting and you have a superb plain bread that gets compliments whenever you serve it. Lovely yellow-pink slices of Tomato Bread, framed with golden crust, always bring praises for their delicate, spicy flavor.

Dainty Brioche from our own Test Kitchens is a true treat. Our rolls made with sour cream also are country specials—Holiday Cream Twists, to name one. Potato Puffs, Bran Rolls and Perfect Buns are among other favorites. Hot Cross Buns await the Easter season. What a shame not to mention all of these hot rolls, which truly are miniature loaves of yeast bread, but made with a softer dough and baked faster and oftener at a higher temperature.

We can't leave out our crisp pizza crust. Our teen taste-testers voted this the best they ever had. You can make it ahead and freeze it; bake it when you want to serve pizza. Different fillings are described.

The many coffee breads from faraway places, adapted to the American scene, deserve a spotlight. Every woman can find at least a dozen kinds she'd be happy to feature at a coffee party. Reading recipes for them is something like taking a trip abroad: Grecian Feast Loaf, Austrian Gugelhupf, Norwegian Jule Kage, Glazed Danish Twist, German Stollen and Russian Kulich.

Quick breads—the kind you frequently bake when you say to a caller, "Stay for supper"—make up about a third of the book. We've found easy ways to make traditional kinds. For instance, if you don't want to spend time steaming our Boston Brown Bread to serve at your bean supper, try our Oven-Baked Brown Bread.

Quick breads, like yeast-leavened types, have a history. Many of them are descendants of the coarse hearth breads primitive people made. The "cakes" King Alfred forgot to watch in his peasant hut were among the forerunners of today's highly refined and delicious hot breads.

We hope you'll get as much pleasure and satisfaction in baking, serving and eating breads made by recipes in this cookbook as we enjoyed preparing them for you. And we also hope you'll bake breads frequently for your family—that you won't save them only for guests. Homemade breads deliver big batches of cheer to the dining table. They're a symbol of home. Good luck. And many bakings!

YEAST BREADS

Conventional Method
for Baking Bread

There's more than one way to bake good yeast bread. This section deals with today's Conventional Method. Home economists sometimes call it the straight-dough method because you combine all the ingredients at one time. It's quite different from the sponge method of our grandmothers—after supper on the farm, a frequent remark of women once was: "I must set the sponge." These earlier bread bakers stirred together dry, slow-acting yeast, liquid and some of the flour and put the sponge-like batter in a warm place overnight. Next morning they added the remaining ingredients to the spongy, bubbling mixture to make their dough.

Recently there has been a revolution in breadmaking techniques. Many companies—flour milling companies and yeast manufacturers—have been working on short cuts for breadmaking. Each manufacturer's test kitchens have produced new recipes following their timesaving techniques, and we present them to you in this book.

We also, however, give you an excellent collection of breads made by the Conventional Method—treasures from farm and ranch kitchens all over the country. Even though you switch to newer ways of bread baking, hold onto your best-liked recipes that follow the Conventional Method and add our collection in this section. Progress, after all, is keeping the best of the old and accepting the best of the new.

With a few simple changes in combining the ingredients, you can use these Conventional Method recipes with the Rapidmix and Instant Blend Methods, in which the active dry yeast is not predissolved in water and the electric mixer does a lot of the work.

Whichever method you use, read the pointers on bread baking which follow, especially if you're inexperienced in handling yeast doughs.

Pointers for Baking Perfect Bread

How to Recognize Top Quality. The loaf is plump and it has a tender, golden crust. The crust may be crisp, but if you brush a little soft or melted butter on it while the loaf is warm, it is shiny and soft. Along the sides of the loaf, just below the top crust, there's an even, slight break, often called the shred. The texture is fine-grained. If you feel a slice of the loaf, it is soft, springy and a little moist. The bread tastes good when cold and when warm.

Flour. The kind used in the recipes in this cookbook is all-purpose flour, which is milled from blended soft and hard wheats. In some supermarkets, flours, labeled "high protein" and "for breadmaking" are available and they may be used. They are especially desirable for CoolRise breads, which are described in the section Newer Ways to Bake Bread (see Index).

We recommend sifting the flour before measuring in both quick breads and conventional breads to get uniform results. But we stir, rather than sift, whole wheat and rye flours. Most of the rye flour in national distribution is medium rye. This is what our recipes in this book call for.

Yeast. There are two kinds of yeast in some markets, active dry and compressed. Since active dry yeast is available almost every place, we list it in our recipes. You can substitute a cake of compressed yeast for a package of active dry yeast in breads made by the Conventional Method, but dissove it in lukewarm water

(85°) instead of the warm water (110 to 115°) used for active dry yeast. You can dissolve compressed yeast in lukewarm water, milk, potato water, diluted evaporated milk, reconstituted nonfat dry milk or a combination of these liquids. The trend is away from predissolving active dry yeast in water, as recipes in Newer Ways to Bake Bread indicate.

Yeast is a plant; in its rapid growth it produces carbon dioxide gas, or bubbles, that causes dough to rise. Yeast grows best at a temperature of 80 to 85°. This is the ideal temperature for dough during the rising processes.

Liquids. Water, milk and potato water are the most common liquids. Unpasteurized milk must be scalded and cooled until lukewarm to destroy an enzyme that makes bread gummy. Generally pasteurized milk need not be scalded. Buttermilk does not require scalding. Water produces a bread with crisp crust and wheaty flavor. Bread made with milk has a more velvety grain, creamy white crumb and browner crust than that made with water. Potato water adds a characteristic flavor and moisture to bread; it gives a loaf of a little greater volume, but slightly coarser in texture.

Sugar. It contributes flavor to bread. Sugar also helps yeast to manufacture gas bubbles and the crust to brown beautifully during baking.

Salt. It contributes flavor, and helps control the action of yeast; if you use too much it checks the growth. Measure it accurately because altering the amount may throw the recipe out of balance.

Fat. Use lard, butter, margarine, vegetable shortening or salad oil, as the recipe suggests. It makes for tenderness, improves the keeping quality and flavor and aids in the browning. Fat also lubricates the gluten meshwork so the dough can expand easily.

How Much Flour to Add. Add enough flour at mixing or kneading time to prevent the dough from sticking to your hands—keep it as soft as you can handle it. If you add flour after the dough has risen, it may make dark streaks and coarsen texture.

To Knead. Turn dough out on lightly floured board or other surface (sticks less to a board). Flatten it with the palms of your hands. Then pick up the edge farthest from you and fold it over to the edge nearest you. Curve your hands over the dough and push gently, but firmly, three or four times with the heel of your hands. Turn the dough a quarter of the way around, fold it over on itself again and push. Repeat this folding, turning and pushing until the dough is smooth and elastic. Use a rocking-rolling motion as you knead. The dough, when kneaded enough, not only looks very smooth, but it also no longer has a sticky feel. (If you are kneading dough that contains fruits, like raisins, for instance, and nuts, look at the dough between the bits of fruit and nuts to see if it is smooth.)

To Rise. The correct temperature is necessary and humidity helps. Place dough in lightly greased bowl; turn it over to grease top. Cover with a sheet of waxed paper and a clean towel to prevent dried crust from forming. Let rise in a warm, humid place (80 to 85°) free from drafts. An unheated oven is an ideal place. Set a pan on the lower rack or the bottom of the oven and fill it with hot water. Or place the bowl of dough in an empty cupboard and set pans of warm water around it. Another way to keep yeast dough and batter warm during rising is to fill a large saucepan or bowl about two thirds full of hot water. Place a wire cooling rack over the top and set the bowl of dough on the rack. In very hot weather, it may be desirable to set the bowl of dough in a pan of cool, but not cold, water. Let dough rise until doubled. To test when it is doubled, press with the tips of two fingers lightly and quickly ½″ into the dough. If the dent stays, the dough is doubled.

To Punch Down. Plunge fist into dough to collapse it; fold edges over to center. Turn dough over in bowl. Let rise again until doubled if recipe so directs.

How to Shape an Oblong Loaf. Turn risen dough onto board; divide and let rest as recipe directs. Flatten dough with hands. Then with rolling pin roll it into a rectangle the size recommended in the recipe. Starting at the narrow side farthest from you, roll tightly like a jelly roll, sealing with each turn. Seal the long seam well; then seal ends of loaf by pressing firmly with sides of hands to make a thin, sealed strip. Use care not to tear dough. Fold sealed ends under. Place loaf, seam side down, in a greased loaf pan of the size specified in the recipe. You may lightly brush top of loaf with salad oil or melted butter. Cover and let rise until doubled or until dent made by gently pressing sides of dough with finger does not disappear. Do not let bread rise too much or it may crumble, be coarse-grained and have a yeasty flavor.

Baking Tips. Place loaves on center shelf in a preheated oven unless recipe directs otherwise. If you are baking 2 loaves, leave at least 2″ between pans. If you are baking 3 or 4 loaves, stagger them on 2 shelves. When you bake a large loaf, you can keep the top from browning too much by baking it on the shelf placed at the lowest oven level. Or you can cover the bread loosely, if it starts to brown too fast, with aluminum foil during the last 20 minutes of baking.

For loaves with sides browned like the top and bottom crusts, use anodized aluminum (dull finish), oven-proof glass or darkened metal loaf pans. Shiny metal pans reflect the heat away from the bread. When baking bread in glass pans, the oven temperature needs to be 25° lower than for metal. Recipes in this cookbook indicate when glass baking pans are used, and the temperature given in such recipes is correct. When there is no mention of the pan, other than size, it is a metal pan. The standard loaf pan sizes are 9×5×3″ and 8½-×4½×2½″.

When baking time is up, remove one loaf from pan and tap the bottom or side of the loaf with forefinger. If there is a hollow sound, the bread is done. If there is no such hollow sound, return bread to oven and bake 5 minutes longer, then test again.

To Cool Bread. Remove bread from pans or baking sheet as soon as baked to prevent steam forming and making bread soggy. Place on wire racks. Cool in place free from drafts to prevent cracking of crust.

The Big Three Breads

The big three yeast-leavened, loaf breads, no matter how you bake them, are white, whole wheat and rye. In this cookbook, we give you several recipes for each that produce the kind of homemade breads farm people rate superior (see Index for those not in this section). Then we also give you recipes for specialty breads—raisin, cheese, orange, prune, cracked wheat, herb and potato, to name a few. Try several of them to find out which kinds are the most praised by your family and friends. It's quite an exciting game to play and one that brings a lot of eating pleasure to your table.

BEST-EVER WHITE BREAD

This is a 2-loaf recipe—dough is easy to handle, loaves are plump

2   c. milk
2   tblsp. sugar
2   tsp. salt
1   tblsp. lard or shortening
1   pkg. active dry yeast
¼   c. warm water (110 to 115°)
6 to 6½ c. sifted all-purpose flour

• Scald milk. Stir in sugar, salt and lard. Cool to lukewarm.
• Sprinkle yeast on warm water; stir

to dissolve. Add yeast and 3 c. flour to milk mixture. Beat with spoon until batter is smooth and sheets off spoon. Or beat with electric mixer at medium speed until smooth, about 2 minutes, scraping bowl occasionally.

• Add enough remaining flour, a little at a time, first by spoon and then with hands, to make a dough that leaves the sides of the bowl. Turn onto lightly floured board; cover and let rest 10 minutes.

• Knead until smooth and elastic, 8 to 10 minutes. Round up into a ball and put into lightly greased bowl; turn dough over to grease top. Cover and let rise in warm place until doubled, about 1½ hours. Punch down, cover and let rise again until almost doubled, about 45 minutes.

• Turn onto board and shape into ball. Divide in half. Shape into loaves and place in 2 greased 9×5×3″ loaf pans. Cover and let rise until doubled, about 1 hour.

• Bake in hot oven (400°) 35 minutes, or until deep golden brown. Place on wire racks and let cool away from drafts. Makes 2 loaves.

Note: Just double the recipe for Best-Ever White Bread if you want to bake 4 loaves.

Roll Out the Bubbles

When you get ready to shape dough into loaves, roll it with rolling pin. This removes the big bubbles that otherwise would make holes in the bread. Pay special attention to rolling out bubbles in edges of dough.

RICH WHITE BREAD

This bread makes superlative toast

1 c. milk
2 tblsp. sugar
2 tsp. salt
2 tblsp. lard or shortening
2 pkgs. active dry yeast
½ c. warm water (110 to 115°)
2 eggs
5½ to 6 c. sifted all-purpose
    flour

• Scald milk; stir in sugar, salt and lard. Cool to lukewarm.

• Sprinkle yeast on warm water; stir to dissolve. Add yeast, eggs and 2¾ c. flour to milk mixture. Beat with spoon until batter is smooth and sheets off spoon. Or beat with electric mixer at medium speed until smooth, about 2 minutes, scraping bowl occasionally.

• Add enough remaining flour, a little at a time, first with spoon and then with hands, to make a dough that leaves sides of bowl. Turn onto lightly floured board, cover and let rest 10 minutes.

• Knead until smooth and elastic, 8 to 10 minutes. Round up into ball and place in lightly greased bowl; turn dough over to grease top. Cover and let rise in a warm place until doubled, 1 to 1½ hours.

• Punch down, cover and let rise until almost doubled, about 30 minutes. Turn onto board and shape into ball; divide in half. Shape into loaves and place in 2 greased 9×5×3″ loaf pans. Cover and let rise in warm place until dough reaches top of pan on sides, fills corners and top is rounded above pan.

• Bake in hot oven (400°) 30 to 40

minutes, or until golden brown. Place on wire racks and cool away from drafts. Makes 2 loaves.

ZUCCHINI MARMALADE

Serve as spread on toasted home-made bread—zucchini adds crunch

2 lbs. young zucchini squash
Juice of 2 lemons
1 tsp. grated lemon peel
1 (13½ oz.) can crushed
  pineapple, drained
1 (1¾ oz.) pkg. powdered fruit
  pectin
5 c. sugar
2 .tblsp. finely chopped
  crystallized ginger

• Peel squash and cut in thin slices. Measure 6 c. sliced zucchini into a large kettle.
• Add lemon juice, peel and crushed pineapple. Bring to a boil. Lower heat and simmer, uncovered, until squash is tender but holds its shape, about 15 minutes.
• Add fruit pectin. Place over high heat and bring to a boil. Stir in sugar and ginger. Bring to a full rolling boil and boil hard 1 minute, stirring constantly.
• Remove from heat; skim off any foam. Stir and skim 5 minutes to cool slightly and prevent fruit from floating.
• Ladle into hot, sterilized jars; seal with hot paraffin. Makes 5 half pints.

To Slice Warm Bread

Lay the fragrant, hot loaf on its side on bread board. Cut in neat slices with an electric knife.

WHOLE WHEAT BREAD

Homemade bread at its best—this has a rich wheat flavor and is light

1   pkg. active dry yeast
¼   c. warm water (110 to 115°)
½   c. brown sugar
1   tblsp. salt
2½ c. lukewarm water
¼   c. shortening
3½ c. whole wheat flour
4   c. sifted all-purpose flour

• Sprinkle yeast on ¼ c. warm water; stir to dissolve.
• Dissolve brown sugar and salt in lukewarm water. Add with shortening, whole wheat flour (stirred before measuring) and 1 c. all-purpose flour to yeast. Beat thoroughly to mix well.
• Stir in remaining flour to make a dough that leaves the sides of the bowl. Turn out on floured board, cover and let rest for 10 to 15 minutes. Knead until smooth and elastic, about 10 minutes.
• Place in greased bowl; turn dough over to grease top. Cover and let rise in warm place until doubled, about 1½ hours.
• Punch down. Turn onto board and divide in half; round up each half to make a ball. Cover and let rest 10 minutes.
• Shape into loaves and place in 2 greased 9×5×3″ loaf pans. Let rise until dough reaches top of pan on sides and the top of loaf is well rounded above pan, about 1¼ hours.
• Bake in moderate oven (375°) about 45 minutes, covering loosely with sheet of foil the last 20 minutes if necessary, to prevent excessive browning. Makes 2 loaves.

HONEY WHOLE WHEAT BREAD

A group of Nebraska wheat growers voted this their favorite—recipe from our Freezing & Canning Cookbook

2 pkgs. active dry yeast
5 c. warm water (110 to 115°)
6 tblsp. lard or other shortening
¼ c. honey
4 c. whole wheat flour
½ c. instant potatoes (not reconstituted)
½ c. nonfat dry milk
1 tblsp. salt
6½ to 8 c. sifted all-purpose flour

• Sprinkle yeast on ½ c. warm water; stir to dissolve.
• Melt lard in 6-qt. saucepan; remove from heat, add honey and remaining 4½ c. warm water.
• Mix whole wheat flour (stirred before measuring), instant potatoes, dry milk and salt. Add to saucepan; beat until smooth.
• Add yeast and beat to blend. Then with wooden spoon mix in enough all-purpose flour, a little at a time, to make a dough that leaves the sides of the pan. Turn onto lightly floured board and knead until smooth and satiny and small bubbles appear, 8 to 10 minutes.
• Place in lightly greased bowl; turn dough over to grease top. Cover and let rise in warm place until doubled, 1 to 1½ hours. Punch down dough, turn onto board and divide in thirds. Cover and let rest 5 minutes. Shape into 3 loaves and place in greased 9×5×3″ loaf pans. Cover and let rise until doubled, about 1 hour.
• Bake in hot oven (400°) about 50 minutes, or until bread tests done. Remove from pans and cool on wire racks. Makes 3 loaves.

Note: You may use 1 c. mashed potatoes in place of instant potatoes. Combine with the honey-water mixture.

Extra-good Rye Bread

Swedish women make many kinds of rye breads, all of them good. Usually they flavor their loaves with grated orange peel, caraway seeds or anise seeds. Our Swedish Rye Bread Supreme recipe comes from a farmer's wife in McPherson County, Kansas, who lived in Sweden until she was of high school age. You have a choice of flavorings. Try all three and see which one gets the most compliments.

SWEDISH RYE BREAD SUPREME

Take your pick of caraway or anise seeds or orange peel for flavoring

¼ c. brown sugar
¼ c. light molasses
1 tblsp. salt
2 tblsp. shortening
1½ c. boiling water
1 pkg. active dry yeast
¼ c. warm water (110 to 115°)
2½ c. rye flour
2 to 3 tblsp. caraway seeds
3½ to 4 c. sifted all-purpose flour

• Combine brown sugar, molasses, salt and shortening in large bowl; pour on boiling water and stir until sugar is dissolved. Cool to lukewarm.
• Sprinkle yeast on warm water; stir to dissolve.
• Stir rye flour (stir before measuring) into brown sugar-molasses mix-

ture, beating well. Stir in yeast and caraway seeds; beat until smooth.

· Mix in enough of the all-purpose flour, a little at a time, first with spoon and then with hands, to make a smooth soft dough. Turn onto lightly floured board; knead until satiny and elastic, about 10 minutes. Place dough in lightly greased bowl; turn dough over to grease top. Cover and let rise in warm place until dough is doubled, 1½ to 2 hours.

· Punch down; turn dough onto lightly floured board and divide in half. Round up dough to make 2 balls. Cover and let rest 10 minutes. Shape into loaves and place in 2 greased 8½ × 4½ × 2½" loaf pans. Cover and let rise in a warm place until almost doubled, 1½ to 2 hours.

· Bake in moderate oven (375°) 25 to 30 minutes, covering with sheet of aluminum foil the last 15 minutes if loaves are browning too fast. Turn onto wire racks to cool. Brush loaves with melted butter while warm if you like a soft crust. Makes 2 loaves.

VARIATIONS

Orange-Flavored Rye Bread: Omit caraway seeds and use instead 2 tblsp. grated orange peel.

Anise-Flavored Rye Bread: Omit caraway seeds and in their place use 1 tsp. anise seeds.

Round Loaf Rye Bread: Shape the 2 balls of dough by flattening them slightly instead of shaping into oblongs. Place loaves on opposite corners of greased baking sheet instead of in loaf pans. Let rise and bake as as directed for Swedish Rye Bread Supreme.

Dark Rye Bread

Practically every country in Europe has its own version of rye bread. Most of the breads are darker and coarser than the preceding Scandinavian recipe produces. Pumpernickel is a good example. This bread carries the name of the Swiss baker. Pumper Nickel, who first made it to stretch the limited amount of flour during a wheat shortage. You will notice that our recipe calls for cornmeal, mashed potatoes and whole wheat flour, in addition to rye flour. You can add caraway seeds if you like.

PUMPERNICKEL

A dark moist bread full of flavor— excellent for cheese sandwiches

3   c. cold water
¾   c. cornmeal
¼   c. dark molasses
1   tblsp. caraway seeds
2   tblsp. shortening
4   tsp. salt
1   pkg. active dry yeast
¼   c. warm water (110 to 115°)
2   c. mashed potatoes, made
      with packaged instant mix
5   c. rye flour
6½ to 7 c. whole wheat flour

· Combine cold water and cornmeal in saucepan. Bring to a boil and cook until thick, about 2 minutes, stirring constantly. Remove from heat, add molasses, caraway seeds, shortening and salt. Pour into a large mixing bowl.

· Sprinkle yeast over warm water; stir to dissolve. Add cold potatoes and yeast to cornmeal mixture. Gradually add rye flour and then whole wheat flour (stirred before measuring), to form a stiff dough. Knead on well-floured board until no longer sticky, 10 to 15 minutes (be sure not to underknead).

• Place in greased bowl; turn dough over to grease top. Cover and let rise in warm place until doubled, 2 to 2½ hours. Punch down dough. Knead on board sprinkled with whole wheat flour until dough no longer is sticky, adding more flour if necessary. Divide into 4 equal portions. Shape into round or oblong loaves. Place 2 loaves on each of 2 greased baking sheets, sprinkled liberally with cornmeal. Cover and let rise again in warm place 45 minutes (dough will not double in volume).

• Bake in moderate oven (375°) 40 to 45 minutes. Remove from oven and cool on wire racks. Makes 4 loaves.

Note: For a crisp crust, brush top of loaves with cold water just before baking. For a tender crust, brush with melted butter.

Specialty Breads Start with Raisins

Raisin loaves are international bread favorites. Their goodness depends to no small extent on using soft, plump raisins. If you've had your supply in the cupboard some little time and the raisins seem a little dry, pour boiling water over them. Let stand a few minutes and drain well. Or you may place raisins in a sieve and steam over boiling water.

Toasted raisin bread enjoys continuous popularity. Spread liberally with butter and orange or apricot marmalade, it's mighty inviting alongside a cup of hot tea or coffee. One of our good farm cooks tells how she prevents the glaze or frosting from melting in the electric toaster and making an annoying clean-up job. She inserts two or three wooden toothpicks in each slice of bread just under the top crust. The picks hold the sweet topping above the toaster, away from the heat.

ORANGE-NUT-GLAZED RAISIN BREAD

Rich golden loaves, so delicious . . .
The orange glaze contains walnuts

1	c. milk
1½	tsp. salt
½	c. sugar
½	c. soft butter or shortening
2	pkgs. active dry yeast
¼	c. warm water (110 to 115°)
5¼ to 5¾	c. sifted all-purpose flour
2	eggs
1	tsp. grated orange peel
1	tsp. ginger
1½	c. raisins

Orange-Nut Glaze

• Scald milk. Pour over salt, sugar and butter in large bowl. Blend and cool to lukewarm.

• Sprinkle yeast on warm water; stir to dissolve. Add to milk mixture with 2½ c. flour. Beat 2 minutes with electric mixer at medium speed, scraping bowl occasionally. Or beat with spoon until smooth, about 100 strokes.

• Beat in eggs, orange peel, ginger,

raisins and ½ c. flour. Then mix in enough remaining flour, a little at a time, first with spoon and then with hands, to make a soft dough that leaves the sides of bowl.
• Turn onto lightly floured board. Knead just until smooth, about 50 strokes. Round up in ball. Place in a lightly greased bowl; turn dough over to grease top. Cover and let rise in warm place until doubled, 1 to 1½ hours.
• Punch down and let rest for 15 minutes. Divide in half. Shape into loaves and place in 2 greased 8½ × - 4½ × 2½″ or 9 × 5 × 3″ loaf pans. Make 3 diagonal slashes ¼″ deep across top of each loaf.
• Cover and let rise in warm place only until doubled, about 1 hour.
• Bake in moderate oven (375°) 40 to 50 minutes. Cover with sheet of foil after first 20 minutes of baking if loaves are browning too fast. Remove loaves from pans; place on wire racks. Spread Orange-Nut Glaze on tops, then cool. Makes 2 loaves.

Orange-Nut Glaze: Blend 1 c. sifted confectioners sugar, 2 tsp. soft butter and ½ c. finely chopped walnuts; add 2 to 4 tblsp. orange juice to make glaze of spreading consistency.

CINNAMON TWIST BREAD

Lovely to look at—wonderful to eat

1 c. milk
¼ c. shortening
½ c. sugar
2 tsp. salt
2 pkgs. active dry yeast
½ c. warm water (110 to 115°)
6 c. sifted all-purpose flour
2 eggs, slightly beaten

½ c. sugar
1 tblsp. cinnamon
1 tblsp. soft butter

• Scald milk; stir in shortening, ½ c. sugar and salt. Cool to lukewarm.
• Sprinkle yeast on warm water in large bowl; stir to dissolve. Stir in 3 c. flour, eggs and milk mixture. Beat with electric mixer 2 minutes at medium speed, scraping bowl occasionally. Or beat by hand until batter sheets off spoon. Mix in enough remaining flour with hands, a little at a time, to make a soft dough that cleans the sides of bowl. Turn out onto lightly floured board; knead until smooth, about 10 minutes. Place in lightly greased bowl; turn dough over to grease top. Cover and let rise in warm place until doubled, about 1½ hours.
• Punch down; cover and let rise again until almost doubled, about 30 minutes. Turn onto board; divide in half. Round up each half to make a ball. Cover and let rest 10 minutes.
• Roll each half into a 12 × 7″ rectangle. Combine ½ c. sugar and cinnamon; save out 1 tblsp. for topping. Sprinkle dough rectangles evenly with sugar-cinnamon mixture. Sprinkle 1 tsp. cold water over each rectangle. Spread smooth with spatula. Roll as for jelly roll, starting at narrow end. Seal long edge; tuck under ends. Place, sealed edge down, in 2 greased 9 × 5 × 3″ loaf pans. Cover and let rise until almost doubled, 45 to 60 minutes.
• Brush tops of loaves with soft butter and sprinkle with reserved sugar-cinnamon mixture.
• Bake in moderate oven (375°) 35 to 40 minutes. Cover tops of loaves

with aluminum foil the last 15 minutes of baking, if necessary, to prevent excessive browning. Remove from pans and cool on wire racks. Makes 2 loaves.

WHEAT GERM BREAD

Good for you and extra-good tasting

1 ¾ c. milk
2   tblsp. sugar
1   tblsp. salt
¼   c. shortening
2   pkgs. active dry yeast
½   c. warm water (110 to 115°)
⅓   c. wheat germ
5   to 6 c. sifted all-purpose
       flour
Melted butter or margarine
Sesame seeds

• Scald milk; add sugar, salt and shortening. Stir and cool to lukewarm.
• Sprinkle yeast on warm water; stir to dissolve.
• Combine milk mixture, yeast, wheat germ and 2½ c. flour. Beat with electric mixer at medium speed, scraping bowl occasionally, 2 minutes. Or beat by hand until batter is smooth.
• Mix in enough remaining flour with spoon and hands to make a dough that leaves the sides of bowl. Turn onto board and knead until smooth and elastic, about 10 minutes. Place in lightly greased bowl; turn dough over to grease top. Cover and let rise in warm place until doubled, about 1 hour. Punch down; cover and let rise until doubled, about 30 minutes.
• Turn dough onto board; divide in half. Round up to make 2 balls. Cover and let rest 10 to 15 minutes. Shape into 2 loaves and place in greased 9×5×3" loaf pans. Cover and let rise until almost doubled, 50 to 60 minutes. Brush tops of loaves with butter and sprinkle with sesame seeds.
• Bake in hot oven (425°) 25 to 30 minutes, or until bread tests done. Makes 2 loaves.

OLD-FASHIONED OATMEAL BREAD

Loaves with tempting homemade look and taste go fast at bake sales

2   c. milk
2   c. quick rolled oats, uncooked
¼   c. brown sugar, firmly packed
1   tblsp. salt
2   tblsp. shortening
1   pkg. active dry yeast
½   c. warm water (110 to 115°)
5   c. sifted all-purpose flour
       (about)
1   egg white
1   tblsp. water
Rolled oats

• Scald milk; stir in 2 c. rolled oats, brown sugar, salt and shortening. Remove from heat and cool to lukewarm.
• Sprinkle yeast on warm water; stir to dissolve.
• Add milk mixture and 2 c. flour to yeast. Beat with electric mixer on medium speed, scraping the bowl occasionally, 2 minutes. Or beat with spoon until batter is smooth.
• Add enough remaining flour, a little at a time, first with spoon and then with hands, to make a soft dough that leaves the sides of the bowl. Turn onto floured board; knead until dough is smooth and elastic, 8 to 10 minutes. Place in lightly greased bowl; turn dough over to grease top. Cover and

let rise in warm place until doubled, 1 to 1½ hours. Punch down and let rise again until nearly doubled, about 30 minutes.
• Turn onto board and divide in half. Round up to make 2 balls. Cover and let rest 10 minutes. Shape into loaves and place in greased 9×5×3″ loaf pans. Let rise until almost doubled, about 1 hour and 15 minutes. Brush tops of loaves with egg white beaten with water and sprinkle with rolled oats.
• Bake in moderate oven (375°) about 40 minutes. (If bread starts to brown too much, cover loosely with sheet of aluminum foil after baking 15 minutes.) Makes 2 loaves.

Cracked Wheat Bread Sells Fast

A Minnesota farm woman grinds some of their new crop of wheat every year to make a dark bread, flecked with crunchy bits of cracked wheat. Her family and friends are fond of her tasty loaves. She also bakes them for her church's food sales, and customers buy them almost as soon as they arrive.

She wraps each loaf in clear plastic wrap to keep it fresh and to show off its golden beauty. She cuts some loaves in half and wraps them separately so that everyone can see the interesting color and texture of the inside of the loaves. Families of two buy up these half loaves, which look so good that they encourage more people to buy whole loaves.

Once you bake this bread and taste it, you'll not wonder at its popularity.

If you don't have your own wheat to grind, you can buy cracked wheat in packages at health food stores.

CRACKED WHEAT BREAD
Disappears fast at church bake sales

1   c. milk
1 ½ tblsp. shortening
1 ½ tsp. salt
1 ½ tblsp. molasses
1   pkg. active dry yeast
1 ¼ c. warm water (110 to 115°)
1   c. rye flour
1   c. cracked wheat
4   to 4 ½ c. sifted all-purpose flour

• Scald milk; add shortening, salt and molasses. Cool to lukewarm.
• Sprinkle yeast on warm water in large mixing bowl; stir to dissolve. Stir in rye flour, cracked wheat, 1½ c. all-purpose flour and milk mixture. Beat with electric mixer at medium speed for 2 minutes, scraping bowl occasionally.
• Stir in remaining flour, a little at a time, to make a dough that leaves the sides of the bowl. Turn onto lightly floured board and knead until satiny and elastic, about 10 minutes.
• Place in lightly greased bowl; turn dough over to grease top. Cover and let rise in warm place until doubled, 1 to 1½ hours. Punch down, cover and let rise again until doubled, about 45 minutes.
• Turn dough onto board; divide in half. Round up in balls, cover and let rest 10 minutes. Shape into loaves and place in 2 greased 9×5×3″ loaf pans. Cover and let rise again until doubled, about 1 hour.

· Bake in moderate oven (375°) 45 minutes, covering with foil last 10 minutes to prevent excessive browning. Turn from pans onto wire racks. Brush tops of warm loaves with melted butter if desired. Makes 2 loaves.

Roadside Potato Bread

Plump, richly browned loaves of potato bread are farm kitchen specialties. Many women treasure their mothers' recipes for them, but almost every home baker now simplifies her recipes by using packaged instant potatoes. This eliminates the work of peeling, cooking and mashing. Frequently milk substitutes for potato water; it gives the bread increased nutritional value and helps ovens to brown the crusts beautifully.

The recipe that follows comes from a Pennsylvania farmer's wife; she calls the loaves Roadside Potato Bread. That's because her mother used to sell them at a roadside market.

"When September nights have a cidery fragrance of orchards and vineyards and the smell of new-mown hay," she says, "I start thinking of the cold weather ahead. I visualize my kitchen filled with the aroma of baking bread. By the time the first frosts swagger across the fields, I have my bread recipe file on the counter top. Roadside Potato Bread will be one of my first bakings. We like it toasted and spread with homemade jelly or jam. It's just the change we need at breakfast to start busy, chilly days in good spirits."

Here is her version of the heirloom recipe.

ROADSIDE POTATO BREAD

Dusting cornmeal inside greased pans gives crust an interesting look

3½ c. milk
6 tblsp. sugar
6 tblsp. lard or butter
2 tsp. salt
¼ c. instant mashed potatoes (not reconstituted)
2 pkgs. active dry yeast
½ c. warm water (110 to 115°)
10 to 11 c. sifted all-purpose flour
3 tblsp. cornmeal

· Scald milk; pour into large bowl and stir in sugar, lard, salt and instant mashed potatoes. Cool to lukewarm.
· Sprinkle yeast on warm water; stir to dissolve.
· Add yeast and 4 c. flour to milk mixture. Beat 2 minutes with electric mixer at medium speed, or until batter is smooth. Or beat by hand. Mix in just enough of remaining flour, a little at a time, first with spoon and then with hands, to make a dough that leaves the sides of bowl.
· Turn onto lightly floured board; cover and let rest 10 to 15 minutes. Knead until smooth, about 10 minutes. Place in greased bowl; turn dough over to grease top. Cover and let rise in warm place until doubled, 1½ to 2 hours. Punch down dough; cover and let rise again until doubled, about 45 minutes.
· Turn onto board and divide in 3 equal parts; round up in balls, cover and let rest 10 minutes.
· Meanwhile, grease 3 (8½ × 4½ × 2½") loaf pans. Sprinkle bottoms and sides of pans with cornmeal (1 tblsp. to each pan).

· Shape dough into loaves; place in pans, cover and let rise until doubled, 50 to 60 minutes.

· Bake in moderate oven (375°) 45 minutes, or until loaves are rich brown and have a hollow sound when tapped with fingers. Remove from pans; cool on wire racks. Makes 3 loaves.

ITALIAN BREAD

Long kneading gives this the characteristics of Italian—and French— loaves

2   pkgs. active dry yeast
2½ c. warm water (110 to 115°)
7¼ to 7¾ c. sifted all-purpose
         flour
1   tblsp. salt
Yellow cornmeal
1   egg white, slightly beaten
1   tblsp. cold water

· Sprinkle yeast on warm water; stir to dissolve.

· Add 2 c. flour and beat thoroughly; stir in salt. Stir in 4½ c. flour (about) a cupful at a time; the dough will be stiff.

· Turn onto a lightly floured board, cover with a clean towel and let rest 10 to 15 minutes. Knead 15 to 25 minutes, until dough is smooth and very elastic, working in ¾ to 1¼ c. more flour. Do not underknead.

· Place in lightly greased bowl; turn dough over to grease top. Cover and let rise in a warm place free from drafts until doubled, about 1½ hours. Punch down, let rise again until doubled, about 1 hour.

· Turn onto lightly floured board, divide in half, cover and let rest 10 minutes.

· Roll each half in a 15×12″ rectangle; the dough will be about ¼″ thick. Starting with the long side, roll up tightly, sealing each turn well with the hands. Roll the ends between hands to taper them and place diagonally, seam side down, on greased baking sheet sprinkled with cornmeal. Cut slits ⅛″ deep and 2″ apart on tops of loaf. Combine egg white and cold water. Brush on tops and sides of loaves. Cover with towel wrung from water, but do not let it touch the bread; prop it with iced tea glasses turned upside down. Let rise in warm place until doubled, 1 to 1½ hours.

· Place a large, shallow pan on the floor or low rack of a moderate oven (375°); fill with boiling water. Bake loaves about 20 minutes, or until light brown. Brush tops and sides again with egg white-water mixture. Bake 20 minutes longer, or until loaves are a golden brown. Cool. Makes 2 loaves.

VARIATIONS

Italian Bread—Round Loaves: Shape each half of dough into a ball instead of into a long loaf. Place on baking sheet, sprinkled with cornmeal, and with sharp knife make 3 or 4 cuts ⅛″ deep on tops of loaves. Brush with egg white-water mixture and let rise and bake like Italian Bread.

French Bread: Much French Bread is made exactly like Italian Bread, but sometimes either 1 tblsp. sugar or 1 tblsp. melted shortening is added.

Summer Flour Storage

If space permits, keep flour in freezer during the extremely hot weather.

PIZZA SANDWICHES

Make these appetizing sandwiches with Italian Bread for a teen treat

• Cut 1 loaf Italian Bread in half lengthwise. Spread with butter. Combine ¾ c. lean ground beef, ½ c. grated Parmesan cheese, ½ tsp. dried orégano leaves, 1 tsp. salt, ⅛ tsp. pepper, 1½ tblsp. minced onion and 1½ (6 oz.) cans tomato paste.

• Spread mixture on cut sides of bread. Place, cut side up, on baking sheet. Top with thin slices of 2 ripe tomatoes. Bake in moderate oven (350°) 20 minutes.

• Remove from oven; top with 8 slices process American cheese. Return to oven until cheese melts, about 5 minutes. Cut to make 8 to 10 servings.

BREAD STICKS

Sticks are jaunty served from a tall glass—serve with Italian dishes

¾ c. milk
1 tblsp. sugar
2 tsp. salt
1 tblsp. soft shortening
1 pkg. active dry yeast
¼ c. warm water (110 to 115°)
3 to 3¼ c. sifted all-purpose
      flour
Bread Stick Topping

• Scald milk. Remove from heat and add sugar, salt and shortening. Blend and cool to lukewarm.

• Sprinkle yeast over warm water; stir to dissolve.

• Add the milk mixture and 1½ c. flour to the yeast. Beat with electric mixer at medium speed until smooth, scraping the bowl occasionally (100

strokes by hand). Add more flour, a little at a time, first with spoon and then with hand, until dough leaves the sides of bowl.

• Turn dough onto lightly floured board. Knead until smooth and elastic, about 8 minutes. Place in lightly greased bowl; turn dough over to grease top. Cover and let rise in warm place until doubled, about 45 minutes.

• Turn dough onto board and roll to a 16×6″ rectangle. From wide side, cut into ½″ strips. Roll each strip under hand to make pencil shape. Dough str   will be 8″ long. Place a little apart on 2 greased baking sheets. Let rise in warm place 15 minutes. Brush sticks with Topping.

• Bake in hot oven (400°) 10 to 15 minutes, or until golden brown. Cool on wire racks. Makes 32 bread sticks.

Bread Stick Topping: Mix 1 egg white with 1 tblsp. water. Brush on bread sticks just before baking; sprinkle with poppy or sesame seeds or coarse salt.

VARIATION

Crunchy Bread Sticks: Place the cooled sticks on 2 ungreased baking sheets. Place in very slow oven (250°), turning occasionally, for 45 to 60 minutes, or until evenly browned. Cool on racks.

Hold That Air

When slashing or scoring the tops of loaves, as for French and some rye breads, use care not to drive out the air and flatten the loaf. Make shallow cuts with a very sharp knife or a safety razor blade.

CHEESE BREAD

A favorite from our Country Cookbook; *excellent for toasting, as a base for creamed foods*

1 ¾ c. milk
¼   c. sugar
2   tsp. salt
2   tblsp. butter
3   c. shredded process cheese
1   pkg. active dry yeast
¼   c. warm water (110 to 115°)
5 ½ c. sifted all-purpose flour

• Scald milk; remove from heat and stir in sugar, salt, butter and 2 c. cheese. Stir constantly until cheese melts. Cool to lukewarm.
• Sprinkle yeast on warm water; stir to dissolve.
• Combine cheese mixture, yeast, 2½ c. flour and remaining 1 c. cheese. Beat with electric mixer at medium speed, scraping the bowl occasionally, 2 minutes. Or beat by hand until batter is smooth.
• Add enough remaining flour, a little at a time, first by spoon and then with hands, to make a dough that leaves the sides of bowl. Turn onto lightly floured board and knead until smooth and elastic, 8 to 10 minutes. Place in lightly greased bowl; turn dough over to grease top. Cover and let rise until doubled, about 1½ hours.
• Turn onto board; punch down and divide into thirds. Round up to make 3 balls, cover and let rest 10 minutes. Shape into loaves and place in 3 greased 9×5×3″ loaf pans. Cover

and let rise until almost doubled, about 1 hour.
• Bake in moderate oven (375°) about 40 minutes. (Bread browns easily. If it starts to brown too much, cover loosely with sheet of aluminum foil the last 20 minutes of baking.) Makes 3 loaves.

ONION BREAD

Bread has beef-onion taste; team it with vegetable salad or soup

2   c. water
1   (1 ⅜ oz.) pkg. onion soup mix
2   tblsp. sugar
1   tsp. salt
2   tblsp. grated Parmesan cheese
2   tblsp. shortening
1   pkg. active dry yeast
¼   c. warm water (110 to 115°)
5 ½ to 6 c. sifted all-purpose flour

• Bring 2 c. water to boiling in saucepan; add soup mix and simmer, covered, 10 minutes. Stir in sugar, salt, cheese and shortening; cool to lukewarm.
• Sprinkle yeast on warm water in large bowl; stir to dissolve. Stir in onion soup mixture and 2½ c. flour. Beat with electric mixer at medium speed, scraping the bowl occasionally, 2 minutes, or by hand until batter sheets from spoon. Mix in remaining flour, a little at a time, first with spoon and then with hands, until

BREAD 'N' JAM—Homemade spreads team beautifully with fresh-baked bread (recipe for white bread, page 12). We even include recipe for this Zucchini Marmalade (page 14) which has a pleasant crunch.

dough leaves the sides of bowl. Dough will be moderately stiff. Turn onto lightly floured board.

• Knead until dough is smooth, place in lightly greased bowl and turn dough over to grease top. Cover and let rise in warm place until doubled, about 1½ hours. Punch down, turn onto board and divide in half. Cover and let rest 10 minutes. Shape into loaves and place in 2 greased 9×5×3″ loaf pans. Cover and let rise until doubled, about 1 hour.

• Bake in hot oven (400°) 30 to 40 minutes, or until browned. Makes 2 loaves.

ORANGE BREAD

Favorite from our Freezing & Canning Cookbook; *spread with ground dates and nuts for party sandwiches*

2 pkgs. active dry yeast
½ c. warm water (110 to 115°)
1½ c. warm orange juice (110 to 115°)
5 to 6 c. sifted all-purpose flour
½ c. sugar
2 tsp. salt
¼ c. soft lard or butter
¼ c. grated orange peel

• Sprinkle yeast on warm water in large bowl; stir to dissolve. Add orange juice and 2 c. flour. Beat with electric mixer at medium speed 2 minutes, scraping bowl occasionally, or beat by hand until smooth. Stir in sugar, salt, lard and orange peel. Mix in enough remaining flour, a little at a time, first with spoon and then with hands, to make a dough that leaves sides of bowl.

• Turn out on lightly floured board and knead until satiny and elastic, 5 to 8 minutes. Place in lightly greased bowl; turn dough over to grease top. Cover and let rise in warm place until doubled, about 1½ hours.

• Punch down. Turn onto board and divide in half. Cover; let rest 5 minutes. Shape into 2 loaves and place in greased 8½×4½×2½″ loaf pans. Brush tops lightly with butter, cover and let rise until doubled, about 1 hour.

• Bake in moderate oven (375°) about 45 minutes (watch bread—it browns quickly). Cover with foil after baking 30 minutes if loaves start to brown too much. Cool. Makes 2 loaves.

VARIATION

Orange-Cinnamon Swirl: Roll half of dough into rectangle ¼″ thick, 6″ wide, 20″ long. Brush with 1 tblsp. melted butter. Mix 3 tblsp. sugar and 1½ tsp. cinnamon. Sprinkle evenly over dough, reserving 1 tblsp. for top of loaf. Roll like jelly roll, starting at narrow end. Seal ends. Place, seam side down, in a greased 8½×4½×2½″ loaf pan. Sprinkle with reserved sugar-cinnamon mixture. Cover and let rise until a little more than doubled, about 1¼ hours.

• Bake in moderate oven (375°) about 45 minutes. Cool on wire rack. Makes 1 loaf.

PIZZA SANDWICHES—Made with homemade Italian Bread (recipe page 22), these are hearty and colorful—popular with men and teens. Serve them for lunch or supper or when friends come to spend the evening.

GOLDEN PUMPKIN BREAD

Cheerful yellow color with brown crust—it has faint pumpkin pie taste

1   c. milk
1   c. canned pumpkin
¼   c. shortening
¼   c. sugar
2   tsp. salt
1   tsp. cinnamon
½   tsp. ginger
½   tsp. cardamom
2   pkgs. active dry yeast
½   c. warm water (110 to 115°)
6½   c. sifted all-purpose flour
2   eggs

• Scald milk; stir in pumpkin, shortening, sugar, salt and spices. Cool to lukewarm.
• Sprinkle yeast on warm water; stir to dissolve.
• Add 3 c. flour, milk mixture and eggs to yeast. Beat with electric mixer at medium speed 2 minutes, scraping the bowl occasionally. Or beat by hand until batter is smooth.
• Mix in enough remaining flour, a little at a time, first with spoon and then with hands, to make a dough that leaves the sides of bowl.
• Turn onto lightly floured board. Knead until smooth and elastic, 8 to 10 minutes. Place in lightly greased bowl and turn dough over to grease top. Cover and let rise in warm place until doubled, 1 to 1½ hours. Punch down. Turn onto board, divide in half and round up to make 2 balls. Shape in loaves and place in 2 greased 9×5×3″ loaf pans. Brush tops of loaves with melted butter. Cover and let rise until almost doubled, about 50 minutes.
• Bake in moderate oven (375°) about 35 minutes, or until bread tests done. Makes 2 loaves.

VARIATION

Spiced Pumpkin Raisin Bread: Stir 1½ c. seedless raisins into batter before adding second portion of flour with spoon and hands when making Golden Pumpkin Bread.

PRUNE BREAD

Another popular bread from our Freezing & Canning Cookbook—moist loaves are excellent for toast

2   pkgs. active dry yeast
2   c. warm water (110 to 115°)
½   c. nonfat dry milk (not reconstituted)
½   c. sugar
1½   tsp. salt
1   tsp. cinnamon
8   to 9 c. sifted all-purpose flour
½   c. soft butter or lard
3   eggs, beaten
2   tblsp. grated lemon peel
2   c. cooked, pitted and chopped prunes

• Sprinkle yeast on ½ c. warm water in big bowl; stir to dissolve. Add remaining water, dry milk, sugar, salt, cinnamon and 3 c. flour. Stir until smooth.
• Add 3 c. flour and remaining ingredients. Stir until well blended. Mix in enough remaining flour, a little at a time, first with spoon and then with hands, to make a dough that leaves the sides of bowl. Dough will be soft.
• Turn onto board; knead thoroughly, about 5 minutes. Add more flour, if needed, to prevent dough sticking to board.

• Place in lightly greased bowl; turn dough over to grease top. Cover and let rise in warm place until doubled, about 1½ hours. Punch down, turn onto board and divide dough in thirds. Cover and let rest 5 minutes. Shape into 3 loaves and place in greased 8½ × 4½ × 2½″ loaf pans. Brush with melted fat; let rise until doubled, about 1 hour.

Bake in moderate oven (375°) about 50 minutes. Remove from pans and cool on wire racks. Makes 3 loaves.

HUNGARIAN WHITE BREAD

Here's a delicious way to use herbs—they provide a subtle fine flavor

2   pkgs. active dry yeast
2   c. warm water (110 to 115°)
6   to 7 c. sifted all-purpose flour
3   tblsp. sugar
2   tsp. salt
2   tblsp. salad oil
¼   tsp. anise
½   tsp. fennel

• Sprinkle yeast on warm water; stir to dissolve.
• Blend in 3 c. flour, sugar, salt, oil and herbs. Beat with electric mixer on medium speed about 2 minutes, scraping the bowl occasionally, or until batter is smooth. Or beat about 100 strokes with a spoon.
• Add enough remaining flour, a little at a time, first with a spoon and then with hands, to make a dough that leaves the sides of bowl. Turn onto lightly floured board, let rest 10 minutes and knead until dough is smooth and elastic (little bubbles will show beneath surface).
• Place in lightly greased bowl; turn dough over to grease top. Cover with clean towel and let rise in a warm place free from drafts until doubled, 45 minutes to 1 hour.
• Punch down dough, turn over in bowl, cover and let rise 15 minutes more. Turn out onto board, divide in half, and shape into 2 round loaves. Cover and let rest 10 minutes. Cut 3 or 4 slits ⅛″ deep on top of each loaf. Place on opposite corners of a greased 15½ × 12″ baking sheet, or on 2 baking sheets. Cover and let rise in a warm place until almost doubled, 40 to 50 minutes.
• Bake in hot oven (400°) 30 to 40 minutes, or until well browned. Remove from baking sheet and cool on racks. Makes 2 round loaves.

Note: If you like a soft crust, brush tops and sides of loaves while hot with butter or shortening.

TOMATO BREAD

Pretty pink bread —a meat and cheese sandwich special

2   c. tomato juice
2   tblsp. butter
3   tblsp. sugar
1   tsp. salt
¼   c. tomato ketchup
1   pkg. active dry yeast
¼   c. warm water (110 to 115°)
7   c. sifted all-purpose flour
     (about)

• Heat tomato juice and butter together until butter is melted. Add sugar, salt and ketchup. Let cool to lukewarm.
• Sprinkle yeast on warm water; stir to dissolve.
• Add tomato mixture and 3 c. flour to yeast. Beat with electric mixer at

medium speed, scraping the bowl occasionally, 2 minutes. Or beat by hand until smooth.

· Mix in enough remaining flour, a little at a time, first with spoon and then with hands, to make a soft dough that leaves the sides of bowl. Turn onto lightly floured board and knead until smooth and elastic, 8 to 10 minutes. Place in lightly greased bowl; turn dough over to grease top. Cover and let rise in warm place until doubled, 1 to 1½ hours. Punch down and divide in half. Cover and let rest 10 minutes. Shape into loaves and place in greased 9×5×3" loaf pans. Cover and let rise until almost doubled, about 1 hour.

· Bake in hot oven (425°) about 25 minutes, or until bread tests done. Makes 2 loaves.

· Mix in remaining flour, a little at a time, until dough leaves the sides of bowl.

· Turn onto lightly floured board and knead until smooth and elastic, 8 to 10 minutes. Place in lightly greased bowl; turn dough over to grease top. Cover and let rise in warm place until doubled, 1 to 1½ hours. Punch down; cover and let rise again until almost doubled, about 45 minutes.

· Turn dough onto board, divide in half and round up to make smooth balls. Cover and let rest 10 to 15 minutes. Shape into loaves and place in 2 greased 9×5×3" loaf pans. Cover and let rise until doubled, about 1 hour.

· Bake in hot oven (400°) 35 minutes, or until bread tests done. Makes 2 loaves.

HERB BREAD

Perfect companion for chicken

1 ½ c. milk
¼ c. sugar
1 tblsp. salt
2 tsp. celery seeds
1 tsp. ground sage
2 pkgs. active dry yeast
½ c. warm water (110 to 115°)
¼ c. shortening
2 eggs, slightly beaten
7 ½ c. flour (about)

· Scald milk; stir in sugar, salt, celery seeds and sage. Cool to lukewarm.

· Sprinkle yeast on warm water; stir to dissolve.

· Combine milk mixture, shortening, eggs and 3 c. flour; add yeast. Beat with electric mixer at medium speed, scraping bowl occasionally, 2 minutes. Or beat with spoon until smooth.

Feather-light, Tender Rolls

The country hostess knows what piping hot, homemade rolls do for guest meals. When she passes hot rolls, whatever else she has on the table seems special, too. A Hoosier farmer's wife says: "Because my homemade rolls attract so much favorable attention, I try to get double duty out of them. I like to have them ready to bake so that I can run them in the oven when guests drive into the yard. That heavenly, yeasty aroma of baking bread greets them at the door and is a promise of something wonderful to come. It works like a charm. The anticipation is great, and there's no letdown at mealtime."

Excellent rolls are simple to bake. The important point is to keep the dough soft—as soft as you can handle. You can take a choice of rolls that you knead briefly, those you don't knead at all or refrigerator rolls. We give you recipes for all.

To dramatize your hot rolls, form the dough in different shapes. It may take a litte practice, but we tell you how. Pass a napkin-lined basket or tray of cloverleafs, knots and braids, for instance.

Serve the rolls so hot that the butter spread on melts pronto. If you need to warm them at mealtime, put them in a brown paper bag in a moderate oven (350°) for 15 to 20 minutes. Or if they're frozen, wrap them in aluminum foil and heat in a hot oven (400°) about 20 minutes. One more point to heed—after baking, remove rolls at once from pans or baking sheet. Cool on wire racks if you do not serve right away.

HOW TO SHAPE ROLLS

Cloverleafs: Shape dough in long rolls 1″ in diameter. Cut off 1″ pieces and form each into a small ball. Place 3 balls in each greased muffin-pan cup. Balls should touch bottom of cups and fill them half full. Brush with melted butter or margarine.

Four-Leaf Clovers: Place 2″ ball of dough in each greased muffin-pan cup. With scissors cut surface of each ball in half and then across again to make fourths.

Butterhorns: Roll dough ¼″ thick, brush with melted butter or margarine and cut in 12″ circle. Cut circle in 16 pie-shaped pieces. Starting at wide or curved end, roll up. Place, point end down, on greased baking sheet, 2″ apart.

Crescents: Make like Butterhorns, but curve ends of each roll on baking sheet to make crescent shapes.

Fan-Tans. Roll dough ⅛″ thick into an oblong. Brush with melted butter or margarine. Cut in strips 1½″ wide. Stack 6 strips; cut in 1½″ pieces. Place cut side down, in greased muffin-pan cups.

Pan Rolls. Shape dough in 2″ balls. Dip in melted butter or margarine. Place in greased round layer cake pans, letting balls just touch one another.

Dinner Rolls: Shape dough in 2″ balls. Roll each ball with floured hands until 4″ long. Roll ends between hands to taper. Place on greased baking sheet, 2″ apart.

Parkerhouse Rolls: Roll dough ¼″ thick on lightly floured board; cut in rounds with 2½″ floured biscuit or cookie cutter. Brush with melted butter. Make a crease in each round just off center with back of table knife. Fold larger side of each round over other side, overlapping slightly. Seal end edges. Brush with melted butter; place rolls about 1″ apart on greased baking sheet.

Butterfly Rolls: Roll dough into rectangle about ¼″ thick, 6″ wide. Brush with melted butter or margarine and roll like a jelly roll. Cut in 2″ widths. Make a depression down center of each with a small wooden handle. Place on greased baking sheet.

Easter Bunnies: Shape dough into long ropes ¾ to 1″ in diameter; cut in 10 to 12″ lengths. Tie in loose knots, bringing ends straight up to make ears. Press in raisins for eyes. Brush with 1 egg yolk beaten with 1 tblsp. water. Let rise on greased baking sheet. After baking and while still warm, frost lightly with Confectioners Sugar Frosting (see Index), tinting some of frosting a pale pink for bunnies' ears.

Roll dough into an oblong about 12" long and a scant ½" thick. Cut in strips ½" wide, 6" long, and shape rolls as follows:

Snails: Hold one end of strip on greased baking sheet and twist. Wind strip round and round to make coil. Tuck end under.

Figure 8s: Hold one end of strip in one hand; twist other end, stretching strip slightly until the two ends, when placed together on greased baking sheet, make a Figure 8.

Twists. Make like Figure 8s, but give each circle of Figure 8 an additional twist before placing on greased baking sheet.

Knots: Form loop of strip and ease one end through loop to make a knot. Press ends down on greased baking sheet.

Rosebuds: Form twisted strip into a loop; pull one end up through center of loop (making a knot) and bring other end over the side and under.

Braids: Form several ropes of dough ½" in diameter. Braid 3 ropes into a long braid. Repeat with other ropes. Cut braids into 3½" lengths. Pinch together at both ends; then gently pull to lengthen braids. Lay on greased baking sheets; brush lightly with melted butter.

RICH HOT ROLLS

Light, tender, rich, delicious

¾ c. milk
½ c. shortening
½ c. sugar
1 tsp. salt
2 pkgs. active dry yeast
½ c. warm water (110 to 115°)
4¼ to 4¾ c. sifted all-purpose flour
2 eggs

· Scald milk; add shortening, sugar and salt. Cool to lukewarm.
· Sprinkle yeast on warm water; stir to dissolve.
· Add 1½ c. flour to milk mixture; beat well by hand or with electric mixer at low speed 1 minute. Beat in eggs and yeast.
· Gradually stir in enough remaining flour, a little at a time, to make a soft dough that leaves the sides of bowl. Turn onto lightly floured board; knead until smooth, satiny and no longer sticky, 5 to 8 minutes.
· Place in lightly greased bowl; invert to grease top. Cover and let rise in warm place until doubled, 1 to 1½ hours. Punch down and turn onto board. Divide in half and shape as desired (see How to Shape Rolls).
· Brush tops lightly with melted butter; let rise until doubled, 30 to 45 minutes.
· Bake in moderate oven (375°) 12 to 15 minutes, or until golden brown. Makes about 30 rolls, exact number depending on shape and size.

VARIATIONS

Plain Rolls (less rich): Reduce sugar to ¼ c. and shortening to ⅓ c. in recipe for Rich Hot Rolls.

Cinnamon Rolls: Divide risen dough for Rich Hot Rolls in half. Roll each half into a 16×8″ rectangle. Combine 1 c. sugar, ½ c. melted butter and 1 tblsp. cinnamon. Spread half of mixture on each rectangle. If you like, scatter ⅓ c. raisins over each rectangle. Roll lengthwise as for jelly roll; seal edges. Cut in 1″ slices. Place, cut side down, in 2 well-greased 9×9×2″ pans. Cover and let rise until doubled, 30 to 40 minutes. Bake in moderate oven (375°) 20 to 25 minutes. Remove to wire racks. Makes 32 rolls.

Note: Frost rolls with Confectioners Sugar Frosting, if you like.

Butterscotch Rolls: Use one half of risen dough for Rich Hot Rolls. Roll dough into a 16×8″ rectangle. Brush with ¼ c. melted butter. Sprinkle with ⅓ c. brown sugar combined with 1 tsp. cinnamon. Roll lengthwise as for jelly roll; seal edges. Cut in 1″ slices.
• Pour ¼ c. melted butter into a 9×9×2″ pan; grease sides of pan. Stir ½ c. brown sugar and 1 tblsp. light corn syrup into butter in pan; mix well. Heat slowly, stirring constantly, until mixture is syrupy and spreads evenly over bottom. Remove from heat. Sprinkle with ⅓ c. finely chopped pecans.
• Place rolls, cut side down, over syrup mixture. Cover and let rise until doubled, 30 to 45 minutes. Bake in moderate oven (375°) about 20 minutes. Cool 3 minutes in pan; then invert on rack (place waxed paper under rack to catch any drippings). Makes 16 rolls.

EVERYDAY ROLLS

Rolls are not rich—they taste like warm fresh-baked loaf bread

1 c. milk
2 tblsp. sugar
1 tsp. salt
2 tblsp. shortening
1 pkg. active dry yeast
¼ c. warm water (110 to 115°)
3½ c. sifted all-purpose flour
1 egg
Melted butter

• Scald milk; add sugar, salt and shortening. Cool to lukewarm.
• Sprinkle yeast on warm water; stir to dissolve.
• Combine milk mixture and 1 c. flour; beat 1 minute with electric mixer at low speed. Add yeast and egg. Beat again with electric mixer until smooth.
• Stir in remaining flour, a little at a time, beating after each addition, until you have a soft dough. Cover and let rise in warm place until doubled, 1 to 1½ hours. Turn out onto lightly floured board, toss to coat with flour and knead about 15 strokes to force out large bubbles and to smooth dough.
• Shape in 2″ balls and place close together in greased 9″ layer cake pan. Brush tops with melted butter. Cover and let rise until doubled, 30 to 45 minutes.
• Bake in moderate oven (375°) 25 to 30 minutes, or until golden. Turn out onto wire rack. Serve hot. Makes 16 rolls.

For Soft Golden Crusts

Brush yeast bread or rolls right after baking with melted butter.

Crusty Brown Rolls

There are four important rules to heed in baking crusty rolls:
· Use water for the liquid. Milk makes soft crusts.
· Brush rolls with water or Egg Wash during the rising and before baking. We give you directions for each type of roll.
· Bake rolls in a steam-filled oven (see recipe).
· Rub no shortening on the rolls before or after baking.

CRUSTY BROWN ROLLS

Hard, chewy, delicious—so popular we reprinted recipe from Cooking for Company

    2   pkgs. active dry yeast
    1¾ c. warm water (110 to 115°)
    4   tsp. sugar
    2   tsp. salt
    2   tblsp. melted shortening
    6½ to 7 c. sifted all-purpose flour
    3   egg whites, beaten stiff
    Egg Wash

· Sprinkle yeast on warm water; stir to dissolve. Add sugar, salt, shortening and 2 c. flour; beat well. Add egg whites. Add remaining flour until dough leaves the sides of bowl when you stir it.
· Turn out on lightly floured surface. Knead until dough is smooth and elastic, and tiny blisters show on the surface (about 5 minutes).
· Place in a lightly greased bowl; turn dough over to grease top. Cover with a damp cloth.
· Let rise in a warm place until doubled, about 1 hour. Punch down.

· You may shape the dough at this point. For superior results, let the dough rise again until doubled; then punch it down and shape.
· Follow directions for shaping given with each type roll (see Variations).
· Place rolls on greased baking sheets sprinkled lightly with cornmeal. Brush with Egg Wash or with water. Cover and let rise until doubled, about 20 minutes. Brush again with Egg Wash or water.
· Bake in a hot oven (425°) 20 minutes, or until brown and crusty. Place a large shallow pan of boiling water on the bottom of oven to provide steam while the rolls bake. This makes the rolls crusty. Makes about 3 dozen rolls.

Egg Wash: Beat slightly 1 egg white with 1 tblsp. water. Brush on rolls.

VARIATIONS

French Rolls: Shape raised dough in 3″ balls; flatten under hands to make 4″ circles or 6″ tapered oblongs ¾″ thick. Use a very sharp knife or razor to make shallow cuts about ¼″ deep on top. Place on baking sheet, brush with Egg Wash; sprinkle with poppy or sesame seeds. Let rise until doubled, brush again with Egg Wash and bake.

Onion Rolls: Shape raised dough in 3″ round rolls ½″ thick; make hollow in centers with fingers. Fill with an onion mixture made by soaking 3 tblsp. instant minced onion in 3 tblsp. cold water, then drained and mixed with 1 tblsp. poppy seeds. Brush with Egg Wash; let rise until doubled; brush again with Egg Wash. Bake.

Salty Caraway Crescents: Divide the raised dough into 4 portions. Roll each portion into a very thin 16" square; cut each into 16 (4") squares. Roll each, starting at a corner, diagonally to opposite corner; seal, curve ends and roll gently under the palms of the hands to lengthen slightly. Place on baking sheet. Brush with Egg Wash. Let rise until doubled; brush again with Egg Wash. Sprinkle with coarse salt crystals and caraway seeds. Bake 10 minutes; brush again with Egg Wash; bake 5 minutes more, or until browned.

Note: Table salt may be used, but coarse salt such as that used for pickling and curing meat gives better results. It is available in nearly all food stores.

Italian Bread Sticks: Divide raised dough into 4 portions; roll out each portion to 7×4" rectangle. Cut lengthwise in ½" strips. Roll under hands to make strips 8" long. Place on baking sheet 1" apart. Brush with water; let rise and brush again with water before baking.

POTATO PUFF ROLLS

Try these piping hot, feather-light rolls next time there's company

½ c. mashed potatoes
1 c. milk
¼ c. shortening
¼ c. sugar
1 tsp. salt
1 pkg. active dry yeast
¼ c. warm water (110 to 115°)
4 to 4½ c. sifted all-purpose
    flour
1 egg

• Prepare potatoes from packaged instant mashed potatoes (do not season).

Recipe for 1 serving usually makes ½ c. Or cook potatoes and mash, but do not season.
• Scald milk. Add shortening, sugar, salt and potatoes. Cool to lukewarm.
• Sprinkle yeast on warm water; stir to dissolve. Combine milk mixture, yeast, 2 c. flour and egg. Beat well by hand or with electric mixer at medium speed, scraping the bowl occasionally, to make smooth mixture, about 2 minutes. Stir in enough remaining flour, a little at a time, to make a soft dough that leaves the sides of bowl.
• Turn onto lightly floured board and knead until satiny and elastic, 5 to 10 minutes. Place in lightly greased bowl; turn dough over to grease top. Cover and let rise in warm place until doubled, 1 to 1½ hours. Punch down.
• Turn onto board. Shape into a ball, cover and let rest 10 minutes. Pinch off small pieces of dough and shape in balls to half fill greased muffin-pan cups. Cover and let rise until almost doubled, about 1 hour.
• Bake in hot oven (400°) 10 to 12 minutes. Makes about 34 rolls.

Baking in High Country

Yeast doughs rise faster in high altitudes and many breads are coarse-grained. To bake fine-textured loaves with our recipes, make one of these changes:
• *Let dough rise a shorter time—just until it is barely doubled.*
• *Use less yeast than the recipe specifies.*
• *Punch down the dough two times, instead of once, so the dough will rise three times, instead of two.*

PERFECT BUNS

*Buns are uniform in size and shape
if you bake them in 4" foil tart pans*

½   c. milk
2   tblsp. sugar
1 ½   tsp. salt
¼   c. shortening
1   pkg. active dry yeast
½   c. warm water (110 to 115°)
3   c. sifted all-purpose flour
1   egg, beaten
1   egg (for glaze)
2   tblsp. water
½   tsp. sesame or poppy seeds
    (optional)

• Scald milk; pour into bowl over
sugar, salt and shortening. Stir; cool
to lukewarm.
• Sprinkle yeast on warm water; stir
to dissolve.
• Add yeast, 1½ c. flour and beaten
egg to milk mixture. Beat with electric
mixer at medium speed until batter is
smooth, about 2 minutes; or beat by
hand. Mix in remaining flour, a little
at a time, with spoon or hands. Cover
and let rest 15 minutes.
• Toss dough onto floured board until
it no longer is sticky. Divide into 12
equal portions. Shape each portion
into a smooth ball. (Dough may be
somewhat sticky and difficult to shape
into a ball. If so, toss each ball into
a little flour on the board.)
• Place each ball in a greased 4"
foil tart pan (the disposable kind).
Flatten tops of buns by pressing
dough down gently with fingertips. Set
pans on two baking sheets; cover, let
rise in warm place until doubled. (If
you do not have tart pans, you can
bake the buns on greased baking
sheets, but their shape may not be

uniform.) If oven is not in use, place
buns in oven with pan of boiling water
on oven floor.
• Brush with mixture of 1 egg, beaten
with 2 tblsp. water. If desired, sprinkle each bun with sesame or poppy
seeds.
• Bake in hot oven (400°) 12 minutes, changing position of baking
sheets during baking. Cool 5 minutes;
turn out on wire racks. Buns may be
frozen. Serve warm or cool. Makes
12 buns.

BRAN ROLLS

*These tender, light rolls go together
fast—there's no kneading or shaping*

1   pkg. active dry yeast
½   c. warm water (110 to 115°)
½   c. boiling water
½   c. shortening
⅓   c. sugar
½   c. whole bran
¾   tsp. salt
1   egg
3   c. sifted all-purpose flour

• Sprinkle yeast on warm water; stir
to dissolve.
• Pour boiling water over shortening in mixing bowl; stir in sugar, bran
and salt. Cool to lukewarm. Beat egg
with rotary beater and add to bran
mixture. Stir in yeast and mix well.
• Stir in flour, ½ c. at a time. Cover
and let rise in warm place until almost doubled, about 2½ hours. Punch
down. Drop dough from spoon into
greased muffin-pan cups, filling cups
half full. Cover and let rise until
doubled, about 1 hour.
• Bake in moderate oven (375°) 15
minutes. Makes 2 dozen rolls.

REFRIGERATOR
WHOLE WHEAT ROLLS

*Serve piping hot with plenty of butter
—we guarantee compliments*

1 ¾ c. milk
½ c. sugar
1 tblsp. salt
3 tblsp. shortening
2 pkgs. active dry yeast
½ c. warm water (110 to 115°)
4 to 4 ½ c. whole wheat flour
3 c. sifted all-purpose flour
2 eggs, beaten

• Scald milk; add sugar, salt and shortening. Cool to lukewarm.
• Sprinkle yeast on warm water; stir to dissolve.
• Combine milk mixture, 1 c. whole wheat flour (stirred before measuring) and 1 c. all-purpose flour. Beat well with electric mixer at medium speed, scraping bowl occasionally, 2 minutes. Or beat by hand. Add yeast mixture and eggs and beat well. Stir in enough remaining flours, a little at a time, to make a soft dough that leaves the sides of bowl. Place in greased bowl; turn dough over to grease top. Cover and place in refrigerator (dough will keep in refrigerator about 3 days).
• Remove from refrigerator about 2 hours before you wish to serve rolls. Turn dough onto floured board; knead very lightly a few times. Shape as desired and place in greased pans or on baking sheets. Cover, let rise in warm place until doubled, 1 to 1½ hours.
• Bake in hot oven (400°) 15 to 20 minutes. Brush with melted butter. Makes 4 dozen rolls.

Note: See Index for Rich Refrigerator Dough and recipes made with it.

Coffee Breads and Rolls
for All Occasions

You can take a bread tour of Europe without leaving home. Just sit down in a comfortable chair and relax while you read the pages that follow. Travel with me from the north —Norway, Sweden, Denmark and Finland—to Vienna, the waltz capital and a city of fabulous breads; to Greece, Russia, Yugoslavia, Hungary, Czechoslovakia, Germany, France, Italy and England—the Grand Tour!

As you read about the Easter, New Year, Christmas and other festive sweet breads, you won't want to wait for a holiday to treat your family and friends to the world's great classic breads. Bake them the year round —they're good any time. For the holiday seasons most women like to dress them up a little more with frosting, nuts and candied fruit.

Many of these recipes come from farm and ranch kitchens. Most of them started out as heirlooms handed from mother to daughter for several generations. American homemakers adapted the recipes to the ingredients available, to improved new breadmaking techniques and to the modern equipment in their kitchens. Their imagination and skill have resulted in tasty breads made in less time. Notice how a Minnesota farm woman makes a basic mix to speed holiday and special-occasion baking.

Turn the pages and stimulate your appetite with the recipes for our splendid collection of these sweeter, richer breads and rolls, the kind you serve with coffee and tea and even sometimes for dessert. Some are the new versions of breads from faraway places; others are favorite breads originated in U.S. country kitchens. These yeast breads are easier to bake than you may think.

Honeyed Danish Twist

An unusual shape adds interest to a loaf of bread. Glazed Danish Twist is a good example; it resembles a big, fat pretzel. Hunt up the pretzels in your supermarket and take some home with you to use as a guide when you shape the dough.

Our Danish Twist has a rich brown crust that glistens with Honey Glaze, which contributes a delicate sweet flavor and a shiny coating to the golden loaf.

GLAZED DANISH TWIST

A shiny, nut-sprinkled coffee bread shaped like a giant golden pretzel

½   c. milk
¼   c. sugar
1   tsp. salt
2   tblsp. shortening
1   pkg. active dry yeast
¼   c. warm water (110 to 115°)
2¾ c. sifted all-purpose flour
       (about)
1   egg
1   tblsp. softened butter
3   tblsp. sugar
½   tsp. cinnamon
Honey Glaze
Chopped nuts

• Scald milk; pour into large bowl and add ¼ c. sugar, salt and shortening. Cool to lukewarm.
• Sprinkle yeast on warm water; stir to dissolve.
• Add 1 c. flour, egg and yeast to milk mixture; beat with electric mixer at medium speed, scraping the bowl occasionally, for 2 minutes, or until smooth; or beat vigorously with spoon. Stir in remaining flour, a little at a time, until soft dough is easy to handle. (Add more flour if needed.)
• Sprinkle about 2 tblsp. flour on board and turn out dough. Knead about 5 minutes, or until dough is smooth, satiny and elastic.
• Shape dough in smooth ball and place in lightly greased bowl; turn dough over to grease top. Cover with a clean towel and let rise in a warm place free from drafts until doubled, about 2 hours. Punch down dough and shape into a ball. Cover and let rest 5 minutes.
• Flatten dough and roll out to make a narrow strip 6" wide, ¼" thick and 23" long. Spread with softened butter and sprinkle with 3 tblsp. sugar blended with cinnamon.
• Roll up from long side to make a long, slender roll; seal edges by pressing firmly. Leave roll on board and twist by rolling one end away from you, the other toward you. Lift carefully to baking sheet to avoid untwisting; shape like a pretzel, tucking ends of dough under "pretzel" to prevent untwisting. Cover and let rise in a warm place free from drafts until doubled, about 1 hour.
• Bake in moderate oven (350°) 25 to 30 minutes.
• Remove from oven and immediately brush on Honey Glaze;

sprinkle with chopped walnuts or slivered almonds. Then place loaf on wire rack to cool. Makes 1 large loaf.

Honey Glaze: Combine 2 tblsp. sugar, ¼ c. honey and 1 tblsp. butter in small saucepan. Bring to a boil, stirring occasionally. Brush hot mixture over Danish Twist.

Beautiful Viennese Striezel

Every country on the map of Europe boasts of beautiful braided loaves of yeast bread. The Viennese call theirs Striezel. Sometimes the bakers stack the braids three or four stories high; other times they use only two braids, one on top of the other. Our Striezel has two braids topped off with a plump twist of dough.

The secret of keeping the braids from slipping out of place while the dough rises and bakes is to make a depression with the hands lengthwise down the center of the loaf. You lay the braid in this "trench."

Try our recipe, even if you've never attempted to make a braided loaf, and see if you don't find it's easier than you believed it would be. Our Striezel contains raisins, candied cherries and orange peel, but you can omit these flavorful fruits if you prefer a plainer loaf made with the basic sweet dough. You also can leave off the frosting, but spreading it on is no chore (after cooling or freezing the Striezel), and sprinkling on nuts (chopped candied cherries, too, for the holidays) gives the fascinating brown loaf a gala look.

VIENNESE STRIEZEL

This 3-story braided loaf is handsome, and it tastes as good as it looks

½   c. milk
¼   c. sugar
1   tsp. salt
2   tblsp. shortening
1   pkg. active dry yeast
¼   c. warm water (110 to 115°)
2 ¾ to 3 c. sifted all-purpose
      flour
1   egg
¼   c. raisins
¼   c. chopped candied cherries
2   tblsp. chopped candied
      orange peel
¼   tsp. nutmeg
Frosting
Chopped nuts

· Scald milk; pour into a large bowl and add sugar, salt and shortening. Cool to lukewarm.
· Sprinkle yeast on warm water; stir to dissolve.
· Add 1 c. flour, egg and yeast to milk mixture; beat with electric mixer at medium speed, scraping the bowl occasionally, for 2 minutes, or until smooth. Or beat vigorously with spoon. Stir in raisins, cherries, orange peel and nutmeg. Stir in enough remaining flour, a little at a time, to make a soft dough, easy to handle.
· Sprinkle about 2 tblsp. flour on board and turn out dough. Knead about 5 minutes or until dough is smooth, satiny and elastic.
· Shape dough into a ball and place in lightly greased bowl; turn dough over to grease top. Cover with clean towel and let rise in a warm place free from drafts until doubled, about 2¼ hours.

• Punch down. Cover and let rest 5 to 10 minutes.
• Divide dough into 9 pieces of equal size. Shape each piece into a ball, cover and let rest 5 minutes. Roll each ball under the hands to make a strand 15" long. Place 4 strips on lightly greased baking sheet and braid, starting at the center and braiding to each end. With the sides of the hands make a depression down the center of the braid. (This helps to keep the next braid in place.)
• Braid 3 strands loosely, again braiding from the center to both ends. Lay this braid on top of braid on baking sheet. Make a depression down the center of this braid.
• Twist the 2 remaining strands loosely around each other. Lay the twist in the depression on the second tier of braids. Bring the ends of twist down over ends of loaf; tuck ends of twist under the loaf. Cover with towel and let rise in warm place free from drafts until doubled, about 1½ hours.
• Bake in moderate oven (350°) 35 to 40 minutes. Remove from baking sheet and place on wire rack. When cool, spread with Frosting and sprinkle with chopped nuts. Makes 1 large loaf.

Viennese Striezel Frosting: To ½ c. sifted confectioners sugar add ¼ tsp. vanilla and enough milk or cream (about 2½ tsp.) to make a smooth frosting.

When Freezing Bread

Bake yeast breads to be frozen to a light golden brown. This prevents the separation of the crust from the inside of loaf.

A Farm Woman's Baking Plan

A clever Minnesota farm woman fixes a Sweet Dough Basic Mix for her own style of coffee breads and rolls. It's her solution to the problem of finding time to bake different kinds. She gets the mix ready a day or several days ahead, divides it into 4 portions, which she covers and stores in a cool place. The idea started in a visit with her county Extension home economist.

"It's a real blessing," she says, "to have the mix ready to go, especially at exciting times, such as the holidays, when there's so much I want to do in the kitchen. Because I work with a comparatively small amount of dough at a time, I do all the mixing with a spoon and my hands. I don't get out the mixer, which is such a big help when I bake larger batches of bread."

Taste-testers gave the breads made by her recipes a vote of excellence. Try them and see if you don't rate their judgment as superior.

SWEET DOUGH BASIC MIX

A fix-ahead mix—so handy for making delicious coffee breads and rolls

8½ c. sifted all-purpose flour
⅓   c. nonfat dry milk
½   c. sugar
4   tsp. salt
¼   c. lard

• Combine flour, dry milk, sugar and salt; stir to mix thoroughly.
• Cut in lard with pastry blender.

Divide in 4 equal portions. Each portion makes approximately 2 c. plus 2 tblsp. Basic Mix.

TO USE SWEET DOUGH BASIC MIX

1 portion Sweet Dough Basic
   Mix
1 pkg. active dry yeast
⅔ c. warm water (110 to 115°)
1 egg, beaten

• Place Basic Mix in large bowl; make a hollow in center.
• Sprinkle dry yeast on warm water; stir to dissolve. Add egg and pour into hollow in dry ingredients. Beat with spoon until smooth and satiny. If the dough is too soft to handle, work in a little more flour.
• Turn onto lightly floured board and knead until smooth and satiny, 3 to 5 minutes. Place in lightly greased bowl; turn dough over to grease top. Cover with a clean towel and let rise in a warm place free from drafts until doubled, 1 to 1½ hours.
• Punch down. Let rise again until doubled, 45 minutes to 1 hour. You are ready to make a coffee bread or rolls with this light dough.

NORWEGIAN JULE KAGE

Slices of this Christmas bread display a tempting sprinkling of fruits

1 portion risen dough from
   Sweet Dough Basic Mix
2 tblsp. currants
¼ c. seedless raisins
¼ c. cut-up candied fruits
¼ tsp. ground cardamom
Egg Yolk Glaze

• Place dough on lightly floured board; roll gently to flatten. Sprinkle currants, raisins, candied fruits and cardamom on half of the dough; fold other half over on the fruits. Knead gently to mix fruits through the dough, about 3 minutes. Shape into a ball, cover and let rest 10 minutes.
• Place dough on a greased baking sheet, cover and let rise in warm place until doubled, about 1 hour and 15 minutes. Brush with Egg Yolk Glaze.
• Bake in moderate oven (350°) 30 minutes. Makes 1 round loaf.

Egg Yolk Glaze: Mix with fork 1 egg yolk and 2 tblsp. cold water.

HOUSKA

This braided Bohemian Christmas bread is a treat to see and to eat

1 portion risen dough from
   Sweet Dough Basic Mix
1 tsp. grated lemon peel
2 tblsp. cut-up mixed candied
   fruits
2 tblsp. raisins
2 tblsp. slivered almonds
Confectioners sugar

• Place dough on lightly floured board. Flatten gently with rolling pin. Sprinkle half of dough with lemon peel, candied fruits, raisins and almonds. Fold other half of dough over fruit and nuts and knead gently, 3 to 5 minutes, to distribute fruits and nuts through dough.
• Divide the dough in half. Cut one half in 4 pieces, the other half in 5 pieces. Roll strips under hand to make slender rolls about ½″ thick and 12″ long. Place 4 strips on greased baking sheet and braid, starting at the

center and braiding to each end. Make a depression with sides of hands lengthwise down the center of the braid. Braid 3 strips, from center to each end, and lay on top of braid on baking sheet. Twist remaining 2 strips and lay on top of braids, tucking ends under loaf. Let rise until doubled, about 1 hour and 15 minutes.
· Bake in moderate oven (350°) 25 minutes. Cool on wire rack. Before serving sprinkle with sifted confectioners sugar. Makes 1 loaf.

MINCEMEAT COFFEE BREAD

As American as the Fourth of July and wonderfully good—pretty, too

1   portion risen dough from
       Sweet Dough Basic Mix
1½ c. ready-to-use mincemeat
Lemon-Orange Butter Frosting
Nuts, coarsely chopped
Maraschino cherries, sliced and
       well drained

· Place risen dough on lightly floured board; divide in half. Cover with clean towel and let rest 20 minutes.
· Roll out each half to make a 14×8" rectangle. Place each on a greased baking sheet. Spread ¾ c. mincemeat lengthwise in a strip 3½" wide down center of each rectangle. Bring sides of dough to top over the mincemeat. Pinch edges together firmly to seal.
· Carefully invert loaves (sealed edge will be down) on baking sheets. Make 2" diagonal cuts, 1" apart, on top of loaves (over mincemeat). Cover and let rise in warm place until doubled, about 1 hour and 15 minutes.
· Bake in moderate oven (350°) 20 to 25 minutes. Remove from baking

sheets and place on wire racks. While still slightly warm, spread with Lemon-Orange Butter Frosting and sprinkle with nuts and slices of maraschino cherries. Makes 2 loaves.

Lemon-Orange Butter Frosting: Combine 2 tblsp. soft butter, 1½ c. sifted confectioners sugar, ⅛ tsp. salt, ¼ tsp. grated lemon peel, ¼ tsp. grated orange peel, 1 tsp. lemon juice and enough orange juice to make a frosting of spreading consistency. Beat until smooth and creamy.

ORANGE TWISTS

They'll disappear like magic at coffee time or whenever you serve them

1   portion risen dough from
       Sweet Dough Basic Mix
½ c. sugar
2 tsp. grated orange peel (1
       orange)
2 tblsp. softened butter

· Place dough on lightly floured board. Divide in half and shape in balls. Cover and let rest 20 minutes.
· Meanwhile combine sugar and grated orange peel.
· Roll each half of dough in a 12×9" rectangle. Spread center third of each rectangle with butter and sprinkle with one fourth of the sugar-orange peel mixture.
· Fold one third of dough rectangle over sugar-orange strip in center. Butter top and sprinkle with one fourth of sugar-orange mixture. Fold remaining one third of dough over sugar-orange mixture and seal dough. Repeat with other rectangle.
· Cut each rectangle into 12 strips. Twist shapes and place them on

greased baking sheets. Cover and let rise in a warm place about 40 minutes.

• Bake in moderate oven (375°) about 15 minutes. Makes 24 twists.

Christmas Bread That Pleases

This is an Americanized version of what the Greeks call Christopsomo, which means Christmas Bread.

One of the home economists who helped test readers' recipes for this cookbook gave this bread to her neighbors for a Christmas present. She baked the loaves ahead and froze them so that all she had to do the day before Christmas was to deliver them to nearby holly-decorated doors. She was pleased at the reception for the festive bread and her friends raved about it.

CHRISTMAS BREAD

A cross of dough strips adorns the top of this mildly sweet golden loaf

¾ c. milk
6 tblsp. sugar
2 tsp. salt
⅛ tsp. ground anise
2 pkgs. active dry yeast
½ c. warm water (110 to 115°)
¾ c. butter, melted and cooled
6¾ to 7¼ c. sifted all-purpose
    flour
4 eggs
1 beaten egg
2 tblsp. water
2 tsp. sesame seeds

• Scald milk; add sugar, salt and anise. Cool to lukewarm.

• Sprinkle yeast on warm water; stir to dissolve.

• Combine yeast, milk mixture, melted butter, 4 c. flour and 4 eggs. Beat until smooth. Stir in enough remaining flour, a little at a time, until dough leaves the sides of bowl. Turn onto lightly floured board. Knead until smooth and elastic, about 8 minutes.

• Place in lightly greased bowl; turn dough over to grease top. Cover and let rise in warm place until doubled, 1½ to 2 hours. Punch down.

• Turn onto board; divide in half. Cover and let rest 10 minutes. Take a piece of dough the size of a golf ball from each portion of dough. Divide each small ball of dough in half and roll each piece into a strand 5 to 6″ long. Shape remaining dough into 2 loaves and place in greased 9×5×3″ loaf pans. Place strands of dough on top of loaves to form a cross on each. Cover and let rise in warm place until doubled, 1 to 1½ hours.

• Combine beaten egg and water. Brush over tops of loaves. Sprinkle 1 tsp. sesame seeds on each loaf.

• Bake in moderate oven (350°) 40 to 45 minutes, until golden brown. Remove from pans and cool on racks. Makes 2 loaves.

Fascinating Easter Egg Bread

Almost every European country along Mediterranean shores, as well as nearby Switzerland and faraway Brazil, boasts of a traditional Easter bread festive with color-bright eggs. You see these tempting loaves during the Eastern season in the neighborhood bake shops of our great cities, like New York and San Francisco, especially where people of Italian descent live. There's no reason, though, why you can't bake this seasonal bread in your own kitchen. One of our readers sent us a recipe for a meal-in-one breakfast. What joy either the large or individual "eggs in a bread nest" will bring the children! Grownups will enjoy them, too, if they're young at heart.

EASTER EGG BREAD

Make this traditional in your family —a memory of home

12 eggs in shell, uncooked
Easter egg coloring
½ c. milk
½ c. sugar
1 tsp. salt
½ c. shortening
Grated peel of 2 lemons
2 pkgs. active dry yeast
½ c. warm water (110 to 115°)
2 eggs (at room temperature)
4½ c. sifted all-purpose flour
     (about)
1 egg, beaten
Tiny colored candies

• Wash 12 uncooked eggs. Tint shells with egg coloring; set aside.
• Scald milk; add sugar, salt, shortening and lemon peel. Cool to lukewarm.
• Sprinkle yeast on warm water; stir to dissolve. Add to milk mixture with the 2 eggs, slightly beaten, and 2½ c. flour. Beat until smooth.
• Stir in enough remaining flour, a little at a time, to form a dough that is easy to handle. Turn onto lightly floured board and knead until smooth and elastic, 5 to 8 minutes. Place in

lightly greased bowl; turn dough over to grease top. Cover and let rise in warm place free from drafts until doubled, about 1 hour.
• Punch down; cover and let rise again until almost doubled, about 30 minutes.
• Make 2 large braided rings or 12 individual rings as follows:

Large Rings: Divide dough into 4 parts. Form each part into a 36" rope. On a greased baking sheet, shape 2 of the ropes into a very loosely braided ring, leaving space for 6 eggs (see photo elsewhere in book). Repeat with other 2 ropes of dough for second ring. Insert 6 tinted eggs in spaces in each ring.

Individual Rings: Divide dough into 12 parts. Form each part into a ring around a tinted egg.

• Cover; let rise until doubled.
• Brush evenly with beaten egg. Sprinkle with tiny decorating candies.
• Bake in moderate oven (375°) 15 minutes for individual rings, 20 minutes for large rings, or until lightly browned. Serve warm. Makes 2 large or 12 individual rings.

Note: Easter Egg Bread can be baked the day before. Refrigerate. At serving time, reheat in moderate oven (350°) 8 minutes.

Wonderfully Rich Gugelhupf

Slices of Gugelhupf (pronounced gōōǵlehŭpf), toasted and served with butter and jam, are an Austrian Christmas breakfast special. It's a cake-like bread that is also a favorite Vienna dessert. Coffee is its best accompaniment. The light, delicious bread will please your guests as much as it does Europeans. The loaf is beautiful, especially if you bake it in a fancy-shaped mold. Austrian women and bakeries use heavy tube molds similar to what we call a Turk's head, but our recipe suggests that you can use an angel food cake pan.

Perhaps you've heard of this bread by another name—Kugelhupf, for instance. Just as the bread differs in some ways from one home or country to another, its name also varies. But all the versions are delicious.

GUGELHUPF

A cake-like bread on the sweet side with a subtle lemon-almond flavor

½ c. milk
1 pkg. active dry yeast
¼ c. warm water (110 to 115°)
½ c. sugar
¼ c. butter
2 eggs
2½ c. sifted all-purpose flour
¼ tsp. salt
½ c. chopped golden raisins
1½ tsp. grated lemon peel
1 tblsp. melted butter
¼ c. finely ground almonds
15 to 18 whole blanched almonds (optional)

• Scald milk; cool to lukewarm.
• Sprinkle yeast on warm water; stir to dissolve.
• Cream sugar and ¼ c. butter with electric mixer until light and fluffy. Add eggs, one at a time, beating after each addition. Add yeast and milk, then flour and salt, which have been sifted together. Beat with electric mixer at medium speed until smooth, scraping bowl occasionally.
• Stir in raisins and lemon peel; cover and let rise in warm place free from drafts until doubled, about 2 hours.
• Meanwhile generously grease a heavy 1½-qt. mold with a tube, such as a Turk's head or a 10″ angel food cake pan, with 1 tblsp. melted butter. Be sure to grease tube well. Shake mold or pan to coat sides thoroughly with finely ground almonds. Arrange pattern of whole blanched almonds on bottom of pan.
• Stir down light dough. Spoon batter into mold or pan carefully to avoid disturbing almonds. Cover and let rise in warm place free from drafts until doubled, about 1 hour.
• Bake in moderate oven (350°) 25 to 30 minutes, or until cake tester inserted in bread comes out clean. (Look at bread when it has baked 15 minutes. If it has started to brown, cover loosely with aluminum foil. The bread browns easily.)
• Remove from oven and let stand in pan 10 minutes. Loosen sides and turn bread onto wire rack. Sift a little confectioners sugar over top. Makes about 12 servings.

Fruited and Frosted Stollen

Christmas morning in Germany brings Stollen to the breakfast table. The sweet, fruit-filled bread, with sugar and cinnamon between the layers and frosting on top, decorated with nuts and candied cherry rings, is an important part of the holiday. German hostesses also offer thin slices of Stollen to Yuletime callers.

Recipes for Stollen are many, but they are alike in one way. That's the folded-roll shape. Our recipe eliminates the chopping of candied fruits and citron—it calls for the convenient packaged kind. And as a step to superior flavor, we soak the mixed candied fruits and raisins in orange juice.

When you put the big roll on the baking sheet, there are two things to do to guarantee an attractive shape. One is to curve the Stollen a little to give it a shape slightly suggestive of a crescent. The other is to press the folded edge, never the open one, to encourage the bread to hold its shape when the yeast gets busy and expands the dough in the rising and baking.

Our recipe recognizes the popularity of Stollen—it makes 2 loaves.

STOLLEN

Make these big fold-over rolls for Christmas and other special occasions

1 c. raisins
1 (8 oz.) jar mixed candied
   fruits (1 c.)
¼ c. orange juice
½ c. milk
½ c. sugar
1 tsp. salt
1 c. butter or margarine (2
   sticks)
2 pkgs. active dry yeast
½ c. warm water (110 to 115°)
5 c. sifted all-purpose flour
   (about)
2 eggs
1 tsp. grated lemon peel
¼ tsp. mace
1 c. chopped blanched almonds

2 tblsp. sugar
½ tsp. cinnamon
Creamy Frosting
¼ c. slivered almonds (optional)
12 candied cherries (optional)

• Combine raisins, candied fruits and orange juice in a small bowl. Set aside.
• Scald milk; add ½ c. sugar, salt and ½ c. butter. Cool to lukewarm.
• Sprinkle yeast on warm water; stir to dissolve.
• Combine yeast, milk mixture, 2 c. flour, eggs, lemon peel and mace. Beat with electric mixer on medium speed 2 minutes, scraping the bowl occasionally, until batter is smooth. Stir in chopped almonds and fruits. Stir in enough remaining flour, a little at a time, to make a dough that leaves the sides of bowl and that you can handle easily.
• Turn onto lightly floured board; knead until smooth and satiny, about 5 minutes. Place in lightly greased bowl; turn dough over to grease top. Cover and let rise in warm place free from drafts until doubled, about 2 hours.
• Punch down dough; turn onto board, knead a few times and divide in half. Cover and let rest 5 minutes. Roll each half into a 15×9" oval.
• Melt remaining ½ c. butter; brush part of it over each oval, saving what you do not use for frosting. Sprinkle with 2 tblsp. sugar mixed with cinnamon and sprinkle over the buttered dough.
• Fold each oval lengthwise in half to make a big Parkerhouse roll. Carefully lift folded-over rolls to a greased baking sheet and curve the ends slightly; press down the folded side

slightly (not the open edges) to help the loaf keep its shape during rising and baking.

• Cover and let rise until doubled, 1 to 1½ hours.

• Bake in moderate oven (350°) 30 to 35 minutes, or until loaves are golden. While hot, brush with Creamy Frosting and decorate with slivered almonds and sliced candied cherries. Cool on racks. Makes 2 loaves.

Creamy Frosting: To 1 c. sifted confectioners sugar add 1 tblsp. cream or milk and ¼ c. melted butter. Stir until smooth.

FINNISH COFFEE BREAD

You can divide dough and make 1 coffee bread and 1 plain round loaf

2   pkgs. active dry yeast
2   c. warm water (110 to 115°)
1   egg (room temperature)
6   to 7 c. sifted all-purpose flour
½   tsp. ground cardamom
⅓   c. sugar
2   tsp. salt
¼   c. soft butter or shortening
Thin Confectioners Sugar Icing

• Sprinkle yeast on warm water; stir to dissolve.

• Blend in egg, 3 c. flour, cardamom, sugar and salt. Beat with electric mixer at medium speed about 2 minutes (or about 100 strokes by hand), until batter is smooth. Add butter and enough remaining flour, a little at a time, first with spoon and then with hand, to make a fairly soft dough that leaves the sides of bowl.

• Turn onto lightly floured board. Knead until smooth and elastic, about 8 minutes. Place in greased bowl and

turn dough over to grease top. Cover and let rise in warm place until doubled, about 1 hour. Punch down dough, turn over, cover and let rest 10 minutes.

• Turn out onto board; divide in half. Cut each half into 3 equal parts.

• Roll each part under hand to make a strip 11 to 12″ long. Braid 3 strips, starting from the center and braiding to each end, pinching ends to seal. Place in greased 9×5×3″ loaf pan. Repeat with remaining 3 strips.

• Cover and let rise in warm place until doubled, about 45 minutes.

• Bake in hot oven (400°) 40 to 50 minutes, covering with sheet of foil during last 15 minutes to prevent browning too much. Remove from pans and place on wire cooling racks. After loaves are slightly cooled, brush with Thin Confectioners Sugar Icing. Makes 2 loaves.

Thin Confectioners Sugar Icing: Add 1 tblsp. plus 2 tsp. light cream to 1 c. sifted confectioners sugar, and stir until icing is smooth.

VARIATIONS

Finnish Bread—Round Loaves: Turn risen dough onto board; divide into 2 parts. Shape into 2 round loaves and place in 2 greased 9″ round layer cake pans. Make 3 or 4 slashes on tops of loaves with very sharp knife. Cover, let rise until doubled; bake and cool like Finnish Coffee Bread. Omit icing. Makes 2 round loaves.

Finnish Braids: Turn risen dough onto board; divide in half. Cut one half into 4 parts. Shape 3 parts into strands 12″ long. Place on greased baking sheet and braid, starting at center and braiding to each end. Seal ends. Cut remaining part into 3 parts; shape into strands 9″ long; braid and place on top of large braid, tucking ends into large braid. Repeat with other half of dough. Cover, let rise until doubled; bake (20 to 25 minutes), cool and frost like Finnish Coffee Bread. Makes 2 braids.

Prize-winning Breads

An Oklahoma farm woman won blue ribbons at the county fair on her Classic Sweet Dough. It's a three-from-one recipe. You divide the dough in thirds and use each one to make a different bread. It might be any of the four treats for which we give recipes—Apricot Crescents, Date Braid, Swedish Tea Ring and Grecian Feast Bread. All are good.

CLASSIC SWEET DOUGH

Starting point for wonderful breads

    2   c. milk
    ½   c. butter or margarine
    ½   c. sugar
    2   tsp. salt
    2   pkgs. active dry yeast
    ½   c. warm water (110 to 115°)
    2   eggs, beaten
    9½ to 10 c. sifted all-purpose
        flour

· Scald milk; stir in butter, sugar and salt. Cool to lukewarm.
· Sprinkle yeast on warm water; stir to dissolve.
· Add milk mixture, eggs and 4½ c. flour to yeast; beat until smooth. Stir in enough remaining flour, a little at a time to make a slightly stiff dough.

(If you want to make Grecian Feast Loaf, remove one third of dough at this point.)
· Turn dough onto lightly floured board, cover and let rest 5 minutes. Knead until smooth and elastic, about 5 minutes. Put in greased bowl; turn dough over to grease top. Cover and let rise until doubled, about 1 hour.
· Punch down, turn onto board, divide into thirds and use to make the following breads.

APRICOT CRESCENTS

Twin loaves with hearts of gold

    ⅓   of Classic Sweet Dough
    2   c. Apricot Filling
    2   tblsp. melted butter
    2   tblsp. sugar

· Divide dough in half. Roll each half into a 12×8″ rectangle. Spread each with 1 c. Apricot Filling. Starting at long edge, roll as for jelly roll. Seal edge.
· Place on greased baking sheet and shape in crescents. Make slashes on tops with scissors 1½″ apart. Brush with butter; sprinkle with sugar.
· Cover; let rise in warm place until doubled, about 30 minutes.
· Bake in moderate oven (350°) 25 to 30 minutes. Remove to wire racks to cool. Makes 2 loaves.

Apricot Filling: Combine in a heavy saucepan 2 c. dried apricots (11 oz. pkg.) and 1 c. water. Cover and simmer until apricots are tender. Add ¼ c. butter or margarine, stir and mash until butter is melted. Add 1½ c. sugar and stir to dissolve; beat well. Cool and add 1 c. chopped walnuts. Makes 3 cups.

DATE BRAID

Filling peeks through slits in loaf

⅓ of Classic Sweet Dough
2 c. Date Filling

• Roll dough into a 14×8″ rectangle. Place on greased baking sheet.
• Reserve ¼ c. Date Filling. Spread remaining filling in 3″ strip lengthwise on center of rectangle. At each side of filling cut from edge of dough to filling at 2″ intervals. You will have 7 strips on each side.
• Bring strips from opposite sides to center, crossing them and then tucking in on sides. Spoon reserved filling into the open spaces. Cover and let rise in a warm place until doubled, 30 to 45 minutes.
• Bake in moderate oven (350°) 25 to 30 minutes. Place on wire rack to cool. Frost with Confectioners Sugar Frosting (see Index) while still warm.

Date Filling: Combine in heavy saucepan 1 (8 oz.) pkg. dates, chopped or finely cut with scissors, 1 c. chopped pecans, ¼ c. brown sugar, ⅔ c. water and 1 tblsp. lemon juice. Cook, stirring constantly, until of spreading consistency, 3 to 5 minutes. Cool before using. Makes 2 cups.

SWEDISH TEA RING

For Yuletide centerpiece put candle in center of pretty bread wreath

¼ c. soft butter or margarine
¼ c. sugar
1 tsp. grated lemon peel
½ c. ground almonds
⅓ of Classic Sweet Dough
1 c. mixed candied fruits, chopped

• Cream butter and sugar; stir in lemon peel and almonds. Mix well.
• Roll dough into a 14×10″ rectangle. Sprinkle sugar mixture evenly over dough. Arrange candied fruits evenly over the top. Roll up from the long side as for jelly roll; seal edge. Place, sealed edge down, in ring on lightly greased baking sheet. Seal ends together firmly. Snip dough with scissors from edge of circle three fourths of the way to center every 1½″. Turn cut pieces on their sides. (If you're making this bread for Christmas, place greased custard cup in center to keep hole round for non-drip candle.)
• Cover and let rise until doubled, 45 minutes to 1 hour.
• Bake in moderate oven (350°) 25 to 30 minutes. Cool on wire rack.

Note: You can frost Swedish Tea Ring with Confectioners Sugar Frosting (see Index).

Attractive Grecian Feast Bread

The world owes much to Greece for many things, including the country's festive breads. Among the great loaves is this one with three petals. It's really three small loaves baked as one. It wouldn't be Easter in many Grecian homes without this bread, which also appears in meals and refreshments on other church holidays, such as Christmas.

The three loaves represent Trinity. Grecian hostesses frequently bring the uncut bread to the table and thinly slice the small loaves. The custom is for each person to eat a slice from all three.

While Grecian Feast Bread frequently glistens with a shiny, brown glaze, as our recipe provides, sometimes it is frosted. The traditional way to add the Thin Confectioners Sugar Icing (see Index) is to pour it over each of the miniature loaves while still warm, letting it run down the sides. Flowers of three petals made of almonds and/or sliced candied cherries decorate the white tops.

GRECIAN FEAST LOAF

The 3-leaf-clover loaf is an Easter and Christmas tradition in Greece

⅓ of Classic Sweet Dough
    (before kneading)
½ c. currants
1 tsp. grated lemon peel
¼ tsp. ground mace
1 egg, beaten (for glaze)

• Remove one third of Classic Sweet Dough when mixed, before kneading. Work in the currants, lemon peel and mace; knead until dough is smooth and elastic, 3 to 5 minutes. Place in lightly greased bowl; turn dough over to grease top. Cover, let rise in warm place until doubled, about 1 hour.
• Punch down, turn onto floured board and divide into 3 equal parts. Shape each part into a smooth ball and arrange on greased baking sheet to form a 3-leaf clover. Leave ¾″ between the 3 balls.
• Cover and let rise in warm place until doubled, about 1 hour. Brush each ball of dough with beaten egg.
• Bake in moderate oven (350°) about 25 minutes. Cool on wire rack.

Kulich—A Traditional Easter Bread

Kulich, the traditional Easter bread of old Russia, tastes good any time of year. We baked this dough in No. 2 (1 lb. about 4 oz.) cans in which you buy pineapple or other fruits. During the baking, the dough rises above the tops of the cans and forms a dome that resembles the domes of old Russian churches.

Most Americans like to spread the "dome" of the baked loaves with a Confectioners Sugar Frosting (see Index) and add tiny colored decorating candies or slivered nuts and sliced candied cherries. Some women omit the frosting but save out a little of the dough and shape it into four tiny short ropes. They arrange two dough strips on top of each loaf to make a cross just after they place the dough in the cans to rise. They brush the loaf tops with butter and sprinkle on sugar.

The top slice, sugared or frosted, traditionally goes to the guest of honor or to the eldest member of the family. Whipped butter is a splendid accompaniment, and Honeyed Butter also tastes wonderful on this Easter bread.

KULICH

The shape of this tasty holiday bread always promotes lots of conversation

½ c. milk
¼ c. sugar
1 tsp. salt
2 tblsp. shortening
1 pkg. active dry yeast

¼ c. warm water (110 to 115°)
2 ¾ to 3 c. sifted all-purpose
          flour
1 egg
¼ c. raisins
¼ c. chopped almonds
1 tsp. grated lemon peel
Snowy Frosting

• Scald milk; pour into a large bowl and add sugar, salt and shortening. Cool until lukewarm.
• Sprinkle yeast on warm water; stir to dissolve.
• Add 1 c. flour, egg and yeast to lukewarm milk mixture. Beat hard with spoon or with electric mixer at medium speed 1 minute. Stir in raisins, almonds and lemon peel. Add remaining flour, a little at a time, until you can easily handle the soft dough.
• Sprinkle about 2 tblsp. flour on board and turn out dough. Knead until dough is satiny and elastic, about 5 minutes. Shape in smooth ball and place in lightly greased bowl; turn dough over to grease top. Cover and let rise in warm place until doubled, 2 to 2½ hours. Punch down.
• Turn dough onto board and divide in half. Let rest 10 minutes. Place each half in a greased No. 2 (1 lb. about 4 oz.) can. Cover and let rise until doubled, 1 to 1¼ hours.
• Bake in moderate oven (350°) 30 to 35 minutes, or until well browned. Remove from cans at once and cool on rack before spreading tops of loaves with Snowy Frosting. Whipped butter and Honeyed Butter are excellent accompaniments. Makes 2 loaves.

Snowy Frosting: Mix ½ c. sifted confectioners sugar with 2 tsp. milk or cream to make a smooth frosting. Spread over tops of loaves. Decorate tops with tiny multi-colored decorating candies, or with 2 tblsp. slivered almonds and 2 candied cherries, sliced.

Honeyed Butter: Whip ½ c. butter (1 stick) with spoon or electric mixer until fluffy. Gradually whip in ¼ c. honey and beat until mixture is smooth. For a new note, whip 1 to 2 tsp. grated orange peel into it.

ALMOND-STREUSEL COFFEE BREAD

Almonds, lemons, sugar and butter fill bread with luscious flavors

1 pkg. active dry yeast
½ c. warm water (110 to 115°)
1 ¾ to 2 ¼ c. sifted all-purpose
          flour
1 egg
3 tblsp. sugar
½ tsp. salt
2 tblsp. soft butter
Streusel Topping (recipe follows)

• Sprinkle yeast over warm water; stir to dissolve.
• Add 1 c. flour, egg, sugar, salt and butter. Beat with spoon until smooth.
• Add enough remaining flour, a little at a time, first with spoon and then with hands, to make a dough that leaves the sides of bowl.
• Turn out onto lightly floured board. Grease fingers lightly and knead until smooth. Round up and place in greased bowl; turn dough over to grease top. Cover and let rise in warm place until doubled, 45 minutes to 1 hour. (Dent remains when finger is pressed deep into side of dough.)
• Meanwhile prepare topping.

• Punch down dough. Press evenly into greased 9" square pan. Sprinkle evenly with Streusel Topping, then with fingers make dents all over the top, pressing to the bottom of the pan to distribute topping evenly.
• Cover pan and let rise until doubled, about 45 minutes.
• Bake in moderate oven (375°) 25 to 35 minutes, or until browned. Remove from pan and cool on rack. Makes 1 (9" square) coffee bread.

STREUSEL TOPPING

Almonds give bread its superb taste

½ c. sugar
½ c. flour
2 tsp. grated lemon peel
½ tsp. vanilla
⅓ c. melted butter
⅓ c. ground unblanched almonds

• Blend together all the ingredients well, using fork. Sprinkle over dough as directed.

Election Coffee Cake

It's called a cake, but it's a yeast-leavened coffee bread. More than a century ago this fruit- and nut-studded loaf, according to legend, was the pay-off of Connecticut politicians to men who voted the straight party ticket. Today its only connection with politics is that many hostesses, especially in New England, serve it at informal parties on election day. It's a good choice if you're looking for something tasty to serve with coffee to guests in front of your television set, while listening to vote counts.

You can bake the bread days ahead and freeze it (but then omit the frosting). To use, thaw the loaf in its wrapper at room temperature for several hours; frost shortly before serving. Or if you prefer, wrap the frozen bread in aluminum foil and heat it in a hot oven (400°) 30 minutes to 1 hour. Cool slightly before you spread the frosting on top, letting it dribble temptingly down the sides of the loaf.

ELECTION DAY CAKE

Historic coffee bread as good as ever with coffee for election day parties

2   pkgs. active dry yeast
1 ½ c. warm water (110 to 115°)
2   tsp. sugar
4 ½ c. sifted all-purpose flour
¾   c. butter or margarine
1   c. sugar
1   tsp. salt
1 ½ tsp. cinnamon
¼   tsp. cloves
¼   tsp. mace
½   tsp. nutmeg
2   eggs
1 ½ c. raisins
½   c. chopped citron
¾   c. chopped nuts
Confectioners Sugar Frosting

• Sprinkle yeast on warm water; stir to dissolve. Add 2 tsp. sugar and 1½ c. flour and beat well by hand, or 2 minutes with electric mixer at medium speed. Cover and let rise in warm place until bubbly, about 30 minutes.
• Meanwhile, cream butter and 1 c. sugar until light and fluffy.
• Sift remaining 3 c. flour with salt, cinnamon, cloves, mace and nutmeg.
• When yeast mixture is bubbly, add

eggs to creamed butter and sugar and beat well. Combine yeast with creamed mixture. Add remaining dry ingredients (flour, salt and spices), a little at a time, beating with spoon after each addition. Beat until smooth.
· Stir in raisins, citron and nuts. Pour into well-greased and floured 10″ tube pan. Cover and let rise in warm place until doubled, about 1½ hours.
· Bake in moderate oven (375°) 1 hour. Cool in pan 5 minutes; turn out on rack to finish cooling. While faintly warm, spread with Confectioners Sugar Frosting. Makes 12 to 16 servings.

Confectioners Sugar Frosting: To 1 c. sifted confectioners sugar add enough milk or light cream to make mixture of spreading consistency. Add ½ tsp. vanilla and a dash of salt (or flavor with ½ tsp. lemon juice and ¼ tsp. grated lemon peel). Stir until smooth. Spread on coffee breads or rolls.

RICH REFRIGERATOR DOUGH

Use in the recipes that follow

¾ c. milk
½ c. sugar
2 tsp. salt
½ c. butter or margarine
2 pkgs. active dry yeast
½ c. warm water (110 to 115°)
2 eggs, beaten
6 c. sifted all-purpose flour

· Scald milk; stir in sugar, salt and butter. Cool to lukewarm.
· Sprinkle yeast on warm water; stir to dissolve.
· Add milk mixture, eggs and 3 c. flour to yeast. Beat until smooth. Stir in remaining flour to make a stiff

dough. Cover and refrigerate for several hours, or overnight. Use in the following recipes as directed.

MINIATURE PINWHEELS

Date filling is sweet and luscious

½ of Rich Refrigerator Dough
1 c. Date Filling (see Index)
½ c. mixed candied fruits
15 candied cherries, cut in halves

· Remove Rich Refrigerator Dough from refrigerator and use immediately.
· Roll to a 12×10″ rectangle. Cut in 2″ squares. Place squares on greased baking sheet. Cover and let rise in warm place 30 minutes.
· Combine Date Filling and ½ c. candied fruits. Place a teaspoonful in center of each square. Cut corners of dough three fourths way to center. Bring corners, one at a time, over filling. Press points together to form a pinwheel. Top each pinwheel with ½ candied cherry.
· Cover; let rise until doubled, about 30 minutes.
· Bake in hot oven (400°) 10 to 15 minutes. Drizzle with Confectioners Sugar Frosting (see above). Makes 30 pinwheels.

DAISY COFFEE BREAD

A tasty flower for your table—ideal to serve with coffee to company

½ of Rich Refrigerator Dough
¼ c. Apricot Filling (see Index)

· Remove dough from refrigerator and use immediately.
· Roll to a 14×7″ rectangle. Cut

crosswise into 14 strips 1″ wide. Braid 2 strips together; coil into snail shape. Repeat with other strips. Arrange 1 coil in center, on greased baking sheet, and the other 6 coils around it to form a flower.
• Cover; let rise in a warm place until doubled, about 1 hour. Make a depression in the center of each coil; fill with spoonful of Apricot Filling.
• Bake in moderate oven (350°) about 25 minutes. Frost, while warm, with Confectioners Sugar Frosting (see Index). Makes 7 servings.

Flaky Danish Pastry

Delicate, flaky Danish pastry! What could taste better? No wonder recipes for it travel far and conquer in many places. The pastry, a Viennese original, captured the Danes, who call it Wienerbrød. Translated into English, it's Vienna bread.

No one can deny that it takes time to bake Danish pastry. Or that the inexperienced baker needs patience! But most women, after baking the pastries and serving them to guests, know that the time is well spent.

One of the glories of Danish pastry is the great number of different shapes you can give the dough. Another is the wide variety of luscious fillings you can use. We describe how to make several of the best-liked shapes and fillings.

And we give you two recipes for the pastry. One is made with butter, the classic style. The other, made with vegetable shortening, comes from a California woman, the wife of a walnut grower. Some women find it the easier of the two recipes, while others insist nothing but butter gives the true flavor. So try them both and decide which one is for you.

About the only trouble you might have is rolling the dough. There's a simple cure: Just chill the dough every time it gets a little hard to manage.

DANISH PASTRY (WITH BUTTER)
Quick way to chill dough: put in freezer for 10 minutes, but do not freeze

1 ½ c. butter (3 sticks)
4 ⅓ c. sifted all-purpose flour
¾ c. milk
¼ c. sugar
1 tsp. salt
2 pkgs. active dry yeast
½ c. warm water (110 to 115°)
1 egg

• Cream butter and ⅓ c. flour thoroughly. Place on sheet of waxed paper and cover with a second sheet of waxed paper. Pat out (or roll) to make a 12×6″ rectangle. Chill until very cold.
• Scald milk, add sugar and salt and cool to lukewarm.
• Sprinkle yeast on warm water; stir to dissolve.
• Add yeast, egg and 1 c. flour to milk mixture; beat vigorously with spoon or electric mixer at medium speed until mixture is smooth. Stir in remaining flour, a little at a time, to make a soft dough. Turn onto lightly floured board and knead until smooth, satiny and elastic, about 5 minutes.
• Roll dough into a 14″ square on lightly floured board. Lay the cold

butter-flour mixture on half the dough, fold the other half over and seal edges by pinching with fingers.
• Roll dough to make a 20×12″ rectangle. Fold in thirds to make 3 layers of dough. If the butter softens, chill dough before rolling again. Roll again to make a 20×12″ rectangle. Repeat folding and rolling 2 times more, chilling dough each time before rolling if it gets too soft.
• Chill about 45 minutes after last rolling.
• Shape and, if you like, fill pastries (directions follow). Place on ungreased baking sheets, cover and let rise in warm place until almost doubled, about 1 hour.
• Brush tops with cold water and sprinkle with sugar. Bake in a very hot oven (450°) 8 to 10 minutes. Drizzle tops of warm pastries, if you like, with Sugar Glaze (see Index). Cool on wire racks. Makes about 35 pastries.

HOW TO SHAPE DANISH PASTRY

Snails: Work with one third of pastry at a time. Roll to make a 12×7″ rectangle (dough will be about ¼″ thick). Cut in strips 6×¾″. Hold one end of strip on baking sheet and twist; then coil strips to make snails.

Knots: Tie twisted strips, as for Snails, into knots.

Rings: Shape twisted strips, as for Snails, into circles.

HOW TO FILL DANISH PASTRY

Envelopes: Cut rolled pastry (one third of it at a time) in 3 to 4″ squares. Place 1 scant tsp. Almond Filling (see Index) or thick apricot, pineapple or berry jam in center of each square. Fold 1 corner of square over filling to about 1″ from opposite corner. Press to seal.

Sheaths: Fill squares as for Envelopes. Fold 2 opposite corners to center, overlapping them slightly. Press to seal.

Packages: Fold all 4 corners of squares, as for Envelopes, over filling to center, overlapping slightly. Press to seal.

DANISH PASTRY
(WITH SHORTENING)

You can make pastries of several fascinating shapes with this dough

1	c. milk
⅓	c. sugar
1	tsp. salt
¼	c. shortening
1	pkg. active dry yeast
¼	c. warm water (110 to 115°)
2	eggs
¼	tsp. nutmeg
½	tsp. vanilla
3 ½ to 4	c. sifted all-purpose flour
1	c. soft shortening
1	egg, beaten

Chopped nuts
Sugar Glaze
Fillings, if desired (recipes
    follow)

• Scald milk; add sugar, salt and ¼ c. shortening. Cool to lukewarm.
• Sprinkle yeast on warm water; stir to dissolve.
• Add 2 eggs, yeast, nutmeg, vanilla and 1 c. flour to milk mixture. Beat with electric mixer at medium speed, scraping the bowl occasionally, 2 minutes, or until smooth. Or beat vigorously with spoon.

• Stir in enough remaining flour, a little at a time, to make a soft dough, easy to handle. Cover with waxed paper and a clean towel; let rise in a warm place free from drafts until doubled.

• Roll dough ¼″ thick on lightly floured board. Dot with ½ c. soft shortening (softened by standing at room temperature), leaving 2″ border without shortening. Fold dough in half and seal edges. Dot dough with remaining ½ c. softened shortening; fold in half again and seal edges. Roll dough ⅓″ thick to make a square; fold in half and fold again to make a square (like a handkerchief). Repeat rolling and folding process 3 more times.

• Place dough in lightly greased bowl, cover, and let rest 20 minutes.

• Roll dough ⅓″ thick on lightly floured board. Shape and, if you like, fill (directions follow). Place on ungreased baking sheets. Cover and let rise in warm place until half doubled in size.

• Brush tops of pastries with beaten egg and sprinkle with chopped nuts. Bake in very hot oven (475°) 8 to 10 minutes. Drizzle while warm with Sugar Glaze, if you like. Cool on wire racks. Makes about 24 pastries.

Sugar Glaze: Combine 1 c. sifted confectioners sugar, 1½ tsp. melted butter and enough milk or dairy half-and-half to make a smooth frosting.

HOW TO SHAPE DANISH PASTRY

Coils or Snails, Rings and Figure 8s: Cut dough rolled ⅓″ thick into strips 8″ long and ¾″ wide. Place strips, one at a time, on ungreased baking sheet. Hold one end on baking sheet and twist. Then shape strip into desired design. (Let rise until half doubled in size, brush with beaten egg and sprinkle with nuts. After baking, while pastries are still warm, drizzle on Sugar Glaze, if you like.)

HOW TO FILL DANISH PASTRY

Foldovers: Cut dough rolled ⅓″ thick into 3″ squares. Place 1 tsp. filling in center. Fold opposite corners to center; press to seal.

Pinwheels: Make like Foldovers, only cut from each corner almost to center. Place 1 tsp. filling in center, if you like. Fold alternating points to center and press to seal.

Cockscombs: Roll half of dough at a time into a 12×8″ rectangle. Cut in 4×2″ rectangles. Place 1 tsp. Almond Filling in center of each rectangle (be sure measurement is level). Fold lengthwise in half and tightly press edges to seal. Curve rolls slightly on baking sheet and with sharp scissors snip side opposite sealed edge at 1″ intervals.

FILLINGS FOR DANISH PASTRY

Golden Apricot Filling: Cook ⅔ c. dried apricots with ⅔ c. water until apricots are very tender. Stir in 6 tblsp. sugar. Rub through strainer, or buzz in electric blender. Filling should be thick.

Prune-Spice Filling: Substitute pitted dried prunes for dried apricots in Apricot Filling and use ¼ tsp. cinnamon. Filling should be thick.

Almond Filling: Cream ¼ c. butter and ¼ c. sugar until light and fluffy. Blend in ¼ c. ground almonds. Add a few drops almond extract if you like.

Cherry Filling: Combine ½ c. canned cherry pie filling and a few drops almond extract.

Apricot Jam Filling: Combine ½ c. thick apricot jam and ½ tsp. grated orange peel.

Brioche—Light Butter Rolls

Brioche is typically French. Legend has it that the rolls originated in the district of Brie. The French serve brioche warm for breakfast. In America, we team the rolls with coffee at any time of the day. They always win applause.

There are many recipes for brioche. We give you one worked out in our FARM JOURNAL Test Kitchens. We think the rolls are extra-good and think you'll agree.

BRIOCHE

Light, delicately yeasty, golden—one of the favorite recipes from our Freezing & Canning Cookbook

    1 c. milk
    ½ c. butter or margarine
    1 tsp. salt
    ½ c. sugar
    2 pkgs. active dry yeast
    ¼ c. warm water (110 to 115°)
    4 eggs, beaten
    1 tsp. grated lemon peel
    5 c. sifted all-purpose flour
       (about)
  Melted butter

• Scald milk; stir in ½ c. butter, salt and sugar. Cool to lukewarm.
• Sprinkle yeast on warm water; stir to dissolve.
• Combine eggs and lemon peel and add with yeast to milk mixture. Beat in flour, a little at a time, to make a soft dough you can handle.
• Turn onto floured board; knead lightly until dough is smooth and satiny. Place in greased bowl; turn dough over to grease top. Cover and let rise in warm place free from drafts until doubled, about 2 hours. Punch down and turn out on floured board. Knead lightly.
• Shape two thirds of the dough into smooth balls about 2″ in diameter. Shape remaining dough in 1″ balls. Place large balls in greased muffin-pan cups. Flatten balls slightly; make a deep indentation in each with finger or the handle of a wooden spoon. Shape small balls like teardrops and set one firmly in the indentation in each ball in muffin-pan cups. Brush with melted butter. Cover and let rise until doubled, about 1 hour.
• Bake in hot oven (425°) about 10 minutes. Remove from pans at once. Place on wire racks. Serve warm; or wrap cold rolls in aluminum foil and heat a few minutes in oven before serving. Makes 3 dozen rolls.

Spring's Hot Cross Buns

Shiny, brown rolls, crowned with white frosting crosses, are as English as roast beef and Yorkshire pudding. The recipes came with the early settlers and caught on from the start. Now the buns come to thousands of breakfast and luncheon tables, especially during the Easter season.

You can bake the rolls ahead and freeze them, providing you omit the frosting. It takes only a few minutes to add it the day of serving. Put the frozen rolls on a baking sheet and run them in a hot oven (400°) for 10 minutes. Cool 5 minutes, add the frosting and serve pronto.

When you bake Hot Cross Buns, you are making bread that has stood the test of time. English people first made them to honor the Goddess of Spring. When the Christian faith came to the country, bakers bowed to changing times and added the cross.

HOT CROSS BUNS

Easter buns with frosting crosses—traditionally served on Good Friday

¼ c. milk
⅓ c. sugar
¾ tsp. salt
½ c. shortening
2 pkgs. active dry yeast
½ c. warm water (110 to 115°)
3 eggs
4 c. sifted all-purpose flour
     (about)
¾ c. currants
1 egg white
1 tsp. cold water
White Frosting

• Scald milk, add sugar, salt and shortening; cool to lukewarm.
• Sprinkle yeast on warm water; stir to dissolve.
• Add eggs, yeast and 1 c. flour to milk mixture; beat with electric mixer at medium speed about 2 minutes, occasionally scraping the bowl. Stir in

currants and enough remaining flour, a little at a time, to make a soft dough that is easy to handle. Beat well. Place in lightly greased bowl; turn dough over to grease top. Cover and let rise until doubled, about 1½ hours. Punch down. Turn onto lightly floured board.
• Roll or pat to ½" thickness. Cut in rounds with 2½" biscuit cutter; shape cutouts in buns. Place about 1½" apart on greased baking sheets. Cover and let rise until doubled, about 1 hour.
• With a very sharp knife, cut a shallow cross on top of each bun. Brush tops with unbeaten egg white mixed with cold water.
• Bake in moderate oven (375°) 15 minutes, or until golden brown. Cool on wire racks about 5 minutes. Then, with tip of knife or teaspoon, fill in crosses on buns with White Frosting. Best served warm. Makes about 18 buns.

White Frosting: Combine 1 c. sifted confectioners sugar, ½ tsp. vanilla and 2 tblsp. hot water. Mix until smooth.

VARIATION

Fruited Hot Cross Buns: With currants stir in 3 tblsp. finely chopped candied orange peel and 3 tblsp. finely chopped citron.

To reheat bread and rolls, wrap in aluminum foil and heat about 10 minutes in a hot oven (400°).

EASTER EGG BREAD–Surprise both children and adults on Easter Sunday with Easter Egg Bread (recipe, page 42). You can bake one large ring, or individual bread rings with an Easter egg in the center of each.

Bohemian Kolaches—
Fruity and Gay

If you want to collect compliments for the bread you bake, do make Kolaches. Arrange the apricot- and prune-filled rolls, dusted with confectioners sugar, on a tray for your next tea or coffee party, or pass to guests with coffee at any time of day.

Some women consider Kolaches tedious to make, but almost everyone believes they're worth the effort. Our recipe comes from a farm woman in northeastern Iowa. It came to her from her mother, as a remembrance of home, from relatives in Czechoslovakia. Frequently she fixes the fillings a day ahead and keeps them, covered, in the refrigerator ready to use.

While the rolls are simply superb when fresh-baked, you can bake them ahead and freeze. Few people can tell the difference if you warm the Kolaches before serving (dust on the confectioners sugar after warming).

BOHEMIAN KOLACHES

No European sweet bread has a more enthusiastic American following than these luscious fruit-filled rolls

½ c. milk
2 pkgs. active dry yeast
½ c. warm water (110 to 115°)
¾ c. butter or margarine (1½ sticks)
½ c. sugar
1 tsp. salt
4 egg yolks
4½ c. sifted all-purpose flour
Fillings
2 tblsp. melted butter
2 tblsp. confectioners sugar

• Scald milk; cool to lukewarm.
• Sprinkle yeast on warm water; stir to dissolve.
• Cream butter, sugar, salt and egg yolks together with electric mixer until light and fluffy. Add yeast, milk and 1½ c. flour. Beat with electric mixer at medium speed 5 minutes, scraping the bowl occasionally. Batter should be smooth.
• Stir in enough remaining flour, a little at a time, to make a soft dough that leaves the sides of bowl. Place in lightly greased bowl, turn dough over to grease top. Cover and let rise in warm place free from drafts until doubled, 1 to 1½ hours.
• Stir down; turn onto lightly floured board and divide into 24 pieces of equal size. Shape each piece into a ball. Cover and let rest 10 to 15 minutes.
• Place 2″ apart on greased baking sheets; press each piece of dough from center outward with fingers of both hands to make a hollow in center with a ½″ rim around edge. Fill each hollow with 1 level tblsp. filling (recipes follow).
• Cover and let rise in warm place until doubled, 30 to 40 minutes.

CHRISTMAS BREADS—Bake these fruit-filled, yeast breads to serve holiday guests and for gifts. Pictured, clockwise, are: Swedish Tea Ring, Date Braid, Grecian Feast Loaf and Apricot Crescent (recipes, pages 46–48).

• Bake in moderate oven (350°) 15 to 18 minutes, or until browned. Brush tops of rolls lightly with melted butter and sprinkle lightly with sifted confectioners sugar. Remove from baking sheets and place on wire racks. Makes 24 kolaches.

FILLINGS FOR KOLACHES

Prune Filling: Cook 30 prunes in water to cover until tender; drain, mash with fork and stir in ¼ c. sugar and ¼ tsp. allspice. Filling should be thick. Makes enough for 14 kolaches.

Thick Apricot Filling: Cook 25 dried apricot halves in water to cover until tender; drain and press through strainer or food mill (or buzz in blender). Stir in ¼ c. sugar. Filling should be thick. Makes enough filling for 10 kolaches.

Prune-Apricot Filling: Simmer 1 c. prunes and ¾ c. dried apricot halves in water to cover until tender; drain, chop and mash with fork. Stir in ½ c. sugar, 1 tblsp. orange juice and 1 tblsp. grated orange peel. Filling should be thick. Makes enough filling for 24 kolaches.

VARIATIONS

Peek-a-boo Kolaches: Flatten balls of dough, after resting 15 minutes, to make 3½ to 4″ squares. Place about 1 tblsp. filling on center of each square. Moisten corners with milk and bring opposite corners over filling, overlapping them about 1″; press to seal. Repeat with 2 opposite corners. Place about 2″ apart on greased baking sheet; let rise and bake like Bohemian Kolaches.

Baby Bunting Kolaches: When dough is doubled, stir it down and divide in half. Let rest 15 minutes. Roll each half into a 12×9″ rectangle; cut each half in 12 (3″) squares. Place 1 tblsp. filling on center of each square. Bring one corner of dough to center over filling; repeat with opposite corner; press to seal. Place 2″ apart on greased baking sheet; let rise and bake like Bohemian Kolaches.

Flag-inspired Crescents

When the Turks, in 1683, found their siege of Vienna failing, they decided to dig tunnels by night through which they could enter the city. Bakers, hearing the digging, gave the alarm to the government officials. The city was saved. As a reward, the bakers were given permission to make rolls in the shape of the crescent, an emblem on the Mohammedan flag. From that long-ago beginning, luscious crescent rolls have captured the hearts of people in many countries—France, where people call them croissants and serve them fresh-baked for breakfast, and the United States.

This cookbook features several recipes for crescents, but none of them surpasses Butter Crescents.

BUTTER CRESCENTS

Have copies of this recipe ready—you may be sure guests will ask for it

½ c. milk
½ c. butter
⅓ c. sugar
¾ tsp. salt
1 pkg. active dry yeast

½ c. warm water (110 to 115°)
1 egg, beaten
4 c. sifted all-purpose flour
   (about)

• Scald milk and pour over butter, sugar and salt. Cool to lukewarm.
• Sprinkle yeast on warm water; stir to dissolve.
• Add egg, yeast and 2 c. flour to milk mixture. Beat with electric mixer at low speed until smooth, about 1 minute. Then beat at medium speed until thick, about 2 minutes (or beat with rotary beater).
• Add enough of remaining flour and mix with spoon or hands to make a dough that leaves the sides of bowl. Turn onto a lightly floured board and knead gently. Put into a greased bowl; invert to grease top of dough. Cover with clean towel and let rise in warm place free from drafts until doubled, about 1 hour.
• Turn dough onto board, divide in half, cover and let rest 10 minutes. Roll each half to make a 12″ circle; cut each circle in 12 wedges. Roll up each wedge from wide end and put, pointed end down, on greased baking sheets (you'll need 2). Curve ends slightly to make crescents. Cover with towel. Let rise until doubled, about 30 minutes.
• Bake in hot oven (400°) 15 minutes, changing position of baking sheets in oven when half baked. Remove from baking sheets and cool on wire racks. Makes 24 crescents.

Note: You can refrigerate the dough overnight before you let it rise. After kneading dough, place in lightly greased bowl and turn dough over to grease top. Cover with a piece of waxed paper, brushed with salad oil, and lay a piece of aluminum foil on top. Place in refrigerator. In the morning, let stand at room temperature until dough rises and is soft enough to roll, then turn dough onto board and proceed as with dough that was not refrigerated.

VARIATION

Peanut Butter Crescents: Follow the recipe for Butter Crescents, but before cutting the circles of dough and rolling the pie-shaped pieces, spread with this mixture: Combine ⅓ c. peanut butter and ⅓ c. honey; add ⅛ tsp. salt and ½ tsp. cinnamon. Proceed as directed for Butter Crescents.

Festive St. Lucia Buns

When it comes to yeast breads, Swedish people know what's good. Among their Christmas season favorites are St. Lucia Buns. Americans also like these rolls. Choose them for a kitchen-made gift to take to neighbors, to serve at a holiday coffee party or to treat your family at breakfast.

The Wisconsin farm woman who shares her recipe for this festive bread believes one reason the rolls taste so good is their cardamom flavor. Scandinavian bakers favor this sweet spice. "Some people prefer saffron to cardamom," she says. "You can use a pinch of it in my recipe, if you like. Dissolve it in the hot milk and omit the cardamom." Then she adds: "Sometimes I omit the raisins from the curled ends of the rolls and instead stick candied red cherries, cut in 4 pieces, in the centers of the coils."

The Swedish custom is for the daughters in the family, dressed in white and wearing holly crowns, to awaken their parents at dawn on St. Lucia's Day, December 13, and serve them St. Lucia Buns and hot coffee. This ceremony signals the opening of the Christmas season.

You can bake the buns ahead and freeze them to get a head start on holiday preparations. To thaw them, wrap the frozen rolls in aluminum foil and place them in a slow oven (325°) for 20 minutes, or place them unwrapped on a baking sheet and run them into a hot oven (400°) for 10 minutes. If it is easier for you, let the wrapped buns thaw at room temperature for 30 to 35 minutes.

ST. LUCIA BUNS

These breakfast buns open Sweden's Christmas season on December 13

¾   c. milk
⅓   c. sugar
2   tsp. salt
½   c. butter or margarine (1 stick)
2   pkgs. active dry yeast
½   c. warm water (110 to 115°)
1   tsp. ground cardamom
4⅓ c. sifted all-purpose flour
1   egg
Raisins
1   egg white

• Scald milk; pour into a large bowl and add sugar, salt and butter. Cool to lukewarm.
• Sprinkle yeast on warm water; stir to dissolve.
• Add cardamom, 1 c. flour, yeast and egg to milk mixture; beat with electric mixer at medium speed, scraping the bowl occasionally, 2 minutes, or until smooth. (Or beat vigorously with spoon.) Stir in enough remaining flour, a little at a time, until dough leaves the sides of bowl.
• Turn onto lightly floured board; knead until smooth and elastic, about 5 minutes.
• Place in lightly greased bowl; turn dough over to grease top. Cover and let rise in a warm place free from drafts until doubled, about 45 to 50 minutes. Punch down; cover and let rest 10 minutes.
• Pinch off balls of dough about 2½″ in diameter and roll into pieces 12″ long and ½″ thick. Place 2 strips together, back to back, on greased baking sheets and curl or coil the ends. Stick a raisin in the center of each coil. (Or form strips of dough in the shape of an S, coiling or curling ends. Stick a raisin in the center of each coil.) Brush tops of buns with egg white beaten until foamy. Sprinkle with sugar, if you wish. Cover and let rise until doubled, about 40 minutes.
• Bake in hot oven (400°) 10 to 12 minutes, or until golden brown. Remove from baking sheet to wire racks. Serve warm or cold. Makes 18 buns.

PRUNE AND APRICOT SQUARES

This is what a Nebraska farm woman serves with coffee to morning callers

¾   c. chopped cooked, drained prunes
¾   c. chopped cooked, drained apricots
½   c. sugar
¼   c. finely chopped nuts
¼   c. milk
1   pkg. active dry yeast

¼ c. warm water (110 to 115°)
½ tsp. salt
2¼ c. sifted all-purpose flour
¼ c. shortening
1   egg
Orange Frosting

• Combine prunes, apricots, ¼ c. sugar and nuts. Set aside.
• Scald milk; cool to lukewarm.
• Sprinkle yeast on warm water; stir to dissolve.
• Combine remaining ¼ c. sugar, salt and flour; stir to mix. Cut in shortening with pastry blender as for pie crust. Add milk, yeast and egg. Stir well until blended. Place in greased bowl; turn dough over to grease top. Cover and let rise until doubled, 1 to 1½ hours.
• Turn onto board and divide in half. Cover and let rest 10 minutes. Roll out each half to make a 16×-12″ rectangle. Place 1 rectangle on greased baking sheet. Spread with prune-apricot mixture. Place other dough rectangle on top. Let rise 1 hour.
• Bake in moderate oven (350°) 30 minutes. Cool 5 to 10 minutes and frost with Orange Frosting. Cut into squares to serve. Makes 15 squares.

Orange Frosting: To 1 c. sifted confectioners sugar add ¼ tsp. grated orange peel and 1 tblsp. orange juice, or enough juice to make a frosting of spreading consistency. (If you prefer, substitute cream or milk for orange juice. Then omit orange peel.)

For Shiny Crisp Crusts

Brush yeast bread or rolls before baking with 1 egg yolk beaten with 2 tblsp. cold water.

Rolls Piquant
with Sour Cream

Give a farm woman a mixing bowl, sour cream and a little time for baking and something wonderful happens. Fragrant and delicious foods come from the oven with that piquant taste that sour cream alone imparts. This holds for yeast-leavened rolls as well as for cookies and cakes.

Sugar-Crusted Rolls and Holiday Cream Twists are adequate proof. These dainty rolls are an American substitute for Danish pastries. They're a lot easier to make.

The sour cream used in most kitchens today is dairy sour cream from the grocery—the kind called for in our recipes. It has an advantage for weight watchers because the fat content is lower than that in heavy cream soured at home and its flavor is often better.

HOLIDAY CREAM TWISTS

Dainty, pretty and tasty for the holidays or any festive occasion

1   pkg. active dry yeast
½ c. warm water (110 to 115°)
4   c. sifted all-purpose flour
1   tsp. salt
1   c. shortening
1   whole egg
2   egg yolks
1   c. dairy sour cream
½ tsp. grated lemon peel
½ c. quartered candied cherries
½ c. broken walnuts
¾ c. sugar

• Sprinkle yeast on warm water; stir to dissolve.
• Sift together flour and salt; cut

shortening into flour mixture with pastry blender.

· Combine yeast, egg, egg yolks, sour cream and lemon peel; mix thoroughly into flour mixture. Stir in cherries and walnuts. Cover and place dough in refrigerator overnight (it will be stiff).

· Sprinkle sugar lightly over rolling surface. Place dough on sugared surface and sprinkle it lightly with sugar. Roll to make a 16×12" rectangle. Fold dough from two opposite sides to make 3 layers. Sprinkle rolling surface and dough with a little sugar and roll and fold again. Sprinkle dough and rolling surface again with sugar and roll, fold and roll again. (Divide the sugar—use about 2 tblsp. at a time—so you will use no more than ¾ c. for the entire process.)

· Cut the 16×12" sheet of dough into strips 4" long and 1" wide. Lift strips with both hands and twist 3 or 4 times. Place 1" apart on ungreased baking sheets.

· Bake in moderate oven (375°) 18 to 20 minutes. Makes 48 rolls.

SUGAR-CRUSTED ROLLS

Sweet rolls that taste like Danish pastry made by a simplified method

1   pkg. active dry yeast
¼   c. warm water (110 to 115°)
3½   c. sifted all-purpose flour
1   tsp. salt
¾   c. sugar
1   c. cold butter
2   eggs, slightly beaten
¾   c. dairy sour cream
2   tsp. vanilla

· Sprinkle yeast on warm water; stir to dissolve.

· Sift flour, salt and ¼ c. sugar into large mixing bowl. Cut in firm butter with pastry blender until mixture looks like fine crumbs. Stir in yeast, eggs, sour cream and vanilla to make a smooth dough. Shape into a ball with hands.

· Wrap dough tightly in plastic wrap and refrigerate overnight. (You can keep it in refrigerator up to 3 days, or you can make the rolls after it has chilled 3 hours.)

· Divide dough in half, wrap and return one half to refrigerator. Roll out other half on lightly floured board to make an 18×12" rectangle. Fold from 2 sides so you will have 3 layers. Roll out again on floured board to make an 18×12" rectangle, repeat folding, then roll out again to an 18×12" rectangle. Fold again in thirds and cut in half to make 2 (6") squares.

· Turn in corners of 1 square of the dough to make a circle. Sprinkle the board with about 2 tblsp. of the remaining sugar. Roll dough to a 12" circle. Cut circle into 8 equal wedges. Roll up each wedge, starting with the broad end. Place on greased baking sheet, point side down. Curve each roll slightly to make a crescent shape.

· On sugared board, roll, cut and shape crescents from the other 6" square of dough in the same way.

· Repeat with other half of dough from the refrigerator, using the last ¼ c. sugar for the rolling of this dough.

· Cover; let rolls rise until puffy, about 45 minutes. Bake in moderate oven (375°) 12 to 15 minutes, or until golden brown. Serve warm or cold. Makes 32 crescents.

BREAKFAST CINNAMON CRISPS

*One farmer's first choice of the many
excellent yeast breads his wife bakes*

1 ¼ c. milk
½ c. sugar
½ c. butter or margarine
1 tsp. salt
1 pkg. active dry yeast
¼ c. warm water (110 to 115°)
2 eggs
5 ½ to 6 c. sifted all-purpose flour
½ c. softened butter
1 ½ c. sugar
1 tblsp. cinnamon

• Scald milk; add ½ c. sugar, ½ c. butter and salt. Cool to lukewarm.
• Sprinkle yeast on warm water; stir to dissolve.
• Combine eggs, 2 c. flour, milk mixture and yeast in large bowl. Beat 1 minute with electric mixer at low speed, then 2 minutes at medium speed. (Or beat with spoon until mixture is smooth.)
• Mix in enough remaining flour, a little at a time, with spoon or hands to make a soft dough that is easy to handle.
• Turn onto lightly floured board; knead until smooth and elastic, about 5 minutes. Round up into ball, place in greased bowl and turn dough over to grease top. Cover and let rise in warm place until doubled, about 1½ hours.
• Turn onto board, divide in half, cover and let rest 10 minutes. Roll each half into a 20×13" rectangle.
• Make a filling by combining ½ c. butter and 1 c. sugar. Divide mixture in half, 1 portion for each rectangle of dough. Spread first rectangle with half of 1 portion butter-sugar mix-

ture (about 4 tblsp.). Fold rectangle in half; roll again to make a 20×13" rectangle; spread with remaining half portion of butter-sugar filling (about 4 tblsp.) Fold in half again and roll out to rectangle 20×13". Repeat procedure with other rectangle of dough, using remaining half of butter-sugar filling.
• Combine remaining ½ c. sugar and cinnamon. Divide in half; set aside one half for topping. Sprinkle the other half evenly over both rolled out rectangles of dough.
• Starting at wide side of rectangles, roll each one like a jelly roll. Seal well by pinching edges of each roll together. Even up rolls by stretching slightly. Cut in 1" slices. Place on greased baking sheets and flatten by pressing down and gently pulling outward with fingers from center of each slice. Sprinkle remaining sugar-cinnamon mixture evenly on tops of rolls.
• Cover and let rise in warm place about 30 minutes. Bake in hot oven (400°) 10 to 12 minutes. Cool on wire racks. Makes 40 rolls.

Peanut Butter Syrup

Mix ⅓ c. peanut butter with ⅔ c. light corn syrup until smooth. Good on pancakes.

Country Yeast Specialties

Sleepy appetites awaken quickly on wintry mornings if yeast-leavened waffles, pancakes or doughnuts come to the breakfast table. These hearty country foods never go out of style. Certainly, no bread cookbook would be complete without them.

Pizza, a supper and snack favorite, joins this group of bread specialties that have a delicate yeasty flavor. Teen-agers first promoted this Italian treat, but it quickly made friends with many grownups. More women make pizzas every year, with the help of their young folks, so that it no longer is necessary to drive to town to visit a "pizza parlor" to enjoy the food as much as the Romans do.

You will also find in this group of specialties a recipe for Sour Dough Starter, an old-time favorite that retains popularity with Western ranch people because of the tangy flavor it gives breads made with it.

YEAST WAFFLES

Change of pace and taste in waffles; recipe is reprinted from our Cooking for Company *cookbook*

2   c. milk
1   pkg. active dry yeast
½   c. warm water (110 to 115°)
⅓   c. melted butter
1   tsp. salt
1   tsp. sugar
3   c. sifted all-purpose flour
2   eggs, slightly beaten
½   tsp. baking soda

· Scald milk; cool to lukewarm.
· Sprinkle yeast on warm water in large bowl; stir to dissolve.
· Add milk, butter, salt, sugar and flour to yeast; mix thoroughly with rotary or electric mixer until batter is smooth. Cover and let stand at room temperature overnight.
· When ready to bake, add eggs and baking soda. Beat well. Bake on pre-heated waffle iron. Makes 6 to 8 waffles.

Yeast-leavened Flapjacks

Surprise nearby neighbors on a blustery winter day by inviting them over for a pancake supper. Make yeast-leavened cakes for a change. They're different. And they taste exceptionally good.

You let the batter stand at least an hour before baking the cakes. If you like to be an early bird when getting ready for company, you can fix the batter hours ahead. It will keep up to 24 hours if covered and stored in the refrigerator.

You can roll the flapjacks, or serve a stack of 2 or 3 on each plate. After the first few bites, guests know they are eating something different and delicious. If there is a home bread baker around the table, she will recognize that the marvelous aroma and taste come from yeast.

YEAST-LEAVENED FLAPJACKS

Easy to fix, tempting, satisfying

1 ¾   c. milk
2   tblsp. sugar
1   tsp. salt
1   pkg. active dry yeast
¼   c. warm water (110 to 115°)
3   tblsp. salad oil (or ¼ c. softened shortening)
3   eggs (room temperature)
2   c. sifted all-purpose flour

· Scald milk; add sugar and salt and cool to lukewarm.
· Meanwhile, sprinkle yeast on warm water; stir to dissolve. Add to cooled milk mixture. Beat in salad oil, eggs and flour with rotary beater or elec-

tric mixer on medium speed until batter is smooth.

• Cover bowl and let rise in warm place at least 1 hour before using. The batter will be light and bubbly. Use at once, or refrigerate (do not refrigerate for more than 24 hours).

• Stir down batter. Dip with a ¼-cup measure and pour onto hot griddle, greasing griddle if necessary. Turn flapjacks as soon as tops are bubbly; bake to golden brown on other side.

• Serve at once with butter or margarine and table syrup, jam or jelly. Or squeeze a little lemon juice on hot cakes, sprinkle with sifted confectioners sugar and spread with canned apple pie slices or applesauce. Roll up flapjacks, sift on a little more confectioners sugar and serve at once. Makes about 18 (5″) flapjacks.

VARIATION

Spiced Yeast-leavened Flapjacks: Add ⅛ tsp. each ginger and nutmeg with the sugar and salt.

Note: You can freeze Yeast-leavened Flapjacks. Place waxed paper between cooled baked cakes and stack in a rigid freezer container. Cover, seal and label. Store up to 3 months in freezer. When ready to use flapjacks, place the frozen cakes under broiler, turning them after a few minutes to thaw and heat thoroughly.

Buckwheat Cakes for Breakfast

A stack of hot buckwheat cakes with plenty of butter and syrup often cheerfully starts a cold, wintry day for country people. These griddlecakes may be old-fashioned, but they taste as good as ever. Farmers, no matter how low the mercury goes in their thermometers, spend considerable time outdoors doing chores and errands. They know buckwheat cakes stick to the ribs and give them that well-fed feeling that defies cold.

Young women, inexperienced in making these yeast-leavened griddlecakes, will find our recipe easy to follow. They and experienced pancake makers will like the results they get with it. You do some of the fixing the night (or several hours) before you bake the cakes. With a few quick additions at mealtime, the batter is ready to bake almost before the coffee is done.

It's an old country custom to stir up enough batter to have some left over to simplify the next baking. Our recipe shows how to do it.

BUCKWHEAT CAKES

To please the men, keep the starter ready and the griddle handy to use

1	c. sifted all-purpose flour
3½	c. buckwheat flour
1	tsp. salt
1	pkg. active dry yeast
4	c. warm water (110 to 115°)
2	tsp. granulated sugar
2	tblsp. dark brown sugar
¾	tsp. baking soda
1	tblsp. salad oil

• Combine all-purpose and buckwheat flours. Stir in salt.

• Sprinkle yeast on ¼ c. warm water; stir to dissolve.

• Dissolve 2 tsp. sugar in remaining 3¾ c. warm water; cool to lukewarm.

Add lukewarm water mixture and yeast to flours. Stir to mix thoroughly. Cover and let stand overnight or several hours at room temperature. Batter should no more than half fill bowl.

• When ready to bake pancakes, stir down batter and add brown sugar, baking soda and oil. Stir to mix.

• Dip batter with ¼-cup measure; bake on lightly greased, preheated griddle (hot enough that a few drops of water dropped on it dance about). Brown on both sides, turning once. Serve hot with butter or margarine and table syrup. Makes 5 cups batter.

STARTER FOR MORE BUCKWHEAT CAKES

• The leftover batter becomes the starter. Pour it into a glass or plastic container with tight fitting lid. Fill container no more than half full of batter. Cover and place in refrigerator. It will keep several days.

HOW TO USE BUCKWHEAT CAKE STARTER

• Remove starter from refrigerator the night (or several hours) before you wish to bake cakes. Pour it into a mixing bowl and add 1 c. lukewarm water for every cup buckwheat flour you add to starter. Stir to blend, cover and let stand at room temperature.

• When ready to bake cakes, stir down batter. Add 1 tsp. salt, 2 tblsp. brown sugar, ¾ tsp. baking soda and 1 tblsp. salad oil. Stir to blend.

• Bake like Buckwheat Cakes, saving out batter to store in refrigerator to make starter for the next batch of pancakes.

Popular Pizza for Impromptu Parties

If you like a crisp pizza crust, this recipe is for you. We tried many different ones, but this one rated highest with taste-testers, among them some teen-agers.

With cans of pizza sauce in the cupboard, mozzarella cheese in the refrigerator and frozen pizza dough in the freezer, you're only minutes away from hearty refreshments that young people really like. Our youthful taste-testers rated pork sausage the most popular for pizza topping; the more highly seasoned pizza sausage, second place. But they enjoyed all the toppings we suggest. You'll almost always have at least one of these on hand.

POPULAR PIZZA

A treat for teens! Keep dough in freezer ready to fill and bake

1   pkg. active dry yeast
1 ¼ c. warm water (110 to 115°)
3 ½ to 4 c. sifted all-purpose flour
½   tsp. salt
Pizza Filling

• Sprinkle yeast on warm water; stir to dissolve. Add 2 c. flour and salt. Beat thoroughly. Stir in remaining flour. Turn onto lightly floured board and knead until smooth and elastic, about 10 minutes.

• Place in lightly greased bowl; turn dough over to grease top. Cover and let rise in warm place until doubled, about 30 minutes.

• Turn onto board and knead just long enough to force out large bubbles. Divide in half. Roll each half

to make an 11″ circle. Stretch each circle to fit an oiled 12″ pizza pan. Add filling (recipes follow).
· Bake in very hot oven (450°) 20 to 25 minutes. Exchange position of pans on oven racks once during baking to brown pizzas the same. Makes 2 pizzas.

Note: If you do not have pizza pans, use baking sheets. Roll each half of dough into a 12×10″ rectangle, or one that almost fills your baking sheet. Place on oiled baking sheets and build up edges slightly. Fill and bake like pizzas in round pizza pans.

PIZZA FILLINGS

Hamburger Filling: Spread 1 (8 oz.) can pizza sauce over dough in each pizza pan (you'll use 2 [8 oz.] cans). Brown 1 lb. ground beef in skillet and drain; divide in half and sprinkle evenly over sauce in pizza dough. Then sprinkle evenly over each pizza 1½ c. shredded mozzarella cheese (about 12 oz. cheese for both pizzas). Bake as directed.

Ham and Salami Filling: Spread 1 (8 oz.) can pizza sauce over dough in each pizza pan. Alternate strips of boiled ham and salami on sauce (about 4 slices ham and 6 slices salami, cut in strips, for both pizzas). Sprinkle each pizza with 1½ c. shredded mozzarella cheese. Bake.

Sausage Filling: Spread 1 (8 oz.) can pizza sauce over dough in each pizza pan. Brown 1 lb. bulk pork sausage in skillet, drain and divide in half. Spread evenly over sauce in pizza dough. Then sprinkle 1½ c. shredded mozzarella cheese over each pizza. Bake as directed.

Choice of Pizza Fillings: Fill dough in each pizza pan with 1 (8 oz.) can pizza sauce and sprinkle on each 1½ c. shredded mozzarella cheese. Cook 1 lb. pizza sausage in skillet, drain and divide in half. Sprinkle evenly over pizza dough in pans filled with sauce and cheese. Or instead of pizza sausage, top with anchovies, mushrooms, sliced ripe olives, sardines or miniature frankfurters. Bake as directed.

To Freeze Pizza Dough: When you divide the risen dough in half, roll each into an 11″ circle. Place in oiled pizza pan with double thickness of waxed paper between circles. (Or roll each half of dough into a 12×10″ rectangle, place on oiled baking sheet with waxed paper between rectangles). Wrap and freeze. Keeps up to 1 week.

To Use Frozen Pizza Dough: Remove from freezer and let stand at room temperature 20 minutes. With fingers pull and stretch circles to cover pizza pans. (Or stretch rectangles of dough almost to edges of baking sheet and make small rim around edge.) Fill and bake as directed.

CINNAMON SWIRLS

Glazed doughnuts that look like cinnamon rolls—perfect with coffee

1 ¾ c. milk
⅓ c. sugar
¼ c. butter
2 tsp. salt
2 pkgs. active dry yeast
½ c. warm water (110 to 115°)
6 to 7 c. sifted all-purpose flour
2 tblsp. sugar
1 tblsp. cinnamon
Cinnamon Glaze

• Scald milk; add ⅓ c. sugar, butter and salt. Cool to lukewarm.
• Sprinkle yeast on warm water; stir to dissolve. Stir into lukewarm milk mixture. Add enough flour gradually to make a stiff dough. Turn onto lightly floured board; knead until smooth and satiny, about 7 minutes. Place in a lightly greased bowl and turn dough over to grease top. Cover and let rise in a warm place until doubled, 1 to 1½ hours.
• Meanwhile, combine 2 tblsp. sugar and cinnamon.
• Turn dough onto board and divide in half. Roll one half to make an 18×8″ rectangle; sprinkle half the sugar-cinnamon mixture evenly over top. Starting at long side, roll up as for jelly roll and seal edges. Cut with strong thread or sharp knife into 1″ slices. Place on ungreased baking sheets. Repeat with remaining half of dough. Do not cover. Let rise in warm place until light, 30 to 45 minutes.
• Fry in deep hot fat (375°) 1 to 2 minutes on each side; do not brown too much. Drain on paper towels. While warm, drizzle from teaspoon with Cinnamon Glaze. Makes 3 dozen.

Cinnamon Glaze: Combine 1 c. sifted confectioners sugar, ½ tsp. cinnamon and 1 tblsp. plus 2 tsp. milk. Stir until smooth.

Doughnuts on Sticks

Thread a few centers cut from doughnuts on a wooden skewer (from the meat market) and fry like doughnuts. Youngsters love them.

POTATO DOUGHNUTS

Keep some of these potato doughnuts in the freezer to serve with coffee.
From Cooking for Company

1 ¾ c. milk
½ c. shortening
½ c. sugar
½ c. mashed potatoes
1 pkg. active dry yeast
½ c. warm water (110 to 115°)
2 eggs, beaten
½ tsp. vanilla
6 ½ to 7 c. sifted all-purpose flour
1 tsp. baking powder
2 tsp. salt

• Scald milk; stir in shortening, sugar and mashed potatoes. Cool to lukewarm. Blend well.
• Sprinkle yeast over warm water and stir until yeast is dissolved. Add to milk mixture. Stir in beaten eggs and vanilla.
• Sift 6½ c. flour with baking powder and salt; add gradually to yeast mixture, mixing well after each addition. Add another ½ c. flour if needed to make a soft dough you can handle (use no more than necessary). Turn into greased bowl; turn dough over to grease top. Cover and let rise in warm place until doubled, about 1½ hours.
• Roll to ½″ thickness on floured board. Cut with floured doughnut cutter, reserving centers to make Pecan Rolls (recipe follows).
• Place cut-out doughnuts on waxed paper; cover with cloth and let rise in warm place until doubled, about 30 minutes.
• Fry a few doughnuts at a time in hot salad oil (375°). Drain on absorbent paper. Spread warm dough-

nuts with a thin glaze made of confectioners sugar and milk, or shake them in a bag containing sugar to coat them. Makes about 4 dozen doughnuts.

Pecan Rolls from Potato Doughnut Centers: Lightly grease 12 medium-size (2½″) muffin-pan cups. In the bottom of each cup, place 1 tsp. brown sugar, 1 tsp. light corn syrup, ½ tsp. water, 3 pecan halves and 3 or 4 raisins. Arrange 4 doughnut centers on top, cover with cloth and let rise in warm place until doubled, about 30 minutes. Bake in moderate oven (350°) 25 to 30 minutes. Makes 12 rolls.

SOUR DOUGH STARTER

This recipe and those for Sour Dough Biscuits and Silver Dollar Hotcakes are from Cooking for Company

½   pkg. active dry yeast (1 ¼ tsp.)
2   c. sifted all-purpose flour
2   tblsp. sugar
2 ½ c. water

• Combine the ingredients in a stone crock or glass or pottery bowl. Beat well. Cover with cheesecloth and let stand 2 days in a warm place.

SOUR DOUGH BISCUITS

These biscuits are light and fluffy— they have that marvelous tangy taste

1 ½ c. sifted all-purpose flour
2   tsp. baking powder
¼   tsp. baking soda (½ tsp. if
        Starter is quite sour)
½   tsp. salt
¼   c. butter or margarine
1   c. Sour Dough Starter

• Sift dry ingredients together. Cut in butter with pastry blender. Add Starter and mix.
• Turn dough out on a lightly floured board. Knead lightly until satiny.
• Roll dough ½″ thick. Cut with floured 2½″ cutter. Place biscuits in well-greased 9″ square baking pan. Brush with melted butter. Let rise about 1 hour in a warm place.
• Bake in hot oven (425°) 20 minutes. Makes 10 biscuits.

Note: To replenish Starter, stir in 2 c. warm (not hot) water and 2 c. flour.

SILVER DOLLAR HOTCAKES

Serve with butter and lots of "lick," the cowboy's term for sweet syrup

1 c. Sour Dough Starter
2 c. unsifted all-purpose flour
2 c. milk
1 tsp. salt
2 tsp. baking soda
2 eggs
3 tblsp. melted shortening
2 tblsp. sugar

• About 12 hours before mealtime, mix Starter, flour, milk and salt; let stand in a bowl covered with cheesecloth. Set in a warm place.
• Just before baking cakes, remove 1 c. batter to replenish Starter in crock. To the remaining batter in the bowl, add baking soda, eggs, shortening and sugar. Mix well.
• Bake cakes the size of silver dollars on a lightly greased, hot griddle. For thinner hotcakes, add more milk to the batter. Makes about 30 cakes.

Newer Ways to Bake Bread

Country people like homemade breads. We have ample proof of this in our visits with members of the FARM JOURNAL Family Test Group and other readers, and in our letters from them. One woman reflected a general attitude when she said it doesn't make too much difference what else she has for a meal if she serves bread she baked. This desire to please with food their husbands and children most enjoy is an important reason why women frequently bake yeast breads.

Time is the problem. Today's living loads women with many duties, not only in the house, but also outside on the farm and in their communities. Sometimes it takes a lot of planning to get yeast breads in the oven and out with just the right lapses for kneading and for baking.

Recognizing this situation, home economists in the test kitchens of flour milling and yeast companies work constantly to develop methods that will shorten the time needed and lessen the work in bread baking. We give you examples of their various methods—Can-Do-Quick, CoolRise, Easy Mixer, Instant Blend and Short-Cut Mixer and Rapidmix Methods.

All these newer yeast bread recipes call for unsifted all-purpose flour measured by spooning into a cup and leveling off with the straight edge of a knife (rye and whole wheat flours are measured the same way). Most specify the use of active dry yeast, which now comes in finer particles than formerly and requires no predissolving in water. The electric mixer takes over most of the work in mixing and helps develop gluten, the protein in flour that enables breads to hold their shape.

Back of these methods is the desire not only to make bread faster and more easily but also to produce loaves, rolls and coffee breads of excellent quality. We believe you will find one method (or more) that seems tailor-made for you and the minutes you have available.

The Conventional Method, featured on the preceding pages, is the basic one—the newer ways are offshoots of it. This section deals with them.

Can-Do-Quick Breads

As with all the newer methods of making yeast breads, this one is faster than the Conventional. You cut time required for making bread by one third. Developed by home economists in Betty Crocker Kitchens, the bread soon won a nickname, C.D.Q.—short for Can-Do-Quick.

Buttermilk is the liquid and you do not scald it. The electric mixer does most of the mixing, you knead the dough 5 minutes and then shape and place it in the pan for its one rising. You let the dough rise until doubled with the center of the loaf about 2" above the pan. Home economists in Betty Crocker Kitchens measure the height with a ruler (they keep rulers handy also for measuring the size of dough rectangles, circles and roll-ups —good idea for your kitchen).

The high-rise loaves that result from this method are beautiful. They brown well and the bread has an even, fine texture. The flavor is somewhat different from that of many yeast breads due to the combination of yeast and baking powder for leavening. Some of the rolls and biscuits of the early West had this same type of leavening. A Colorado rancher, eating with apparent enjoyment a buttered slice from a fresh-baked loaf of C.D.Q. bread, said: "The taste is wonderful. It reminds me of the taste of those bread-like rolls and biscuits we used to have at cattlemen's dinners and sometimes at cow camps."

An Indiana farmer's wife who has tried this method volunteers: "I do hope we'll have a good crop of tomatoes this year so we can make tomato sandwiches with C.D.Q. Cheese Bread. We like the bread for sandwiches, also for toast under creamed chicken, tuna and dried beef. But I get hungry thinking how good the bread will be with sliced, red-ripe tomatoes and curly ribbons of cooked bacon."

C.D.Q. WHITE BREAD

Tall, handsome loaf of white bread

2   pkgs. active dry yeast
¾   c. warm water (105 to 115°)
1¼ c. buttermilk
4½ to 5 c. all-purpose flour
¼   c. shortening
2   tblsp. sugar
2   tsp. baking powder
2   tsp. salt
Soft butter

• Grease a dull aluminum (anodized), glass or darkened metal 9×5×3" loaf pan (these pans encourage browning).
• Dissolve yeast in warm water in large mixer bowl. Add buttermilk, 2½ c. flour, the shortening, sugar, baking powder and salt. Blend 30 seconds with electric mixer on low speed, scraping sides and bottom of bowl. Beat 2 minutes on medium speed.
• Stir in remaining 2 to 2½ c. flour. (Dough should remain soft and and slightly sticky.) Knead 5 minutes, or about 200 turns on a generously floured board.
• Roll dough into an 18×9" rectangle. Roll up from short side as for jelly roll. With side of hand, press each end to seal. Fold ends under

loaf. Place, seam side down, in loaf pan. Brush loaf lightly with butter. Let rise in warm place (85°) until doubled, about 1 hour. (Dough in center comes about 2″ above pan.) • Heat oven to 425°. Oven rack should be in lowest position or bread will brown too quickly. Bake loaf 30 to 35 minutes. Remove from pan and brush with butter; cool on wire rack. Makes 1 loaf. (You can make 2 smaller loaves by using 2 [8½×4½×2½″] loaf pans instead of the 9×5×3″ pan. Divide the dough in half after kneading.)

Note: To make 2 large loaves C.D.Q. White Bread, double all ingredients except the yeast. Blend 1 minute with electric mixer on low speed, scraping sides and bottom of bowl. Beat 4 minutes on medium speed. Stir in remaining flour. Divide in half. Knead each half 5 minutes.

VARIATIONS

C.D.Q. Cheese Bread: Follow recipe for C.D.Q. White Bread, but omit the shortening. Stir in 1 c. shredded sharp natural Cheddar cheese with second addition of flour.

C.D.Q. Whole Wheat Bread: Follow the recipe for C.D.Q. White Bread, except substitute 1½ c. all-purpose flour and 1 c. whole wheat flour for first addition of flour; substitute 2 c. whole wheat flour for second addition of flour.

C.D.Q. Pan Rolls: Follow recipe for C.D.Q. White Bread, but roll dough into a 13×9″ rectangle. Place in greased 13×9×2″ baking pan. Score dough 1″ deep with knife to make 12 rolls. Let rise until doubled. Bake 20 to 25 minutes.

C.D.Q. SWEET DOUGH

For coffee breads and sweet rolls

2   pkgs. active dry yeast
½   c. warm water (105 to 115°)
1¼ c. buttermilk
2   eggs
5½ c. all-purpose flour
½   c. butter or margarine, softened
½   c. sugar
2   tsp. baking powder
2   tsp. salt

• Dissolve yeast in warm water in large mixer bowl. Add buttermilk, eggs, 2½ c. flour, the butter, sugar, baking powder and salt. Blend 30 seconds with mixer on low speed, scraping sides and bottom of bowl. Beat 2 minutes on medium speed.
• Stir in remaining 3 c. flour. (Dough should remain soft and slightly sticky.) Knead 5 minutes, or about 200 turns on a lightly floured board.
• Shape into coffee breads or rolls, as desired (recipes follow). Let rise in warm place (85°) until doubled, about 1 hour. (Dough is ready to bake if slight dent remains when touched with finger.)
• Heat oven to 375°.

C.D.Q. CINNAMON COFFEE BREAD

Make this for your coffee party

1   recipe for C.D.Q. Sweet Dough
½   c. butter, melted
¾   c. sugar
1   tsp. cinnamon
½   c. finely chopped nuts

• Cut dough into 1″ pieces; form each piece into a ball. Roll in butter and then in mixture of sugar, cinnamon and nuts. Place 1 layer of

balls so that they barely touch in well-greased 10″ tube pan. (If pan has removable bottom, line with aluminum foil.) Add another layer of balls.
• Let rise until doubled.
• Bake in moderate oven (375°) 1 hour. Loosen from pan. Invert pan so butter-sugar mixture runs down over loaf. To serve, break apart with 2 forks. Makes 1 loaf.

C.D.Q. CINNAMON ROLLS

Frost these rolls if you like

½ recipe for C.D.Q. Sweet Dough
1 tblsp. soft butter
¼ c. sugar
1 tsp. cinnamon

• Roll dough into a 12×7″ rectangle. Spread with butter. Sprinkle with sugar and cinnamon. Roll up, beginning at wide side. Seal well by pinching edge of dough. Cut into 12 slices.
• Place in greased 9″ round layer cake pan, leaving a small space between each slice. Let rise until doubled.
• Bake in moderate oven (375°) 25 minutes. Remove from pan to wire rack. Makes 12 rolls.

VARIATION

C.D.Q. Pecan Rolls: Make like Cinnamon Rolls, but bake slices in pan coated with ¼ c. melted butter, ¼ c. firmly packed brown sugar and ½ c. broken pecans. Bake 30 to 35 minutes.

Wrap cooled baked bread and rolls in aluminum foil for freezing and you can reheat them without unwrapping.

C.D.Q. CHEESE DIAMONDS

Unusual and distinctive—pretty, too

1 (8 oz.) pkg. cream cheese, softened
¼ c. sugar
3 tblsp. all-purpose flour
1 egg yolk
½ tsp. grated lemon peel
1 tblsp. lemon juice
½ recipe for C.D.Q. Sweet Dough
½ c. jam
Chopped nuts

• Beat cream cheese and sugar until light and fluffy. Stir in flour, egg yolk, lemon peel and juice.
• Roll dough into 15″ square. Cut in 25 (3″) squares. Place on greased baking sheets and put 1 tblsp. cheese mixture in center of each square. Bring 2 diagonally opposite corners to center of each square. Overlap them slightly; pinch together.
• Let rise until doubled.
• Bake in moderate oven (375°) 15 minutes.
• Meanwhile, heat jam until melted. Brush lightly over baked rolls while hot. Sprinkle with nuts. Makes 25 diamonds.

CoolRise Method of Bread Baking

One of the big problems of women who like to bake bread is to find time to carry the process through from start to finish. This is especially true of farm women with many outside chores and errands interrupting their days. The CoolRise Method, developed by home economists in the Robin Hood Flour Kitchens, answers the problem. It takes from 45 minutes to an hour to mix, knead, shape and place the dough in pans; you let it rise from 2 to 24 hours in the refrigerator. During the 45 minutes to an hour you have 20 minutes off while the dough rests on the board. This resting takes the place of the first rising in the Conventional Method.

With new CoolRise recipes the yeast does not need to be dissolved and hot water (hot to the touch, not scalding) is used right from the kitchen tap.

Some women tell us they like to get the dough in the refrigerator right after breakfast when they are in their kitchens attending to other duties. For instance, they say they can get the dishes in the dishwasher while it rests. After shaping the dough and placing it in pans, they refrigerate it until time to get the evening meal. If the oven is not in use, they bake the bread then. Otherwise they bake it while clearing up after dinner or supper. Several women also mentioned that they often refrigerate dough for coffee breads and rolls overnight, baking it in the morning to serve hot for breakfast.

We had good luck when we baked CoolRise breads in our Test Kitchens. We found that those baked with dough refrigerated from 2 to 8 hours had the best volume. However, the bread was acceptable even when we held the dough longer.

For success with this method, follow recipes carefully. They are designed for the CoolRise Method. Resist the temptation to improvise. By changing ingredients, you throw recipes off balance and affect your results. The ideal temperature of the refrigerator is 38 to 41°. It's also important to use the size of pans specified in recipes. Flours labeled "high protein" or "for breadmaking" are good selections for this method. Cover dough loosely when placing in refrigerator for rising—allow space for it to rise.

These breads have a tasty yeast flavor, fine and even texture and golden brown crusts. FARM JOURNAL readers tell us the CoolRise Method enables them to bake the refrigerated dough at the strategic time, just before a meal or coffee party. There's nothing like the aroma of baking yeast bread to make their families and guests hungry and eager to eat!

COOLRISE WHITE BREAD

They'll be glad to come home to this

5½ to 6½ c. all-purpose flour
2 pkgs. active dry yeast
2 tblsp. sugar
1 tblsp. salt
¼ c. soft margarine (½ stick)
2¼ c. hot tap water
Salad oil

• Combine 2 c. flour, undissolved yeast, sugar and salt in large bowl. Stir well to blend. Add soft margarine.
• Add hot tap water to ingredients in bowl all at once.
• Beat with electric mixer at medium speed 2 minutes. Scrape sides of bowl occasionally.
• Add 1 c. more flour. Beat with electric mixer at high speed 1 minute, or until thick and elastic. Scrape sides of bowl occasionally.
• Stir in just enough remaining flour to make a soft dough that leaves the

sides of the bowl. Turn onto floured board. Round up into ball.
• Knead 5 to 10 minutes or until dough is smooth and elastic. Cover with plastic wrap and with towel. Let rest on board 20 minutes. Punch down.
• Divide dough into 2 equal portions. Roll each portion into an 8×12″ rectangle. Roll up tightly into loaves beginning at 8″ side. Seal lengthwise edge and ends well. Tuck ends under.
• Place in greased 8½×4½×2½″ loaf pans. (Correct pan size is important for best results.)
• Brush surface of dough with salad oil. Cover pans loosely with waxed paper, brushed with oil, and then with plastic wrap.
• Refrigerate 2 to 24 hours at moderately cold setting. When ready to bake, remove from refrigerator. Uncover.
• Let stand 10 minutes while preheating oven.
• Puncture any surface bubbles with oiled toothpick just before baking.
• Bake at 400° for 35 to 40 minutes, or until done.
• Remove from pans immediately. Brush top crust with margarine if desired. Cool on rack. Makes 2 loaves.

COOLRISE HONEY LEMON WHOLE WHEAT BREAD

You'll like the taste of lemon

3¼ to 4¼ c. all-purpose flour
2   pkgs. active dry yeast
1   tblsp. salt
¼   c. honey
3   tblsp. softened margarine
    or shortening
1   tblsp. grated lemon peel

2¼ c. hot tap water
2   c. whole wheat flour
Salad oil

• Combine 2 c. all-purpose flour, undissolved yeast and salt in large bowl. Stir well to blend.
• Add honey, margarine and lemon peel.
• Add hot tap water all at once.
• Beat with electric mixer at medium speed 2 minutes. Scrape bowl occasionally.
• Add 1 c. whole wheat flour. Beat with electric mixer at high speed for 1 minute, or until thick and elastic. Scrape bowl occasionally.
• Stir in remaining 1 c. whole wheat flour with wooden spoon. Then gradually stir in just enough remaining all-purpose flour to make a soft dough that leaves the sides of bowl. Turn onto floured board; round up into ball.
• Knead 5 to 10 minutes, or until dough is smooth and elastic. Cover with plastic wrap and then with towel. Let rest 20 minutes. Punch down.
• Divide dough into 2 equal portions.
• Roll each portion into an 8×12″ rectangle. Roll up tightly into loaves beginning at 8″ side. Seal lengthwise edge and ends. Tuck ends under.
• Place in greased 8½×4½×2½″ loaf pans. (Correct pan size is important for best results.)
• Brush surface of dough with oil. Cover pans loosely with waxed paper, and then with plastic wrap.
• Refrigerate 2 to 24 hours at moderately cold setting. When ready to bake, remove from refrigerator. Uncover.
• Let stand 10 minutes while preheating oven.

· Puncture any surface bubbles with oiled toothpick just before baking.

· Bake at 400° for 30 to 40 minutes, or until done. Bake on lower oven rack for best results.

· Remove from pans immediately. Brush top crust with margarine if desired. Cool on racks. Makes 2 loaves.

Higher than 5,000 Feet

If the recipe for CoolRise bread calls for 2 pkgs. active dry yeast, use only 1 pkg. if you live in an area with an altitude of more than 5,000 feet. In other recipes, watch the bread during the rising period. Doughs rise faster at higher elevations.

COOLRISE HEIDELBERG RYE BREAD

Cocoa adds a good flavor you can't recognize—a sandwich special

3   c. all-purpose flour
2   pkgs. active dry yeast
¼   c. cocoa
1   tblsp. sugar
1   tblsp. salt
1   tblsp. caraway seeds
⅓   c. molasses
2   tblsp. softened margarine
      or shortening
2   c. hot tap water
2½ to 3½ c. rye flour
Salad oil

· Combine 2 c. all-purpose flour, undissolved yeast, cocoa, sugar, salt and caraway seeds in large bowl. Stir well to blend. Add molasses and softened margarine.

· Add hot tap water to ingredients in bowl all at once.

· Beat with electric mixer at medium speed 2 minutes. Scrape bowl occasionally.

· Add remaining all-purpose flour. Beat with electric mixer at high speed 1 minute, or until thick and elastic. Scrape bowl occasionally.

· Gradually stir in just enough rye flour with wooden spoon to make a soft dough that leaves the sides of bowl. Turn onto floured board. Round up into ball.

· Knead 5 to 10 minutes, or until dough is smooth and elastic.

· Cover with plastic wrap, then with towel. Let rest 20 minutes. Then punch down. Divide into 2 equal parts.

· Shape each portion into round loaf, or roll each portion into an 8×15″ rectangle on lightly greased board. Roll up tightly like jelly roll, beginning with long side. Seal lengthwise edge and ends well. Tuck ends under. Taper ends by rolling gently with hands.

· Place in greased 8″ pie pans or on greased baking sheets. Brush surface of dough with oil. Cover loosely with plastic wrap.

· Refrigerate 2 to 24 hours at moderately cold setting. When ready to bake, remove from refrigerator. Uncover. Let stand 10 minutes while preheating oven.

· Slash an X in tops of round loaves with sharp knife or slash tops of long loaves diagonally at 2″ intervals just before baking.

· Bake at 400° for 30 to 35 minutes, or until done.

· Remove from pans immediately. Brush top crust with margarine if desired. Cool on racks. Makes 2 loaves.

COOLRISE FRENCH BREAD

Get it ready in the morning and bake for barbecue as guests arrive

5½ to 6½ c. all-purpose flour
2 pkgs. active dry yeast
1 tblsp. sugar
1 tblsp. salt
2 tblsp. softened margarine
   or shortening
2¼ c. hot tap water
Salad oil
Cold water

• Combine 2 c. flour, undissolved yeast, sugar and salt in large bowl. Stir well to blend. Add softened margarine.
• Add hot tap water to ingredients in bowl all at once.
• Beat with electric mixer at medium speed 2 minutes. Scrape bowl occasionally.
• Add 1 c. more flour. Beat with electric mixer at high speed 1 minute, or until thick and elastic. Scrape bowl occasionally.
• Gradually stir in just enough of remaining flour with wooden spoon to make a soft dough that leaves the sides of bowl. Turn out on floured board. Round up to make a ball.
• Cover with plastic wrap, then with towel. Let rest 20 minutes on board. Punch down.
• Divide dough into 2 equal portions.
• Roll each portion into an 8×15″ rectangle on lightly greased board. Roll up tightly like jelly roll, beginning with long side. Seal lengthwise edge and ends well. Tuck ends under. Taper ends by rolling gently with hand.
• Place, seam side down, on greased baking sheets.

• Brush lightly with oil. Cover baking sheets loosely with plastic wrap.
• Refrigerate 2 to 24 hours at moderately cold setting. When ready to bake, remove from refrigerator. Uncover.
• Let stand 10 minutes while preheating oven.
• Brush gently with cold water. Slash tops of loaves diagonally at 2″ intervals with sharp knife just before baking.
• Bake at 400° for 30 to 40 minutes, or until done.
• Remove from baking sheets immediately. Cool on racks. Makes 2 long loaves.

COOLRISE BRIOCHE

Refrigerate overnight and bake for breakfast; serve hot as the French do

6 to 7 c. all-purpose flour
2 pkgs. active dry yeast
½ c. sugar
1½ tsp. salt
½ c. softened butter or margarine
1⅓ c. hot tap water
4 eggs (at room temperature)
1 egg yolk
1 tblsp. milk

• Combine 2 c. flour, undissolved yeast, sugar and salt in large bowl. Stir well to blend. Add softened butter.
• Add hot tap water to ingredients in bowl all at once.
• Beat with electric mixer at medium speed 2 minutes. Scrape bowl occasionally.
• Add the 4 eggs and 1½ c. more flour. Beat with electric mixer at high speed 1 minute, or until thick and elastic. Scrape bowl occasionally.

• Gradually stir in enough of remaining flour with wooden spoon to make a soft dough that leaves the sides of bowl. Turn onto floured board; round up into ball.

• Knead 5 to 10 minutes, or until dough is smooth and elastic. Cover with plastic wrap, then a towel. Let rest 20 minutes; then punch down.

• Divide dough into unequal portions —one about three fourths of dough, the other about one fourth of dough.

• Cut larger portion into 30 equal pieces. Shape into smooth balls. Place in buttered muffin-pan cups; flatten slightly.

• Cut smaller portion into 30 equal pieces. Shape into smooth balls.

• Make deep indentation in center of each large ball. Press rough end of small ball into each indentation.

• Cover pans loosely with plastic wrap.

• Refrigerate 2 to 24 hours at moderately cold setting. When ready to bake remove from refrigerator. Uncover.

• Let stand 10 minutes while preheating oven.

• Bake at 350° for 15 minutes. Remove from oven and brush with egg yolk combined with milk. Return to oven immediately and bake 5 to 10 minutes longer, or until done. Bake on lower rack of oven for best results.

• Remove from pans immediately. Cool on racks. Makes 30 rolls.

Country Christmas Gift

Wrap a loaf of your best coffee bread in plastic wrap to show off its beauty. Present it in a straw basket trimmed with holly or red ribbons.

COOLRISE SWEET DOUGH

This is the start of many good things

5   to 6 c. all-purpose flour
2   pkgs. active dry yeast
½ c. sugar
1 ½ tsp. salt
½ c. softened butter or margarine
1 ½ c. hot tap water
2   eggs (at room temperature)
Salad oil

• Combine 2 c. flour, undissolved yeast, sugar and salt in large bowl. Stir well to blend. Add softened butter.

• Add hot tap water to ingredients in bowl all at once.

• Beat with electric mixer at medium speed 2 minutes. Scrape bowl occasionally.

• Add eggs and 1 c. more flour. Beat with electric mixer at high speed 1 minute, or until thick and elastic. Scrape bowl occasionally.

• Gradually stir in just enough of remaining flour with wooden spoon to make a soft dough that leaves the sides of bowl. Turn onto floured board. Round up into ball.

• Knead 5 to 10 minutes, or until dough is smooth and elastic. Cover with plastic wrap, then a towel.

• Let rest 20 minutes on board. Punch down.

• Divide and shape as desired into 2 coffee cakes or 2½ dozen rolls (recipes follow).

• Place in greased pans or on greased baking sheets. An 8" square pan is ideal for 1 dozen pan rolls, and a 13×9×2" pan for 1½ dozen pan rolls.

• Brush surface with oil. Cover pans loosely with plastic wrap.

• Refrigerate 2 to 24 hours at moderately cold setting. When ready to bake, remove from refrigerator. Uncover.
• Let stand 10 minutes while preheating oven.
• Puncture any surface bubbles with oiled toothpick just before baking.
• Bake in 375° oven 20 to 25 minutes, or until done. Bake on lower oven rack position for best results.
• Remove from pans or baking sheet immediately. Cool on racks.
• Brush with butter, or frost and decorate as desired. Makes 2 coffee cakes or 2½ to 3 dozen pan rolls.

COOLRISE CHERRY NUT COFFEE BREAD

Festive—looks like ribbon candy

1   recipe CoolRise Sweet Dough
¾   c. cut-up maraschino cherries, drained
1   c. chopped walnuts
Sweet Cheese Spread

• Make CoolRise Sweet Dough, but stir in cherries with wooden spoon after adding eggs and 1 c. flour and beating 1 minute at high speed.
• When ready to shape, after punching down dough, divide in half. Roll 1 portion into a 6×20″ rectangle on lightly buttered board. Cut lengthwise into 5 equal strips.
• Shape into a 6×10″ rectangle by placing first strip, cut edge down, on greased baking sheet or in a 15½×-10½″ (jelly roll) pan. Bring one end of strip around to start a second row. Join strips as you go, making rows 10″ long. Tuck loose ends under. The completed coffee bread will look like ribbon candy.

• Sprinkle with ½ c. walnuts. Press together gently to make rows of dough stand up.
• Repeat procedures with the remaining dough and walnuts.
• Cover baking sheets loosely with plastic wrap.
• Refrigerate as recipe for CoolRise Sweet Dough directs.
• Bake at 375° for 25 to 30 minutes, or until done. Bake on lower oven rack position for best results.
• Remove from baking sheets immediately. Cool on racks.
• Frost when cool with Sweet Cheese Spread. Serve remaining spread with coffee bread. Makes 2 coffee breads.

Sweet Cheese Spread: Combine 1 (8 oz.) pkg. cream cheese, softened, and ½ c. confectioners sugar. Stir until smooth.

COOLRISE APRICOT COFFEE BRAID

A beautiful braid—and the apricot-ginger taste is a luscious surprise

¾   c. dried apricots
1½ c. water
⅓   c. sugar
½   tsp. ground ginger
1   recipe CoolRise Sweet Dough

• Simmer apricots in water, uncovered, 20 to 30 minutes, or until tender. Drain; mash fruit well with fork.
• Add sugar and ginger to fruit; stir to mix well. Cool.
• When ready to shape CoolRise Sweet Dough, divide in half. Round up each portion.
• Roll 1 portion into a 9×14″ rectangle on lightly greased board. Cut lengthwise into 3 equal strips.
• Spread 2 tblsp. apricot mixture

down center of each strip. Pinch lengthwise edges of strip together to form a rope.

• Braid 3 ropes together on a lightly greased baking sheet, starting at center and braiding to each end. Tuck ends under braid.

• Repeat procedure with second half of dough and apricot mixture.

• Cover loosely with plastic wrap.

• Refrigerate as recipe for CoolRise Sweet Dough directs.

• Bake at 375° for 25 to 30 minutes, or until done. Bake on lower oven rack position for best results.

• Remove from baking sheets immediately. Cool on racks. Brush while warm with melted butter, frost when cool with Confectioners Sugar Frosting (see Index) or sprinkle with sifted confectioners sugar. Makes 2 coffee braids.

COOLRISE TWIRLS

Taste appeal—morning, noon or night

1 recipe CoolRise Sweet Dough
Confectioners Sugar Frosting
(see Index)

• Prepare CoolRise Sweet Dough as directed. When ready to shape, divide dough into 2 equal portions. Round up each portion into a ball.

• Roll each portion into a 12×15″ rectangle on a lightly greased board. Cut into 15 (1″) strips.

• Twist each strip. Hold one end of twisted strip on lightly greased baking sheet and wind strip around this point. Tuck ends under. Place rolls several inches apart.

• Cover loosely with plastic wrap.

• Refrigerate as CoolRise Sweet Dough recipe directs.

• Bake at 375° for 15 to 20 minutes, or until done.

• Remove from baking sheet immediately. Cool on racks.

• Frost while warm with Confectioners Sugar Frosting. Decorate as desired. Makes 2½ dozen rolls.

COOLRISE MEXICAN SWEET ROLLS

So good you'll want to double the recipe

½ c. sugar
½ c. flour
½ tsp. cinnamon
⅓ c. finely chopped nuts
¼ c. melted butter
1 egg white, beaten until frothy
½ recipe CoolRise Sweet Dough

• Combine sugar, flour, cinnamon, nuts, melted butter and egg white.

• Prepare CoolRise Sweet Dough as recipe directs. When ready to shape, pinch off pieces of dough of equal size and shape into balls 1½″ in diameter. Place on greased baking sheet about 3″ apart. Press each ball down to flatten slightly.

• With finger, make indentation in center of each ball. Top with spoonful of sugar-cinnamon mixture.

• Cover loosely with plastic wrap.

• Refrigerate as CoolRise Sweet Dough recipe directs.

• Bake at 375° for 15 to 20 minutes, or until done.

• Remove from baking sheet immediately. Cool on racks. Makes 18 rolls.

Note: Use 1 recipe for CoolRise Sweet Dough and double amounts of the other ingredients to make 36 rolls for a coffee party.

Easy Mixer Breads

One newer way of making yeast breads and rolls that has caught on with busy women—especially the younger, inexperienced bread bakers —is the Easy Mixer Method developed in the Ann Pillsbury Kitchens. As the name of the bread implies, the electric mixer does lots of the work. There's no milk to scald; you use instant nonfat dry milk. The fat you add is easy-to-measure salad oil.

You toss the dough on the floured board a few times and then you knead it 1 minute. You shape it next and put it in the pans to rise—it rises only once. The fast-fix bread is attractive and of good texture. It has a pleasant, delicate yeasty taste.

A FARM JOURNAL food editor first tasted Easy Mixer Bread on an irrigated farm in western Nebraska. Her young hostess baked and served with pride—the first yeast bread she ever made. Another editor tasted Sunburst Coffee Bread, made by this method, at an Iowa coffee party.

We pass along to you Ann Pillsbury recipes for these two and other Easy Mixer Breads. Do notice the dark Peasant Bread. This cereal-rich loaf is the beginning of marvelous sandwiches, and it's also especially good with cold cuts.

EASY MIXER WHITE BREAD

Correctly named—it's really easy

2½ c. warm water (110 to 115°)
2 pkgs. active dry yeast
½ c. instant nonfat dry milk
2 tblsp. sugar
1 tblsp. salt
⅓ c. salad oil
7 to 7½ c. all-purpose flour

· Pour warm water into large mixer bowl. Sprinkle yeast over top. Add dry milk, sugar, salt, oil and about 3¼ c. flour. Blend well on low speed of mixer, scraping sides and bottom of bowl. Beat 3 minutes on medium speed.

· Gradually add remaining flour by hand to make a very stiff dough. Cover and let rest 15 minutes.

· Toss dough on floured surface until no longer sticky. Knead until smooth, about 1 minute. Divide in half. With rolling pin, roll each half into a 12×6" rectangle. Roll up tightly like a jelly roll, starting with the 6" side. Seal edges and ends. Place, seam side down, in well-greased 8½×4½×3" or 9×5×3" loaf pans.

· Cover and let rise in warm place until doubled, 1 to 1½ hours.

· Bake in hot oven (400°) 30 to 35 minutes. Remove from pans immediately. Cool on wire racks. Makes 2 loaves.

VARIATIONS

Easy Mixer Herb Bread: Substitute brown sugar for white. Add ½ tsp. caraway seeds and ¼ tsp. thyme before adding flour. Shape into 2 long loaves. Place on greased baking sheets. Cover and let rise until doubled; then bake in hot oven (400°) 30 to 35 minutes.

Easy Mixer Patio Loafers: Pat half the dough in each greased 9×5×3" loaf pan. Spread each with ¼ c. barbecue sauce and sprinkle with ⅓ c. quick-cooking rolled oats and

⅓ c. chopped cashew nuts. With blunt knife, cut each loaf into 1" strips crosswise. Cover and let rise 30 to 45 minutes. Bake in hot oven (400°) 25 to 30 minutes. Remove from pans immediately; cool on wire racks. To reheat, wrap in aluminum foil and place on barbecue grill.

EASY MIXER PEASANT BREAD

Looks like pumpernickel but contains no rye flour—a tasty cereal bread

2 ½ c. warm water (110 to 115°)
2   pkgs. active dry yeast
2   c. all-bran cereal
2   c. bite-size shredded wheat
2   tblsp. brown sugar
1   tblsp. salt
1   tblsp. salad oil
2   tblsp. bottled brown bouquet
     sauce
4 ½ to 5 ½ c. all-purpose flour
1   egg white
1   tblsp. water

• Measure warm water into large mixer bowl. Sprinkle yeast over water. Add cereals, sugar, salt, oil, bouquet sauce and 2 c. flour. Blend well. Beat 3 minutes at medium speed of electric mixer.
• By hand, gradually add enough of remaining flour to form a very stiff dough, mixing well after each addition. Cover dough with plastic wrap or waxed paper; let rest 15 minutes.
• Toss on floured surface until dough no longer is sticky. Knead until smooth, about 1 minute.
• Divide dough in half. Roll each half into an 8×15" rectangle. Roll tightly as for jelly roll, starting with longest side. Seal edge and ends; fold under ends. Roll gently to taper ends.

• Place on greased baking sheets. Place in plastic bags and let rise in warm place about 1½ hours (or place in refrigerator overnight).
• Carefully brush dough with egg white diluted with 1 tblsp. cold water.
• Bake at 400° for 25 to 30 minutes. Remove from baking sheets at once and cool on wire racks. Makes 2 long loaves.

Note: If you wish, just after brushing dough with egg white-water mixture, sprinkle loaves with 1 tblsp. caraway seeds.

EASY-DO SWEET DOUGH

First step to coffee breads and rolls

1   c. warm water (110 to 115°)
1   pkg. active dry yeast
¼   c. instant nonfat dry milk
¼   c. sugar
¼   c. salad oil
1   egg
2   tsp. salt
3 ½ to 4 c. all-purpose flour

• Measure warm water into large mixer bowl. Sprinkle yeast over water. Add dry milk, sugar, oil, egg, salt and about 1½ c. flour. Blend well. Beat 3 minutes with electric mixer at medium speed, scraping sides and bottom of bowl.
• By hand, gradually add remaining flour to form a stiff dough, beating well after each addition. Cover; let rest 15 minutes.
• Toss dough on lightly floured board until it no longer is sticky. Knead 1 minute. Shape and bake as following recipes suggest.

Pan Rolls: Pat Easy-Do Sweet Dough into 2 well-greased 8" square pans. Spread dough with soft butter. Using a blunt knife, cut into squares, cutting almost through dough. Let rise until doubled. Bake in hot oven (400°) 20 to 25 minutes. Remove from pans and break rolls apart. Makes about 32 rolls, 16 to a pan.

Cloverleaf Rolls: Divide Easy-Do Sweet Dough into 20 pieces of equal size. Roll quickly into balls and place in greased muffin-pan cups. Brush tops with soft butter. Using a blunt knife or kitchen scissors, cut each ball in half, or in thirds for cloverleafs. Let rise until doubled. Bake in moderate oven (375°) 15 to 20 minutes. Makes 20 rolls.

Parkerhouse Rolls: Roll out Easy-Do Sweet Dough on floured surface to make a 20×8" rectangle. Cut in half lengthwise, making 2 (20×4") strips. Spread lengthwise half of each strip with 1 tblsp. soft butter. With knife handle, crease each strip lengthwise, slightly off center on unbuttered side. Fold along crease. Gently pull and stretch each strip to 24". Cut each into 12 (2") or 8 (3") slices. Place on greased baking sheet. Cover and let rise until doubled. Bake in moderate oven (375°) 10 to 15 minutes. Serve hot. Makes 24 or 16 rolls.

Tiny Tea Rolls: Divide Easy-Do Sweet Dough in half; roll out each half to make a 15×10" rectangle. Spread 1 rectangle with 2 tblsp. butter; sprinkle with mixture of ¼ c. sugar, 2 tblsp. slivered almonds and 1 tsp. grated orange peel.
• Spread second rectangle with 2 tblsp. butter; sprinkle with mixture of

¼ c. firmly packed brown sugar, ¼ c. chopped walnuts and ½ tsp. cinnamon. Starting with long side, roll up each rectangle jelly-roll fashion; seal edges and ends. Place, seam side down, on greased baking sheets. Using a sharp knife, cut rolls halfway through at 1" intervals. Let rise. Bake in moderate oven (375°) 20 to 25 minutes. Makes 30 rolls.

Note: After shaping roll dough and placing on baking sheet or in pans, you can slip pans into loose plastic bags and refrigerate several hours before baking. Bake immediately after removing from refrigerator.

EASY MIXER SUNBURST COFFEE BREAD

Crescent rolls form lovely sunburst

¾ c. shredded coconut
1 c. warm water (110 to 115°)
1 pkg. active dry yeast
¼ c. instant nonfat dry milk
¼ c. sugar
2 tsp. salt
¼ c. salad oil
1 egg
3½ to 4 c. flour
2 tblsp. soft butter
1½ tblsp. grated orange peel
½ c. sugar
Orange Glaze

• Toast coconut by spreading in shallow pan and heating in slow oven (300°) until golden brown, 15 to 18 minutes. Stir occasionally to brown evenly.
• Measure warm water into large mixer bowl. Sprinkle yeast over water. Add dry milk, ¼ c. sugar, salt, salad oil, egg and 1½ c. flour. Beat

3 minutes with electric mixer on medium speed, scraping sides and bottom of bowl.
• Gradually stir in enough remaining flour by hand to form a stiff dough. Beat well after each addition. Cover and let rest 15 minutes.
• Toss dough on lightly floured board until it no longer is sticky. Knead 1 minute. Divide dough in half. Roll each half to make a 12" circle. Spread each circle with 1 tblsp. soft butter. Combine grated orange peel with ½ c. sugar and ½ c. toasted coconut; sprinkle half of mixture over each circle of dough.
• Cut each circle in 12 wedges. Roll up, starting at wide end and roll to the point. Arrange 12 rolls, pointed side down, on greased baking sheet in circle to make a ring or sunburst. Repeat with remaining 12 rolls. Cover and let rise in warm place until doubled, 1 to 1½ hours.
• Bake in moderate oven (350°) until golden brown, 20 to 25 minutes. Loosen rolls with a spatula and gently slide each sunburst onto wire rack. Drizzle Orange Glaze over each sunburst and sprinkle with remaining ¼ c. toasted coconut.

Orange Glaze: Combine 1 c. sifted confectioners sugar, ½ tsp. grated orange peel and 1½ tblsp. orange juice.

Test for Doneness

Tap the loaf of yeast bread with a forefinger. If you hear a hollow sound, the bread is done. If you get a "solid" sound, bake the bread a few minutes longer and test again.

Instant Blend and Short-Cut Mixer Methods

The fragrance of baking yeast bread has been filling many test kitchens recently. And there's an air of excitement akin to that when home economists were discovering you don't always have to cream butter and sugar together to make good cakes. But the emphasis now is on faster and easier ways to make good yeast breads.

Out of Red Star Yeast's Home Service Department come two ways, related to each other, Instant Blend and Short-Cut Mixer Methods. In neither of them do you dissolve the active dry yeast in water before you add it with other ingredients to the mixing bowl. The Instant Blend system enables you to use all your choice Conventional Method recipes, including the treasures of farm and ranch women in this cookbook. This is how you can adapt your recipes to it:
• Measure liquids, including the amount of water formerly used to dissolve yeast (and spices, honey, molasses or oil if these are in the ingredients), shortening, sugar and salt into a saucepan. Heat at low temperature to *warm* (120 to 130°).
• Measure the same amount of flour in cups as total liquid into mixer bowl (count each egg in a recipe as ¼ c. liquid, but do not add yet). Add undissolved yeast to flour in mixer bowl; stir to blend.
• Pour contents of saucepan into dry ingredients. If there are eggs, add now. Beat 30 seconds with electric

mixer at low speed, scraping bowl.
• Beat 3 minutes at high speed,
scraping bowl occasionally. Stop
mixer; stir in fruits, nuts, etc. and
dark flours if used.
• Stir in enough remaining flour, a
little at a time, to make a soft dough
—less flour is needed by this method.
Turn dough onto lightly floured surface. Then follow your conventional
recipe.

The Short-Cut Mixer Method and
the Instant Blend Method are the
same until you turn the dough onto
the board and knead it. Then they
part company. Our recipes from Red
Star Kitchens illustrate the Short-
Cut Mixer way—recipes must be
designed especially for this method—
but here are the highlights: After
kneading the dough, you cover it
with bowl or pan and let rest 20 minutes. Then you shape and place it in
pans or on baking sheets and let rise
until doubled. You bake the bread
after only this one rising!

When we made the first bread by
this method, we used a candy thermometer to test the temperature of
liquids heated to 120 to 130°. A few
drops on the inside of the wrist soon
taught us how to judge the temperature in other bakings without a
thermometer.

The Short-Cut Mixer breads and
rolls are quick and easy to bake,
light and even in texture. The crusts
brown beautifully. Our taste-testers
gave all of them high ratings. And our
home economists adopted the idea of
using a tent of aluminum foil over
rising bread dough instead of covering with a towel.

As the result of our testing experi-
ence, we recommend that you bake

all these fast breads the first chance
you have. We'll be surprised if you
don't get many compliments on them.

SHORT-CUT MIXER WHITE BREAD
*Smaller loaves are fine to slice and
toast, but use the pan size you have*

4½ to 5 c. all-purpose flour
2   pkgs. active dry yeast
1   c. milk
¾   c. water
2   tblsp. shortening
2   tblsp. sugar
2   tsp. salt

• Measure 1¾ c. flour into large
mixer bowl. Add yeast; stir to blend.
• Measure milk, water, shortening,
sugar and salt into saucepan. Blend;
heat until warm (120 to 130°).
• Pour into flour-yeast mixture. Beat
30 seconds with electric mixer at
low speed, scraping bowl constantly.
• Beat 3 more minutes at high speed,
scraping bowl occasionally. Stop
mixer.
• Gradually stir in more flour to form
a soft dough. Knead until smooth,
5 to 10 minutes.
• Cover dough with bowl or pan and
let rest 20 minutes. Grease 2 (8½ ×-
4½ ×2½″) loaf pans or 1 (9×5×-
3″) loaf pan.
• For 2 loaves, divide dough in half
and pat or roll each half into a 7×-
14″ rectangle; for 1 loaf pat into
an 8×16″ rectangle. Roll from narrow side, pressing dough into roll
at each turn. Press ends to seal.
Place in pans or pan. Cover with
aluminum foil tent.
• Let rise on rack over hot water until doubled, 30 to 45 minutes. Center
of small loaves will be about ½″

above pan edges, center of large loaf 2" above pan edges.
• Bake in hot oven (400°) 35 to 40 minutes. Remove from pans to racks. Brush with butter for soft crusts. Makes 1 (2 lb.) loaf or 2 (1 lb.) loaves.

SHORT-CUT MIXER WHOLE WHEAT BREAD

So good it disappears like magic

2 ¾ to 3 ¼ c. all-purpose flour
2   pkgs. active dry yeast
¾   c. milk
¾   c. water
2   tblsp. shortening
2   tblsp. honey
2   tsp. salt
1   egg (room temperature)
1 ½ c. whole wheat flour

• Measure 1¾ c. all-purpose flour into large mixer bowl. Add yeast; blend.
• Measure milk, water, shortening, honey and salt into saucepan. Blend. Heat until warm (120 to 130°).
• Pour into flour-yeast mixture; add egg. Beat 30 seconds with electric mixer at low speed, scraping bowl constantly.
• Beat 3 more minutes at high speed, scraping bowl occasionally. Stop mixer.
• Add whole wheat flour, then gradually add more all-purpose flour to form a soft dough. Turn onto lightly floured board and knead until smooth, 5 to 10 minutes.
• Cover dough with bowl or pan. Let rest for 20 minutes. Grease 2 (8½ × 4½ × 2½") loaf pans or 1 (9 × 5 × 3") loaf pan.
• For 2 loaves, divide dough in half and roll each half into a 7 × 14"

rectangle; for 1 loaf roll dough into an 8 × 16" rectangle. Roll from narrow side, pressing dough into roll at each turn. Press ends to seal. Place in pans. Cover with tent of aluminum foil.
• Let rise on rack over hot water until doubled, 30 to 45 minutes. Dent remains when finger is pressed gently on sides of loaves.
• Bake in moderate oven (375°) 35 to 45 minutes. Remove from pans, brush with butter for soft crusts and cool on racks. Makes 2 (1 lb.) loaves or 1 (2 lb.) loaf.

SHORT-CUT MIXER RYE BREAD

Dill-caraway flavors are delightful

2 ¾ to 3 ¼ c. all-purpose flour
2   pkgs. active dry yeast
1   c. milk
¾   c. water
2   tblsp. shortening
2   tblsp. sugar
2   tsp. salt
2   tsp. caraway seeds
2   tsp. dill weed
1 ½ c. rye flour

• Measure 1¾ c. all-purpose flour into large mixer bowl. Add yeast and blend.
• Measure milk, water, shortening, sugar, salt, caraway seeds and dill weed into saucepan. Blend. Heat until warm (120 to 130°).
• Pour into flour-yeast mixture. Beat 30 seconds with electric mixer at low speed, scraping bowl constantly.
• Beat 3 more minutes at high speed, scraping bowl occasionally. Stop mixer.
• Add all the rye flour, then gradually stir in more all-purpose flour to form

a fairly stiff dough. Knead until smooth, 5 to 10 minutes.

• Cover dough with bowl or pan. Let rest 20 minutes. Grease 1 (12×-15½") baking sheet or 2 (9") round layer cake pans.

• Divide dough in half. Round each part into a smooth ball; place on opposite corners of greased baking sheet or in round layer pans. Slash tops of loaves with sharp knife. Cover with tent of aluminum foil.

• Let rise on rack over hot water until doubled, 30 to 45 minutes. Dent remains when finger is pressed gently on sides of loaves.

• Bake in moderate oven (375°) 35 to 45 minutes. Remove from baking sheet or pans to cooling racks. Brush tops of loaves with cold water for chewy crusts. Makes 2 (1 lb.) loaves.

SHORT-CUT MIXER SWEET DOUGH

Makes superior coffee breads—fast

4 ½ to 5 c. all-purpose flour
2   pkgs. active dry yeast
¾   c. milk
½   c. water
½   c. shortening (part butter)
½   c. sugar
1   tsp. salt
2   eggs (room temperature)

• Measure 1¾ c. flour into large mixer bowl. Add yeast and blend.

• Measure milk, water, shortening, sugar and salt into saucepan. Blend. Heat until warm (120 to 130°).

• Pour into flour-yeast mixture. Add eggs. Beat 30 seconds with electric mixer at low speed, scraping bowl constantly.

• Beat 3 more minutes at high speed,

scraping bowl occasionally. Stop mixer.

• Gradually stir in more flour to make a soft dough. Dough will be rather sticky. Knead on lightly floured board until smooth, 5 to 10 minutes.

• Cover with bowl or pan. Let rest 20 minutes. Shape as desired (see recipes that follow). Cover with tent of aluminum foil.

• Let rise on a rack over hot water until doubled, 40 to 60 minutes. Dent remains when finger is pressed gently on sides of dough.

• Bake as directed in recipe.

SHORT-CUT MIXER STREUSEL COFFEE BREAD

Taste-testers praised this treat

1   recipe Short-Cut Mixer Sweet Dough
½   c. butter
½   c. all-purpose flour
1   c. sugar
2   tsp. cinnamon

• After dough has rested 20 minutes, divide in half. Roll or pat one half into a greased 13×9×2" pan. Divide remaining half in 2 equal parts. Press each piece of dough into 2 greased 8 or 9" round layer cake pans.

• Mix butter, flour, sugar and cinnamon together to make small crumbs. Sprinkle over dough in pans.

• Cover with tent of aluminum foil and let rise over warm water until doubled, 30 to 45 minutes. Dough is doubled if dent remains when finger is pressed gently on side of dough.

• Bake in moderate oven (375°) 25 to 30 minutes. Remove from pans and cool on racks. Makes 1 (13×9×2") and 2 (8 or 9") round coffee breads.

Note: You can bake dough in 2 greased 13×9×2" pans if you like.

SHORT-CUT MIXER
DATE FILLED CRESCENTS

Interesting shape—fine to tote

1 recipe Short-Cut Mixer Sweet
   Dough
2 c. cut-up dates
1 c. cut-up peeled apple
1 c. water
¼ c. orange juice
½ c. chopped nuts

• While Sweet Dough rests on board, combine dates, apple, water and orange juice in saucepan. Cook over low heat, stirring often, until mixture is thickened. Add nuts; cool to luke-warm.
• After dough has rested 20 minutes on board, divide in half. Roll one half into a 12" square. Cut diagonally to make 2 triangles. Spread each with one fourth of the lukewarm date-apple filling. Roll up, starting at wide side. Seal edges well. Place, seam side down, on greased baking sheet; curve ends to make crescents. Repeat with other half of dough and filling.
• Cover with tents of foil and let rise over hot water until doubled, 40 to 60 minutes. Dent remains when finger is pressed gently on side of dough.
• Bake in moderate oven (350°) 25 to 35 minutes, or until well browned.

Remove from pans and cool on racks. Spread with Thin Confectioners Sugar Icing (see Index) or sprinkle with confectioners sugar before serving. Makes 4 crescents (about 12 servings).

SHORT-CUT MIXER SWEET WHIRLS

King-size with color-bright centers

4½ to 5 c. all-purpose flour
2 pkgs. active dry yeast
¾ c. milk
½ c. water
¼ c. butter
¼ c. shortening
½ c. sugar
1 tsp. salt
1 tsp. grated orange peel
¼ tsp. cardamom
2 eggs (room temperature)
Jam or canned fruit pieces
Quick Orange Glaze

• Measure 1¾ c. flour into large mixer bowl. Add yeast; blend.
• Measure milk, water, butter, shortening, sugar, salt, orange peel and cardamom into saucepan. Blend. Heat until warm (120 to 130°).
• Pour into flour-yeast mixture. Add eggs. Beat 30 seconds with electric mixer at low speed, scraping bowl constantly.
• Beat 3 minutes longer at high speed, scraping bowl occasionally. Stop mixer.
• Gradually stir in more flour to make a soft dough. The dough will be

BRIOCHE—When you want to serve rolls that taste as good as they look, bake feather-light Brioche. Recipe (page 55) gives pointers on handling these fluffy puffs of dough so topknots will stay in their proper place.

slightly sticky. Turn onto lightly floured board and knead until smooth, 5 to 10 minutes.

• Cover dough with bowl or pan; let rest 20 minutes. Roll into an 8×16″ rectangle. Cut into 16 strips lengthwise. Roll each on board to make smooth; then twist, holding one end of strip down on greased baking sheet, winding remainder of strip round and round. Tuck end under. Cover with aluminum foil tent.

• Let rise on racks over hot water until doubled, 40 to 60 minutes. Dough is doubled if dent remains when finger is pressed gently on sides of dough. Just before baking, make a small dent in center of each whirl and fill with 1 tsp. jam or with a few pieces of drained, canned fruit, such as peaches, apples or apricots.

• Bake in moderate oven (375°) 12 minutes, or until light brown. Remove from oven and brush with Quick Orange Glaze; return to oven and bake 5 minutes longer. Remove from baking sheets and cool on racks. Makes 16 large rolls.

Quick Orange Glaze: Stir together ¼ c. orange juice and 2 tblsp. sugar.

SHORT-CUT MIXER PEPPERY CHEESE DOUGH FOR ROLLS

Serve rolls made with this dough with salads—they'll make a hit

4½ to 5 c. all-purpose flour
2 pkgs. active dry yeast
1 c. milk
½ c. water
¼ c. shortening
2 tblsp. sugar
1 ½ tsp. salt
2 tsp. coarse black pepper
1 egg (room temperature)
¼ lb. coarsely shredded
     sharp Cheddar cheese
     (1 c.)

• Measure 1¾ c. flour into large mixer bowl. Add yeast; stir to blend.

• Measure milk, water, shortening, sugar, salt and pepper into saucepan. Blend; heat until warm (120 to 130°).

• Pour into flour-yeast mixture; add egg. Beat 30 seconds with electric mixer at low speed, scraping bowl constantly. Beat 3 minutes at high speed. Stop mixer.

• Stir in cheese and gradually add more flour to make a soft dough. Turn onto lightly floured board and knead until smooth, 5 to 10 minutes.

• Cover dough with bowl or pan. Let rest 20 minutes. Shape the rolls (directions follow).

• Place on greased baking sheets, cover with aluminum foil tent and let rise on rack over hot water until doubled, 30 to 45 minutes. Gently press finger into side of dough; if dent remains, dough is doubled.

• Bake in moderate oven (375°) 15 to 20 minutes. Remove to rack at once, brush with butter and cool, or serve warm.

Short-Cut Mixer Peppery Cheese Twists: Roll ½ dough for Peppery Cheese Rolls into a 7×16″ rectangle. Brush half the dough the long way

CRUSTY BROWN ROLLS—You can bake all these golden Crusty Brown Rolls from one recipe (page 32): French Rolls (bottom and left), Salty Caraway Crescents and Bread Sticks (top) and Onion Rolls (right).

with 2 tblsp. softened butter. Fold unbuttered side over buttered side. Cut strips 1" wide from long sides. Twist each strip several times, stretching slightly, until two ends when brought together on greased baking sheet form a figure 8. Place a little apart on baking sheet. Let rise and bake as directed in recipe for Peppery Cheese Dough for Rolls. Makes 16 twists.

Short-Cut Mixer Peppery Cheese Buns: Divide one half Peppery Cheese Dough into 10 equal pieces and shape into balls. Place on greased baking sheet and flatten. Slash an X lightly on tops. Let rise and bake as directed in recipe for Peppery Cheese Dough for Rolls. Makes 10 buns.

The Rapidmix Method

Rapidmix is a short-cut way to combine ingredients for yeast breads. This method was developed by home economists in Fleischmann's Yeast Test Kitchens. You do not dissolve the yeast in warm water. You blend it with other dry ingredients and then add the liquid. If it's more convenient for you, you can mix the dry ingredients a day ahead, or longer if kept in a cool, dry place. This is one way to get a head start on baking day.

If you are already a bread baker, you probably treasure a few recipes for bread made by the Conventional Method. You can use your own favorite recipes and convert them to this newer short-cut method. Also, you can adapt recipes from our Con-

ventional Method to Rapidmix. Here's how to do it:

· Measure all ingredients.
· Pour active dry yeast from the package into the large bowl of your electric mixer. Add one third of the flour called for in the recipe, and all the other dry ingredients. Stir to mix.
· Heat the liquid with the fat— —margarine, lard, butter or shortening—until warm. (When measuring liquid, be sure to add the water called for in Conventional Method to dissolve yeast. Add it to the milk if the recipe calls for milk.)
· Add liquid to the dry ingredients in the bowl. Beat 2 minutes with electric mixer at medium speed, scraping bowl occasionally.
· Add eggs, if used in recipe, and about ½ c. more flour; beat 2 minutes at high speed, scraping bowl occasionally.
· Gradually stir in enough of remaining flour by hand to make a soft dough that leaves the sides of the bowl.
· The dough is ready to turn from the bowl. At this stage you follow the rest of the Conventional Method recipe.

When we baked breads the Rapidmix way, we found the mixing quick and easy. The dough was a joy to work with and the breads were exceptionally light. Their taste was identical to that of the bread made by the same recipe with the Conventional Method.

We tried some of the breads made by long-time popular Fleischmann recipes which their home economists have converted to the Rapidmix Method. We believe you'll like these recipes.

RAPIDMIX WHITE BREAD

This dough really is easy to handle

5 ½ to 6 ½ c. all-purpose flour
3 tblsp. sugar
2 tsp. salt
1 pkg. active dry yeast
1 ½ c. water
½ c. milk
3 tblsp. margarine

• In a large bowl thoroughly mix 2 c. flour, sugar, salt and undissolved yeast.

• Combine water, milk and margarine in saucepan. Heat over low heat until liquids are warm (margarine does not need to melt). Gradually add to dry ingredients and beat 2 minutes with electric mixer at medium speed, scraping bowl occasionally. Add ¾ c. flour, or enough to make a thick batter. Beat at high speed 2 minutes, scraping bowl occasionally.

• Stir in enough remaining flour with spoon to make a soft dough. Turn out onto lightly floured board and knead until smooth and elastic, about 8 to 10 minutes.

• Place in greased bowl; turn dough over to grease top. Cover; let rise in warm place free from draft until doubled, about 1 hour.

• Punch down dough; turn onto lightly floured board. Cover and let rest 15 minutes. Divide dough in half; shape each half into a loaf. Place in greased 8½ × 4½ × 2½″ loaf pans. Cover; let rise in warm place free from draft until doubled, about 1 hour.

• Bake in hot oven (400°) 25 to 30 minutes, or until done. Remove from pans and cool on wire racks. Makes 2 loaves.

RAPIDMIX WHOLE WHEAT BREAD

Loaves have full rich wheaty flavor

4 ½ c. whole wheat flour
2 ¾ c. all-purpose flour (about)
3 tblsp. sugar
4 tsp. salt
2 pkgs. active dry yeast
1 ½ c. water
¾ c. milk
⅓ c. molasses
⅓ c. margarine

• Combine flours. In a large bowl thoroughly mix 2½ c. of the flour mixture with sugar, salt and undissolved yeast.

• Combine water, milk, molasses and margarine in a saucepan. Heat over low heat until the liquids are warm (margarine does not need to melt). Gradually add to dry ingredients and beat 2 minutes with electric mixer at medium speed, scraping sides of bowl occasionally. Add ½ c. flour mixture, or enough to make a thick batter. Beat 2 minutes at high speed, scraping bowl occasionally.

• Stir in enough remaining flour mixture to make a soft dough. (If necessary add additional all-purpose flour to obtain desired consistency.) Turn dough onto lightly floured board. Knead until smooth and elastic, about 8 to 10 minutes.

• Place in greased bowl; turn dough over to grease top. Cover; let rise in warm place free from draft until doubled, about 1 hour.

• Punch down; turn onto lightly floured board. Divide in half. Shape into loaves. Place in 2 greased 8½ ×- 4½ × 2½″ loaf pans. Cover; let rise in warm place free from draft until doubled, about 1 hour.

· Bake in hot oven (400°) about 25 to 30 minutes, or until done. Remove from pans and cool on wire racks. Makes 2 loaves.

RAPIDMIX RYE BREAD

Honey-sweetened loaves full of rye flavor—they're easy to make

2 ½ c. rye flour
2 ½ c. all-purpose flour (about)
1   tblsp. sugar
1   tblsp. salt
1   tblsp. caraway seeds
      (optional)
1   pkg. active dry yeast
1   c. milk
¾   c. water
2   tblsp. honey
1   tblsp. margarine
¼   c. cornmeal
1   egg white
2   tblsp. water

· Combine flours. In large bowl thoroughly mix 1⅔ c. flour mixture, sugar, salt, caraway seeds and undissolved yeast.
· Combine milk, ¾ c. water, honey and margarine in saucepan and heat over low heat until liquids are warm (margarine does not need to melt). Gradually add to dry ingredients and beat 2 minutes with electric mixer at high speed, scraping bowl occasionally. Add 1 c. flour mixture, or enough to make a thick batter. Beat at high speed 2 minutes, scraping bowl occasionally.
· Stir in enough flour mixture to make a soft dough. (If necessary, add additional all-purpose flour to make a soft dough.)
· Turn dough onto lightly floured board; knead until smooth and elastic,

about 8 to 10 minutes. Place in greased bowl; turn dough over to grease top. Cover; let rise in warm place free from draft until doubled, about 1 hour.
· Punch down; turn out onto lightly floured board. Divide in half; form each piece into a smooth ball. Cover and let rest 10 minutes. Flatten each piece slightly. Roll lightly on board under hands to taper the ends.
· Sprinkle 2 greased baking sheets with cornmeal. Place breads on baking sheets. Combine egg white and 2 tblsp. water; brush on breads. Let rise, uncovered, in a warm place free from draft, 35 minutes.
· Bake in hot oven (400°) about 25 minutes, or until done. Remove from baking sheets and cool on wire racks. Makes 2 loaves.

RAPIDMIX FAST-NIGHT CAKES

The Pennsylvania Dutch call these holeless doughnuts Fastnachts. They serve them on Shrove Tuesday, the night before the Lenten season begins

3 ¾ to 4 ¼ c. all-purpose flour
⅓   c. sugar
½   tsp. salt
1   pkg. active dry yeast
¼   c. margarine, softened (½
      stick)
1   c. very hot tap water
1   egg (at room temperature)
Salad oil

· In a large bowl thoroughly mix 1¼ c. flour, sugar, salt and undissolved yeast. Add softened margarine.
· Gradually add very hot tap water to dry ingredients and beat 2 minutes with electric mixer at medium speed, scraping bowl occasionally.

Add egg and ½ c. flour, or enough flour to make a thick batter. Beat at high speed 2 minutes, scraping bowl occasionally.
· Stir in enough flour to make a soft dough. Cover; let rise in warm place free from draft until doubled, about 1 hour.
· Turn dough onto lightly floured board; knead until smooth and elastic, about 8 to 10 minutes. Roll out to make an 8×16" rectangle. Cut into 2" squares. Cut a slit about ¼" deep (almost through the dough) in the top of each square. Place on ungreased baking sheets. Cover; let rise in warm place free from draft until doubled, about 45 minutes.
· Fry in deep hot salad oil (375°) until golden brown on both sides. Drain on paper towels. If desired, dip warm doughnuts in sugar with a little cinnamon added. Makes 32 doughnuts.

RAPIDMIX CHERRY-GO-ROUND

Here's a pretty coffee bread for your February festivities—and it's delicious

3½ to 4½ c. all-purpose flour
½ c. granulated sugar
1 tsp. salt
1 pkg. active dry yeast
1 c. milk
¼ c. water
½ c. margarine (1 stick)
1 egg (at room temperature)
½ c. all-purpose flour
½ c. chopped pecans
½ c. light brown sugar, firmly packed
1 (1 lb.) can pitted tart cherries, well drained
Confectioners Sugar Frosting

· In a large bowl mix 1¼ c. flour, granulated sugar, salt and undissolved yeast.
· Combine milk, water and margarine in saucepan. Heat over low heat until liquids are warm (margarine does not need to melt). Gradually add to dry ingredients and beat 2 minutes with electric mixer at medium speed, scraping bowl occasionally. Add egg and ¾ c. flour, or enough flour to make a thick batter. Beat at high speed 2 minutes, scraping bowl occasionally. Stir in enough additional flour to make a stiff batter. Cover dough tightly with aluminum foil and refrigerate at least 2 hours. (Dough may be kept in refrigerator 3 days.)
· When ready to shape dough, combine ½ c. flour, pecans and brown sugar.
· Turn dough onto lightly floured board; divide in half. Roll one half the dough into a 14×7" rectangle. Spread with ¾ c. cherries; sprinkle with half the brown sugar mixture. Roll up from long side as for jelly roll. Seal edges. Place, seam side down, in circle on greased baking sheet. Seal ends together firmly. Cut slits two thirds through ring at 1" intervals; carefully turn each section on its side. Repeat with remaining dough, cherries and brown sugar mixture.
· Cover; let rise in warm place free from draft until doubled, about 1 hour.
· Bake in moderate oven (375°) about 20 to 25 minutes, or until done. Remove from baking sheets and cool on wire racks. Frost while warm with Confectioners Sugar Frosting (see Index). Makes 2 coffee breads.

No-Knead Batter Breads

If you look through the yellowed pages of old cookbooks, you almost always find a couple of recipes for no-knead yeast breads that require no shaping into loaves. These were the timesavers for our busy grandmothers and the forerunners of today's batter breads, which home economists developed within the last 20 years.

Beating takes the place of kneading. You do not produce loaves with the even, fine texture of well-kneaded loaves, but you do get breads with that wonderful homemade taste. They are at their best when fresh-baked.

Success with these breads depends largely on not letting the dough rise too much. Spread the batter evenly in greased pans and smooth the tops with your hand, lightly floured. You may need to push the batter into pan corners with a rubber spatula. Cover and let rise in a warm place (85°) until almost doubled—never let it rise above the top of the pan. If you do, the bread will fall in the center during baking. In case the batter gets too light, turn it back into a bowl and beat 25 vigorous strokes. Then return it to greased pan, smooth the top and let rise again.

When you take baked loaves from the oven, remove them from pans at once and cool, right side up, on wire racks away from drafts before slicing. Brush tops with softened or melted butter while loaves are warm. The crust will be a dark brown and the surface will be rather rough. Slice batter breads a little thicker than the sliced bread you buy. Slices will be neater that way and will have a tempting home-baked look.

Here are recipes for batter breads and rolls that won the approval of our taste-testers. We include a modernized recipe for a perennial favorite, Sally Lunn Supper Loaf, named for an English girl who baked and sold a similar bread 200 years ago to enthusiastic customers. It's best served warm from the oven, as for supper, with the left over cold bread sliced, toasted and buttered for breakfast. Serve this appetizing treat with plenty of butter and one of your best homemade fruit spreads. Or do as the English do, and pass orange marmalade.

ANADAMA BATTER BREAD

Easy bread to make—no kneading, only one rising—has homemade taste

¾ c. boiling water
½ c. yellow cornmeal
3 tblsp. soft shortening
¼ c. light molasses
2 tsp. salt
1 pkg. active dry yeast
¼ c. warm water (110 to 115°)
1 egg
2 ¾ c. sifted all-purpose flour

• Stir together boiling water, cornmeal, shortening, molasses and salt. Cool to lukewarm.
• Sprinkle yeast on warm water; stir to dissolve.
• Add yeast, egg and 1¼ c. flour to cornmeal mixture. Beat with electric mixer at medium speed 2 minutes, scraping sides and bottom of bowl frequently. (Or beat 300 vigorous strokes by hand.))
• With spoon, beat and stir in remaining flour, a little at a time, until batter is smooth.
• Grease an 8½ ×4½ ×2½″ loaf pan and sprinkle with a little cornmeal and salt. Spread batter evenly in pan and, with floured hand, gently smooth top and shape loaf. Cover and let rise in warm place until batter just reaches the top of the pan, about 1½ hours.
• Bake in moderate oven (375°) 50 to 55 minutes, or until loaf tests done. (Tap with fingers. If there's a hollow sound, the loaf is done.) Crust will be a dark brown. Remove from pan to rack at once, brush top with melted butter. Cool in place free from drafts before slicing. Makes 1 loaf.

Note: You can bake the batter in a greased 9×5×3″ loaf pan. Let batter rise to 1″ from top of pan.

VARIATION

Oatmeal Batter Bread: Follow recipe for Anadama Batter Bread, but substitute ½ c. rolled oats for cornmeal. Omit sprinkling greased pan with cornmeal and salt.

PEANUT BATTER BREAD

Spread with butter and honey or jelly to treat the children

1 pkg. active dry yeast
1 ¼ c. warm water (110 to 115°)
¼ c. chunk style peanut butter
¼ c. brown sugar, firmly packed
2 tsp. salt
3 c. sifted all-purpose flour

• Sprinkle yeast on warm water; stir to dissolve. Beat in peanut butter, brown sugar, salt and 1½ c. flour. Beat 2 minutes with electric mixer at medium speed, scraping sides and bottom of bowl frequently. (Or beat 300 vigorous strokes by hand.)
• With spoon beat and stir in remaining flour, a little at a time. Stir until smooth.
• Cover, let rise in warm place free from drafts until doubled, about 45 minutes. Stir batter down by beating 25 vigorous strokes.
• Spread evenly in greased 9×5×3″ loaf pan. Pat top of loaf with hand, lightly floured, to smooth surface. Cover and let rise until doubled, about 40 minutes.
• Bake in moderate oven (375°) 45 minutes. (If loaf starts to brown too fast, cover loosely with aluminum foil the last 25 minutes of baking.) Or

bake until loaf has a hollow sound when tapped with a forefinger. Remove from pan at once. Cool on rack out of drafts before slicing. Makes 1 loaf.

Note: Add ¼ c. finely chopped peanuts with peanut butter for a more positive peanut flavor.

CHEESE-CARAWAY BATTER BREAD

Wonderful toasted—serve with salads

1 pkg. active dry yeast
1 c. warm water (110 to 115°)
1 c. grated Cheddar
   cheese (4 oz.)
1 tsp. caraway seeds
2 tblsp. shortening or margarine
2 tblsp. sugar
2 tsp. salt
3 c. sifted all-purpose flour

• Sprinkle yeast on warm water; stir to dissolve. Add cheese, caraway seeds, shortening, sugar, salt and 1½ c. flour. Beat with electric mixer at medium speed 2 minutes, scraping bottom and sides of bowl frequently. (Or beat 300 vigorous strokes by hand.)
• With spoon beat and stir in remaining flour, a little at a time. Stir until smooth.
• Cover, let rise in warm place free from drafts until just doubled, about 45 minutes. Stir down batter by beating 25 strokes.
• Spread evenly in greased 9×5×3″ loaf pan. Pat top of loaf gently with floured hand to smooth surface. Cover and let rise until doubled, about 40 minutes.
• Bake in moderate oven (375°) 45 minutes, or until loaf has hollow

sound when tapped with forefinger. Remove from pan at once. Cool on rack out of drafts before slicing. Makes 1 loaf.

SALLY LUNN SUPPER LOAF

Ideal hot bread for company supper

1 c. milk
1 pkg. active dry yeast
¼ c. warm water (110 to 115°)
½ c. butter
¼ c. sugar
3 eggs
4 c. sifted all-purpose flour
1 tsp. salt

• Scald milk; cool to lukewarm.
• Sprinkle yeast on warm water; stir to dissolve. Add to milk.
• Cream butter and sugar well; add eggs, one at a time, beating after each addition.
• Combine flour and salt.
• Alternately add yeast-milk mixture and flour to creamed butter and sugar, beating well after each addition. Beat until smooth. Cover and let rise in warm place until doubled, about 1 hour.
• Beat 25 vigorous strokes. Spread into a well-greased 10″ tube pan; smooth and even top with floured hand. Cover and let rise until doubled, 35 to 40 minutes.
• Bake in moderate oven (350°) about 40 minutes until crusty and brown, or until loaf tests done when tapped with fingers. Remove from pan to rack; brush top with butter. Serve warm. (Cut with electric knife if you have one.) Or slice cold bread, toast and butter. Makes 1 loaf.

DILLY CASSEROLE BREAD

A prize winner in a national baking contest—good for sandwich making

1   pkg. active dry yeast
¼   c. warm water (110 to 115°)
1   c. large curd creamed cottage cheese
2   tblsp. sugar
1   tblsp. instant minced onion
1   tblsp. butter
2   tsp. dill seeds
1   tsp. salt
¼   tsp. baking soda
1   egg
2¼ to 2½ c. sifted all-purpose flour

• Sprinkle yeast over warm water; stir to dissolve.
• Heat cottage cheese until lukewarm; combine in mixing bowl with sugar, onion, butter, dill seeds, salt, baking soda, egg and yeast.
• Add flour, a little at a time, to make a stiff batter, beating well after each addition. Cover and let rise in warm place until doubled, 50 to 60 minutes.
• Stir down with 25 vigorous strokes. Turn into well-greased 1½-qt. round (8") casserole. Cover and let rise in warm place until light, 30 to 40 minutes.
• Bake in moderate oven (350°) 40 to 50 minutes. Cover with foil last 15 minutes of baking if necessary to prevent excessive browning. Makes 1 loaf.

Beat—Don't Knead

In batter breads, beating takes the place of kneading. You have beaten enough when the batter leaves the sides of bowl.

DOUGH FOR BATTER ROLLS

This refrigerator dough promises good eating—just follow recipes

2   pkgs. active dry yeast
2   c. warm water (110 to 115°)
½   c. sugar
¼   c. shortening or margarine
1   egg
2   tsp. salt
6½ c. sifted all-purpose flour (about)

• Sprinkle yeast on warm water in large mixer bowl; stir to dissolve. Add sugar, shortening, egg, salt and 3 c. flour. Beat with electric mixer at medium speed until smooth, about 2 minutes, scraping sides and bottom of bowl occasionally. Or beat by hand until smooth.
• With spoon beat in enough remaining flour, a little at a time, until soft dough is easy to handle. Place in greased bowl; turn dough over to grease top.
• Cover with aluminum foil; place in refrigerator at least 2 hours before using. Dough may be kept as long as 3 days, but punch it down occasionally as it rises. Use in the following recipes.

IRISH PAN ROLLS

Parsley-sprinkled rolls with a light taste of garlic—you'll like these

¼   Dough for Batter Rolls
¼   tsp. garlic salt
1   tblsp. melted butter or margarine
1½ tblsp. finely snipped parsley

• Shape dough in 1" balls. Place in lightly greased 8" round layer cake

pan. Cover; let rise in warm place until doubled, about 35 minutes.
• Combine garlic salt and butter. Brush lightly over tops of rolls. Sprinkle with parsley, cut fine with scissors. Cover; let rise about 5 minutes.
• Bake in hot oven (400°) 15 minutes, or until done. Remove from pan and place on rack. Makes about 18 rolls.

HERB CLAWS

Unusual shape is eye-catching—team rolls with green or tuna salad

¼ Dough for Batter Rolls
1 tblsp. soft butter or margarine
2 tsp. cheese-garlic salad dressing mix

• Roll dough into a 12×9″ rectangle. Spread with butter. Sprinkle evenly with salad dressing mix. Cut in 3″ squares. Roll up each square as for jelly roll; place on lightly greased baking sheet, seam side down.
• With sharp knife make cuts ½″ apart halfway through each roll; curve rolls slightly to separate cuts. Cover and let rise in warm place just until doubled, 25 to 30 minutes.
• Bake in hot oven (400°) 12 minutes, or until done. Makes 12 rolls.

Note: The cheese-garlic flavor is not pronounced; bake the rolls according to recipe the first time to find out if you want to sprinkle on a litle more of the salad dressing mix the next baking.

ITALIAN CRESCENTS

Excellent rolls for barbecue supper with grilled steaks or lamb chops

¼ Dough for Batter Rolls
2 tblsp. ketchup
2 tblsp. grated Parmesan cheese
1 tsp. orégano

• Roll dough into 12″ circle. (Circle will be about ¼″ thick.) Spread with ketchup; sprinkle with cheese and orégano. Cut in 12 or 16 pie-shaped pieces. Beginning at wide or rounded end, roll up. Place, point side down, on greased baking sheet. Curve ends slightly to make crescents.
• Cover and let rise in warm place until just doubled, about 30 minutes.
• Bake in hot oven (400°) 15 minutes, or until done. Makes 12 or 16 rolls.

POPPY SEED CLOVERLEAFS

Fancy looking and good tasting— serve warm to impress your guests

¼ Dough for Batter Rolls
1 egg yolk
2 tblsp. water
Poppy seeds

• Form small pieces of dough into ¾″ balls. Place 3 balls in each greased muffin-pan cup.
• Mix egg yolk and water; brush over tops of rolls. Sprinkle with poppy seeds. Cover and let rise in warm place just until doubled, about 30 minutes.
• Bake in hot oven (400°) 12 minutes, or until browned. Makes about 12 rolls.

Quick Breads for All Occasions

The two important types of bread are yeast and quick breads. So far in our cookbook we have given you descriptions of and recipes for all kinds of yeast breads. Now we'll present the versatile quick breads. Country women rely on them because they are so adaptable—fast enough to make for everyday meals and fancy enough for guests.

Fortunately, there's a quick bread for every kind of occasion. Hot biscuits, muffins, pancakes, coffee bread and waffles brighten breakfasts. They're also at home on luncheon and supper tables. Popovers, like muffins, appear at party luncheons. Waffles, once reserved for special breakfasts, now take the spotlight in guest suppers, frequently with each person pouring batter on the iron and baking his own waffle. Drop small dumplings (also a quick bread) atop the meat-vegetable stew and let everyone enjoy the transformation of an everyday dish into something distinctive.

Nut and/or fruit breads are ideal for sandwich making. Spread thin slices of these moist, luscious loaves with softened butter or cream cheese and you quickly produce appetizing open-face sandwiches.

Quick breads, like yeast breads, depend on bubbles of carbon dioxide gas for their lightness. Yeast breads rise more slowly because, as previously explained, the yeast plants manufacture the bubbles as they multiply. With quick breads, the bubbles start forming in the mixing bowl as soon as you combine the liquid with baking powder and/or baking soda and the acid (such as in molasses, sour milk or buttermilk). These bubbles expand and form tiny air pockets, which make doughs and batters light.

Another difference between the two bread types is that you handle the doughs and mix the batters for the quick varieties as little as possible. You try *not* to develop the gluten in flour, while in yeast doughs you beat, stir and knead for that very purpose. Quick breads are delightfully tender.

These breads definitely are a boon for busy women pressed for time. And baking quick breads is satisfying because you get results fast.

Piping Hot Biscuits

Pass a basket of napkin-wrapped, golden-crusted biscuits so hot that they melt butter as it's spread on them. See that, along with the butter, some honey or jam tags the hot bread around the table. You're off to a good start in serving a successful meal. It upholds an old country kitchen axiom: Hot breads make an otherwise plain-Jane meal special.

Be sure the hot biscuits you serve live up to their name—that they're hot when they reach the table. To help keep them warm, transfer them from the baking sheet to a basket or dish lined with a napkin or foil; cover loosely. Hurry biscuits to the table.

Most farm women keep a package of biscuit mix in their cupboards to use when they're in a hurry. But from-scratch biscuits are particular favorites, and many women bake them for special occasions.

If you are a make-ahead hostess, arrange the cut biscuit dough on a baking sheet and put in the refrigerator. You can hold the dough cutouts ½ to 1 hour before baking the biscuits.

Good Biscuits Every Time

Follow these directions and you'll bake tender, flaky, light biscuits:
· Sift flour, baking powder and salt into a bowl. Cut in shortening with pastry blender until mixture resembles coarse meal or crumbs.
· Make a hollow in dry ingredients and pour in the milk. Stir until dough follows a fork around the bowl.
· Turn dough onto a lightly floured board and gently round up. Knead lightly 12 to 15 strokes, unless recipe specifies otherwise.
· Pat out lightly with hands, or roll to even thickness. The thickness depends on how you like biscuits, which depends to some extent on where you live. Southerners usually prefer thin crusty biscuits. For them you pat or roll the dough about ¼" thick. Many people north of the Mason-Dixon line favor tall biscuits. For them you roll the dough ½" thick.
· Cut the dough with a biscuit cutter dipped lightly in flour. Then fit the scraps together and pat or roll them (do not knead) and cut. For biscuits with soft sides, place the dough cutouts close together on an ungreased (unless recipe specifies greased) baking sheet; for biscuits with crusty sides, arrange dough rounds 1" apart on baking sheet. For a rich brown crust, brush tops of cutouts with milk or light cream, or melted butter.
· Bake in the middle of a very hot oven (450°) 10 to 12 minutes, depending on thickness. Serve at once.

NEVER-FAIL
BAKING POWDER BISCUITS

Flaky, tender biscuits—the highlight of any meal. Do try the variations

2   c. sifted all-purpose flour
1   tblsp. baking powder
1   tsp. salt
¼   c. lard or shortening
¾   c. milk (about)

· Sift together flour, baking powder and salt into bowl. Cut in lard until mixture resembles coarse meal or crumbs.

• Make a hollow in flour-shortening mixture and stir in enough milk to make a soft dough that leaves the sides of the bowl and sticks to the mixing fork.

• Turn onto lightly floured surface and knead with heel of hand 15 times. Roll ¼ to ½″ thick.

• Cut with 2″ cutter; lift cutouts to ungreased baking sheet with broad spatula. Place close together for soft sides, 1″ apart for crusty sides.

• Bake in very hot oven (450°) 10 to 12 minutes, or until golden brown. Serve at once. Makes 12 to 16 biscuits.

Note: If you use self-rising flour, omit baking powder and salt.

ADDITIONS TO NEVER-FAIL BAKING POWDER BISCUITS

• Before combining milk and the flour mixture, add one of the following:

Cheese Biscuits: ¼ to ½ c. grated sharp Cheddar cheese.

Blue Cheese Biscuits: ¼ to ½ c. crumbled blue cheese.

Cheese-Onion Biscuits: ¼ to ½ c. grated sharp Cheddar cheese and 1 tblsp. instant minced onion.

Orange Biscuits: Grated peel of 1 medium orange. (For serving at a salad luncheon, dip ½ cube of loaf sugar in orange juice and press into each biscuit before baking.)

Bacon Biscuits: 4 bacon slices, cooked crisp, drained and finely crumbled (You should have ⅓ c. crumbled bacon).

VARIATIONS

Drop biscuits: Use recipe for Never-Fail Baking Powder Biscuits, and increase milk to 1 c.; drop dough from teaspoon onto greased baking sheet, or into greased muffin-pan cups to fill two thirds full.

Southern Biscuits: Increase lard or shortening to ⅓ c. and reduce milk to ⅔ c. (about).

Whole Wheat Biscuits: Substitute 1 c. whole wheat flour for 1 c. all-purpose flour and add after sifting the other dry ingredients together. Stir to mix well before cutting in lard.

Buttermilk Biscuits: Add ¼ tsp. baking soda to dry ingredients and substitute buttermilk for the milk. Use ⅓ c. lard or shortening.

Cinnamon Pinwheels: Roll dough for Never-Fail Baking Powder Biscuits into a 16×6″ rectangle. Combine ⅓ c. butter or margarine, 1½ tsp. cinnamon and ½ c. sugar. Spread over dough, and starting at long edge, roll up like a jelly roll. Seal edge; cut in 1″ slices. Place in greased muffin-pan cups; brush tops with butter. Bake in hot oven (400°) 15 to 20 minutes. Makes 12 to 16 pinwheels.

Butterscotch Biscuits: Combine ½ c. brown sugar, firmly packed, ¼ c. melted butter or margarine and 1 tblsp. water. Spoon 2 tsp. mixture into 12 well-greased muffin-pan cups. Sprinkle pecan halves on top. Roll dough for Never-Fail Baking Powder Biscuits about ½″ thick; cut with 2″ cutter. Place rounds in prepared muffin-pan cups. Bake in hot oven (425°) 15 to 18 minutes. Invert at once onto waxed paper or foil; remove biscuits at once. Makes 12 biscuits.

Texas Roll-ups: Add ½ c. grated sharp Cheddar cheese to flour-shortening mixture. Roll dough into 18×9″ rectangle, ¼″ thick. Combine ½ c. grated sharp Cheddar cheese and ¾ tsp. chili powder; sprinkle over rolled out dough. Starting at long side, roll up like jelly roll. Seal edges; cut in ¾″ slices. Bake on well-greased baking sheet in very hot oven (450°) about 12 minutes. Makes about 16 biscuits. Excellent with steak.

BISCUIT FAN-TANS

Fancy biscuits that go together fast —perfect with fruit salad and coffee

2 c. sifted all-purpose flour
3 tblsp. sugar
4 tsp. baking powder
½ tsp. cream of tartar
½ tsp. salt
½ c. shortening
⅔ c. milk
2 tblsp. melted butter
¼ c. sugar
1 tblsp. cinnamon

· Sift together flour, 3 tblsp. sugar, baking powder, cream of tartar and salt into mixing bowl.
· Cut in shortening until mixture resembles coarse meal or crumbs. Add milk and stir with fork to moisten all ingredients. Turn onto lightly floured surface and knead gently 20 times.
· Roll dough into a 12×10″ rectangle. Brush with melted butter.
· Combine ¼ c. sugar and cinnamon; sprinkle evenly over dough.
· Cut lengthwise into 5 strips, 2″ wide. Stack strips, one on top of the other. Cut in 12 (1″) pieces. Place cut side down in well-greased muffin-pan cups.
· Bake in hot oven (425°) about 15 minutes. Remove carefully from pan with spatula so fan-tans will hold their shape. Serve while warm. Makes 12 fan-tans.

Biscuits Rich with Wheat Germ

Some of the good wheat taste comes from the germ, the part that grows first when you plant the grain. Flour millers extract, flatten and sift the germ; they package the golden, oily flakes for sale in supermarkets. Since wheat germ contains a bounty of wheat nutrients, baking with it gives the family a bonus. Good eating, too.

Here is a recipe for tasty biscuits made with wheat germ. (Look in the Index for other breads that contain wheat germ.)

WHEAT GERM BISCUITS

Excellent way to use wheat germ. It gives biscuits a nut-like flavor

1½ c. sifted all-purpose flour
½ c. wheat germ
1 tblsp. baking powder
1 tsp. salt
¼ c. shortening
¾ c. milk

· Combine flour, wheat germ, baking powder and salt in mixing bowl. Stir to blend thoroughly.
· Cut in shortening with pastry blender until mixture looks like coarse cornmeal.

• Add milk all at once and stir with a fork just until all ingredients are moistened.
• Turn onto floured board and knead lightly 15 to 20 times.
• Roll dough ½″ thick. Cut with 2″ floured cutter. Place on ungreased baking sheet.
• Bake in very hot oven (450°) 12 to 15 minutes. Makes 12 biscuits.

PUMPKIN BISCUITS

Bring a change to bread basket with these tasty, colorful biscuits

2 c. sifted all-purpose flour
3 tblsp. sugar
4 tsp. baking powder
½ tsp. salt
½ tsp. cinnamon
½ c. butter or margarine
    (1 stick)
⅓ c. chopped pecans
½ c. light cream or dairy
    half-and-half
⅔ c. canned pumpkin

• Sift together flour, sugar, baking powder, salt and cinnamon.
• Cut in butter with pastry blender until mixture looks like coarse meal or crumbs. Stir in pecans.
• Combine cream and pumpkin; stir into flour mixture just enough to moisten dry ingredients. You will have a stiff dough. Turn dough onto a lightly floured board and knead gently a few times.
• Roll out to ½″ thickness. Cut with 2″ cutter. Place 1″ apart on greased baking sheet.
• Bake in hot oven (425°) until golden brown, about 20 minutes. Serve at once. Makes about 20 biscuits.

HAPPY VALLEY BISCUITS

A little cornmeal makes a difference

1 c. sifted all-purpose flour
½ tsp. salt
1 tsp. sugar
¼ tsp. baking soda
¼ tsp. baking powder
⅓ c. cornmeal
⅓ c. lard
⅓ c. buttermilk (about)
Melted butter

• Sift together flour, salt, sugar, baking soda and baking powder into mixing bowl. Add cornmeal, white or yellow, and stir to blend.
• Cut in lard with pastry blender until mixture looks like coarse meal.
• Add buttermilk to make a dough that will hold together and that is not too soft to roll. (Measurement of buttermilk varies from ⅓ to ½ c.)
• Round up dough on lightly floured board and roll about ⅓″ thick. Cut with 2″ cutter. Lift delicate biscuits to baking sheet with broad spatula. Place them about ½″ apart. Brush tops with melted butter.
• Bake in very hot oven (450°) 12 to 15 minutes. Serve piping hot. Makes 15 biscuits.

BEATEN BISCUITS

A Southern masterpiece rarely home-made today, but you might like to try

3 c. sifted all-purpose flour
½ tsp. sugar
½ tsp. salt
3 tblsp. cold butter
3 tblsp. cold lard
½ c. cold milk
½ c. cold water

• Sift flour, sugar and salt into bowl.

• Add butter and lard; blend with pastry blender until mixture looks like coarse cornmeal.

• Add milk and water, tossing mixture with fork.

• Knead 15 minutes; then beat with rolling pin or mallet for 20 minutes, or until blistered. Or put through the coarse blade of a meat chopper several times, folding dough over frequently. Or put dough over and over through the rollers of a beaten-biscuit machine, if you have one. When ready to roll, the dough is smooth and glossy.

• Roll dough ½" thick or a little less; cut with small floured biscuit cutter. Prick tops with fork. Place on baking sheets.

• Bake in slow oven (325°) 30 minutes. Biscuits should be pale brown. Serve cold. Makes at least 36 biscuits.

Freezer to Oven Biscuits

Place cut-out biscuit dough in pan; freeze solid. Store frozen biscuits in plastic bags. Bake as needed in very hot oven (450°) 15 to 18 minutes.

Scones—Breads for All Seasons

Scones (rhymes with on), Scottish originals, are a hot bread for all seasons, but in America they're often summer specials. An Illinois farm woman says: "When the giant sunflowers, with big yellow heads, stand tall by the garage and the morning-glory vines twining around the back fence are a cloud of heavenly blue, I know it's time to get out my electric skillet and bake scones." And a Cali-

fornia rancher's wife writes that she bakes scones on a flat surface over coals when her family cooks supper in the yard.

In the land of heather, scones, a cousin of biscuits and of waffles, usually bake on griddles. Many American women prefer to bake them in the oven. Their choice depends on how warm the weather is.

Regardless of how you bake scones, you split, butter and serve them with honey or a fruit spread. While they're superb when freshly baked, they're almost as tasty when baked ahead or left over if split, buttered and toasted.

Here are American adaptations of Scottish recipes for excellent Summer and Winter Scones. Try them and give your family and friends a treat.

WINTER SCONES

Brighten the supper menu with these cream scones cut in pie-shaped pieces

2   c. sifted all-purpose flour
1   tblsp. baking powder
2   tblsp. sugar
½   tsp. salt
¼   c. lard or shortening
2   eggs
⅓   c. heavy cream
1   tblsp. sugar

• Sift together flour, baking powder, 2 tblsp. sugar and salt into mixing bowl. Cut in lard until mixture resembles coarse meal or crumbs. Make a hollow in the center.

• Save out 1 tblsp. egg white for topping. Beat remaining eggs; combine with cream and add all at once to hollow in flour mixture. Stir to mix —the dough will be stiff.

• Turn onto lightly floured board and knead lightly 5 or 6 times, or until dough sticks together. Divide in half. Roll each half to make a 6″ circle about 1″ thick. Cut each circle in 4 wedges.

• Arrange wedges about 1″ apart on ungreased baking sheet. Brush tops with reserved egg white; sprinkle with 1 tblsp. sugar.

• Bake in hot oven (400°) about 15 minutes, or until golden brown. Serve at once. Makes 8 scones.

SUMMER SCONES

Serve hot for breakfast or any meal —use Sour Cream Scones (see Variations) for shortcake

    2 c. sifted all-purpose flour
    1 tblsp. baking powder
    1 tblsp. sugar
    ½ tsp. salt
    ¼ c. lard or shortening
    2 eggs
    ⅓ c. milk

• Sift together flour, baking powder, sugar and salt into mixing bowl. Cut in lard until mixture resembles coarse meal or crumbs. Make a hollow in center.

• Beat eggs slightly; combine with milk and stir into hollow in flour mixture with fork to moisten all ingredients. Avoid overmixing.

• Turn onto floured board and knead lightly 5 or 6 times. Roll to ½″ thickness and cut with 2″ biscuit cutter.

• Place on ungreased griddle or skillet preheated over medium heat; if you use your electric skillet or griddle, set heat control at 325°.

• Bake about 10 minutes, turn and bake about 10 minutes on the other side. The trick is to bake scones slowly to brown the outside delicately and to cook the inside thoroughly. Serve hot. Makes 18 scones.

VARIATIONS

Raisin Scones: Use recipe for Summer Scones and add ½ c. finely cut-up raisins (cut with scissors) to dry ingredients before cutting in lard. Bake as directed.

Currant Scones: Add ½ c. finely cut-up dried currants to dry ingredients before cutting in lard. Bake as directed.

Buttermilk Scones: Substitute ⅓ c. buttermilk for ⅓ c. milk in recipe for Summer Scones. Reduce baking powder to 2 tsp. and add ¼ tsp. baking soda. Sift baking powder and baking soda with the other dry ingredients before cutting in the lard.

Sour Cream Scones: Increase sugar to 2 tblsp. and substitute ½ c. dairy sour cream for the ⅓ c. milk. Ideal for a quick strawberry shortcake. Exciting for cookouts.

Note: Farm women who have lots of butter use it instead of the lard or shortening.

Gingerbreads

Through years of testing different kinds of gingerbreads and cakes (the dividing line between cakes and breads is not very sharp), a few stand out in food editors' memories. Here are several we call "best."

SPICY GINGERBREAD SQUARES

Serve this warm and unadorned, or serve a week after baking with a hot lemon sauce or whipped cream

2 c. sifted all-purpose flour
½ c. sugar
2 tsp. ginger
1 ½ tsp. cardamom
1 tsp. allspice
1 tsp. baking soda
½ tsp. salt
1 tblsp. grated orange peel
3 eggs
½ c. light molasses
1 c. buttermilk
½ c. melted butter

• Sift dry ingredients together into a large mixing bowl. Stir in orange peel.
• Beat eggs until thick, light and foamy; add molasses in a stream, beating constantly; gradually beat in buttermilk. Add half of the milk-molasses mixture to ingredients in large mixing bowl, and beat with a spoon until well blended. Add remaining buttermilk-molasses mixture to large bowl in two additions, beating after each until blended. Gradually add melted butter, and beat with spoon until batter is blended and smooth. Pour into a buttered 8" square baking pan.
• Bake in moderate oven (350°) 45 to 50 minutes, or until toothpick inserted in center comes out clean. Makes about 9 servings.

WHOLE WHEAT GINGERBREAD

Serve this sturdy, fruited bread warm in 1" slices, or cut cooled bread slightly thinner—spread with butter

½ c. butter
2 tblsp. sugar

¾ c. light molasses
1 c. sifted all-purpose flour
1 c. stirred whole wheat flour
1 tsp. ginger
¾ tsp. baking soda
½ tsp. salt
½ tsp. cinnamon
½ tsp. mace or nutmeg
½ c. chopped walnuts
½ c. raisins
3 tblsp. minced candied
    lemon peel
2 eggs
½ c. milk

• Melt butter in saucepan. Add sugar and molasses and stir to blend.
• Sift together into a large mixing bowl all-purpose flour, whole wheat flour (return chaff to sifted ingredients), ginger, baking soda, salt, cinnamon and mace. Stir in nuts, raisins and lemon peel.
• Beat eggs and milk together until blended, add to mixing bowl along with molasses mixture. Stir to moisten all ingredients. Then beat mixture with a rubber scraper or wooden spoon about 70 strokes, until well blended. Turn into a buttered 8" square baking pan.
• Bake in moderate oven (350°) 40 minutes, or until toothpick inserted in center comes out clean. Serve warm or cool on a rack. Makes about 10 servings.

PECAN GINGER LOAF

This moist, nutted gingerbread has the tender texture of cake; slices of it broil-toast divinely for breakfast

½ c. soft butter
1 ½ c. sugar
2 eggs

1 ⅔ c. unsifted all-purpose flour
2   tsp. ginger
1   tsp. baking soda
¾   tsp. salt
½   tsp. cinnamon
½   tsp. nutmeg
¼   tsp. baking powder
¼   tsp. ground cloves
⅓   c. water
1   c. canned pumpkin
½   c. finely chopped pecans

• With electric mixer, beat butter and sugar together in mixing bowl until creamed. Add eggs, one at a time, and beat until mixture is light and fluffy.

• Sift together dry ingredients; add to creamed mixture alternately with water; beat well after each addition. Add pumpkin and beat until well blended. Stir in nuts. Turn into a buttered 9×5×3″ loaf pan and spread smooth.

• Bake in moderate oven (350°) 60 to 70 minutes, or until toothpick inserted in center comes out clean. Allow to cool in pan 10 minutes, then turn out on wire rack to cool thoroughly. Makes 1 loaf.

Hurry-up Coffee Breads

The speed with which you can bake quick coffee breads or cakes, as they are often called, has something to do with their popularity. A more important reason for their widespread acceptance is the way they go with coffee.

These are the breads farm women often bake in cold weather to serve at midmorning when the men, doing chores near the house, come to the kitchen for a few minutes to warm up and relax. Men also like to share these breads with their business callers. Farmers' coffee breaks are in friendly kitchens, not in a coffee shop around the corner. No wonder they make many business deals around the kitchen table over coffee and a delicious coffee bread.

Women say these hurry-up breads are easy to stir up and bake when neighbors stop in to exchange news on their way home from town. And these breads rate high at coffee parties. Also, farm women often bake them in summer to tote to the field for the men's midmorning break.

You leaven these breads or cakes, whichever name you prefer to call these treats, with baking powder, baking soda or a combination of the two. (You'll find recipes for yeast-leavened coffee cakes in another section of this cookbook. See the Index for them.) Many women go a step farther in simplification and use packaged biscuit mix to make them.

Try the recipes for top favorite coffee breads that follow. They come to you highly recommended.

ORANGE-CINNAMON LOAF

Fast to fix—serve warm with butter and orange or apricot marmalade

2   c. biscuit mix
1   tblsp. grated orange peel
1   tsp. cinnamon
¼   c. orange juice
¼   c. milk
2   tblsp. melted butter or margarine
Honey Glaze

• Combine biscuit mix, orange peel and cinnamon in mixing bowl. Stir

to mix and make a hollow in center.
• Combine orange juice, milk and melted butter. Add all at once to hollow in dry ingredients; stir just to moisten mixture.
• Turn dough onto lightly floured board; knead gently about 8 times. Press evenly into greased 8" square pan. With a sharp knife, make one lengthwise cut, about ½" deep, across center of top. Then make crosswise cuts across top about 1" apart. Drizzle on Honey Glaze.
• Bake in hot oven (400°) about 20 minutes, or until browned. Serve freshly baked. Makes 8 servings.

Honey Glaze: Combine 2 tblsp. honey, 2 tblsp. chopped pecans or other nuts, 1 tblsp. melted butter and ½ tsp. cinnamon.

CINNAMON-ORANGE COFFEE BREAD

Serve this warm bread at your coffee party—you'll reap many compliments

2   c. sifted all-purpose flour
1 ½ tsp. baking powder
⅛   tsp. baking soda
½   tsp. salt
½   c. sugar
1   tsp. cinnamon
½   tsp. nutmeg
⅓   c. shortening
2   tblsp. grated orange peel
⅓   c. chopped nuts
1   egg, well beaten
½   c. milk
Cinnamon Topping

• Sift flour with baking powder, baking soda, salt, sugar and spices into mixing bowl.
• Cut in shortening with a pastry

blender until mixture resembles fine crumbs. Add orange peel and nuts. (If made ahead, cover bowl tightly and store in refrigerator.)
• Combine egg and milk. Add to flour mixture. Mix enough to moisten flour.
• Spread batter evenly in a greased 9×9×2" pan. Sprinkle with Cinnamon Topping.
• Bake in moderate oven (375°) 25 minutes. Cut in squares. Best served warm. Makes 9 servings.

Cinnamon Topping: Combine ½ c. sugar, 2 tblsp. flour, ½ tsp. cinnamon and 2 tblsp. melted butter. Blend to make crumbly mixture.

ORANGE-PRUNE COFFEE BREAD

Fun to make; has a tangy flavor

2   eggs
¼   c. brown sugar, firmly packed
¼   c. granulated sugar
3   tblsp. finely shredded orange peel
4   c. prepared biscuit mix
1 ½ c. chopped, pitted prunes
1   c. fresh orange juice

• Beat eggs; stir in sugars and orange peel.
• Place biscuit mix in a bowl. Add chopped prunes and mix well, separating prune pieces with your fingers. Stir into sugar mixture alternately with orange juice. Beat by hand 1 minute; do not overbeat.
• Pour into a greased bundt pan or 10" tube pan. Bake in moderate oven (350°) 45 minutes, or until bread tests done. Cool 10 minutes. Remove from pan and cool completely. Makes 18 to 24 medium-size servings.

SOUR CREAM COFFEE BREAD

Quick, easy-to-make and extra-good with spiced nuts on top and within

1 c. butter
2 c. sugar
2 eggs
1 c. dairy sour cream
½ tsp. vanilla
2 c. sifted all-purpose flour
1 tsp. baking powder
¼ tsp. salt
4 tsp. sugar
1 tsp. cinnamon
1 c. chopped pecans

• Cream butter and 2 c. sugar until light and fluffy. Beat in eggs, one at a time, to mix thoroughly.
• Beat in sour cream and vanilla.
• Fold in flour sifted with baking powder and salt.
• Combine 4 tsp. sugar with cinnamon and pecans; mix well.
• Spoon about one third of batter into a well-greased 9″ tube pan.
• Sprinkle with about three fourths of pecan mixture. Spoon in remaining batter and sprinkle with remaining pecan mixture.
• Bake in moderate oven (350°) 1 hour, or until done. Remove from pan and cool on wire rack. Makes 10 servings.

APPLE COFFEE CAKE

Browned cream spiral adorns top— bread is best served warm

1½ c. sifted all-purpose flour
½ c. sugar
2 tsp. baking powder
½ tsp. salt
½ tsp. cinnamon
½ c. chopped walnuts
1 large shredded, peeled apple
1 egg, beaten
½ c. milk
3 tblsp. melted shortening or salad oil
½ c. dairy sour cream
½ c. sugar

• Sift together flour, ½ c. sugar, baking powder, salt and cinnamon. Add nuts, saving out 2 tblsp. for topping. Stir in apple.
• Blend together egg, milk and shortening. Add to flour mixture, stirring just to mix. Turn into greased 9″ round cake pan.
• Spoon sour cream over the top in spiral fashion, leaving center uncovered. Sprinkle remaining ½ c. sugar over top; scatter on remaining 2 tblsp. nuts.
• Bake in hot oven (400°) 30 to 35 minutes. Let cool slightly before cutting into wedges. (Also makes a good dessert.) Makes 6 servings.

Luscious Blueberry Kuchen

Blueberries are one of the easiest berries to use. All you have to do is put them in a strainer, spray with cool water and drain thoroughly. There's no hulling or pitting. They do have many seeds, but these are soft and seem to vanish in the mouth. It's the blueberry taste, though, that accounts for all those blueberry fans.

The Ohio farm woman who shares with you her recipe for Blueberry Kuchen says: "The berries do sink down in the batter, but they taste just as good there as anywhere else.

Sometimes I turn the servings upside down and sift confectioners sugar over the top.

"When I have friends in for coffee or for dinner, I frequently double the recipe and bake the coffee bread in a greased 13×9×2″ pan.

"I use the grated peel of one lemon in Blueberry Kuchen. Be sure to brush the peel from the grater with a stiff-bristled brush so you get all of that good lemon flavor."

GERMAN BLUEBERRY KUCHEN

Delicate, fine-grained coffee cake for breakfast or dinner dessert

1 ½ c. sifted all-purpose flour
2   tsp. baking powder
½   tsp. salt
¾   c. sugar
¼   c. soft shortening
⅔   c. milk
1   tsp. vanilla
½   tsp. grated lemon peel
     (½ lemon)
1   egg
1   c. fresh blueberries
3   tblsp. sugar
1   tsp. grated lemon peel

• Sift together flour, baking powder, salt and ¾ c. sugar. Add shortening, milk, vanilla and ½ tsp. grated lemon peel. Beat with electric mixer on medium speed 3 minutes, or 300 strokes by hand.
• Add egg and beat with mixer 2 minutes longer (200 strokes by hand).
• Turn into greased 8×8×2″ pan.
• Lightly stir together blueberries, 3 tblsp. sugar and 1 tsp. grated lemon peel. Sprinkle over batter in pan.
• Bake in moderate oven (350°) 40 to 45 minutes, or until lightly browned.

Cool slightly in pan. Cut in squares and serve faintly warm. Makes 6 to 9 servings.

IRISH SODA BREAD

Casserole loaf borrowed from Irish kitchens—it's wonderful with tea

4   c. sifted all-purpose flour
¼   c. sugar
1   tsp. salt
1   tsp. baking powder
2   tblsp. caraway seeds
¼   c. butter or margarine
2   c. raisins
1 ⅓ c. buttermilk
1   egg
1   tsp. baking soda
1   egg yolk, beaten

• Sift flour, sugar, salt and baking powder into mixing bowl; stir in caraway seeds. Cut in butter until mixture looks like coarse meal; stir in raisins.
• Combine buttermilk, 1 egg and baking soda; stir into flour mixture just enough to moisten dry ingredients.
• Turn onto floured board and knead lightly until dough is smooth. Shape in a ball and place in a greased 2-qt. casserole. With a sharp knife, cut a 4″ cross about ½″ deep in center of dough (this makes a decorative top). Brush with egg yolk.
• Bake in moderate oven (375°) about 1 hour, or until a cake tester or wooden pick inserted in center of loaf comes out clean.
• Cool bread in casserole 10 minutes; remove. Cool on wire rack before cutting. To serve, cut down through loaf to divide in quarters; thinly slice each quarter. Makes 1 loaf.

SUGAR-TOP COFFEE CAKE

A favorite for company breakfasts— from our Cooking for Company *book*

1	egg
¾	c. granulated sugar
1	tblsp. melted butter or margarine
1	c. dairy sour cream
1	tsp. vanilla
1 ½	c. sifted all-purpose flour
2	tsp. baking powder
¼	tsp. baking soda
¾	tsp. salt
½	c. brown sugar
2	tblsp. all-purpose flour
½	tsp. cinnamon
2	tblsp. softened butter

· Beat egg until frothy; beat in granulated sugar and 1 tblsp. melted butter. Cream until light and fluffy. Add sour cream and vanilla; blend well.
· Sift together 1½ c. flour, baking powder, baking soda and salt; add to sour cream mixture. Blend well. Pour into a greased 8″ square pan. Mix together until crumbly, brown sugar, 2 tblsp. flour, cinnamon and 2 tblsp. butter. Sprinkle over top of batter.
· Bake in moderate oven (375°) 25 to 30 minutes, or until cake tests done. Serve warm. Makes 6 servings.

Yesterday's Gems Are Today's Muffins

If you were lucky enough to have a State-of-Maine grandmother who baked graham gems, you remember how wonderful the brown beauties tasted when you broke them apart and spread on lots of butter. Children still visit their grandmothers in farm kitchens and enjoy breads hot from the oven. Instead of feasting on graham gems today, they usually eat whole wheat muffins, which are near enough the original. "Gems" is the old-fashioned name for muffins. It still makes a lot of sense, for a gem, according to Webster's dictionary, is a perfect specimen of its kind. The definition for a muffin is a little muff to keep the hands warm, which the quick bread really does if you hurry it from the oven to the table.

Packaged muffin mixes are available and convenient, but perfect muffins aren't difficult to produce from scratch. They are tender and have slightly pebbled, rounded tops, never peaked ones. Their crust is a shiny brown. If you break a perfect muffin open, you'll see no long holes, called tunnels, and you'll find that the crumb is moist. The secret in making this kind of muffin is to mix the batter just enough to moisten the dry ingredients. The batter should be lumpy, not smooth.

Two Ways to Mix Muffins

There are two ways to mix muffins successfully. One bears the muffin name, the other borrows the biscuit technique. The Muffin Method is simpler and gives a typically coarse and open texture. It is used for muffins containing a large proportion of sugar and shortening. The Biscuit Method, sometimes called the Cake Method, gives a finer, more cake-like texture. This method commonly is used for plainer type muffins. The recipes indicate which method to use.

Muffin Method: Sift the dry ingredients into a bowl and make a hollow in the center. Combine the milk or other liquid, egg and melted shortening; pour it all at once into the hollow.

· Stir just enough to moisten the dry ingredients, not to make a smooth batter.

Biscuit Method: Use a pastry blender to mix the dry ingredients with the shortening until the mixture looks like coarse meal or crumbs about the size of small peas. Make a hollow in the center.

· Beat the egg until foamy; combine it with the milk or liquid and pour it all at once into the hollow.

· Stir the dry ingredients this way: Push them with a spoon to the center of the bowl (to the hollow where you've poured liquid), slowly turning the bowl. When you go around the bowl once, chop *straight through* the center with spoon to mix ingredients.

· Now you are ready to stir. Use as few strokes as possible to moisten all the dry ingredients.

Make the muffins small or big, depending on the size of your muffin-pan cups. Fill the greased cups two thirds full. If you do not fill all the cups, partly fill empty ones with water.

If muffins must wait after you bake them, turn each muffin on its side in the pan to prevent steaming; keep in a warm place, such as a low oven. To reheat leftover muffins, split in half, butter and toast under broiler.

Here are prized muffin recipes from country kitchens. Some are such great favorites in certain areas that they bear geographical names. You will notice that you can use an astonishing variety of ingredients. Bake many kinds of muffins soon and frequently. You'll like the compliments you get.

BUTTERMILK MUFFINS

Favorites made by Muffin Method. One taste explains why they're in favor

1 ¾ c. sifted all-purpose flour
2   tblsp. sugar
1   tsp. baking powder
¼   tsp. baking soda
¾   tsp. salt
1   egg, well beaten
¾   c. buttermilk or soured milk
⅓   c. melted shortening or salad oil

· Sift together flour, sugar, baking powder, baking soda and salt into mixing bowl. Make a hollow in the center.

· Combine egg, milk and slightly cooled shortening. Add all at once to hollow in dry ingredients. Stir with spoon just enough to moisten dry ingredients (batter will not be smooth).

· Fill greased muffin-pan cups or paper bake cups two thirds full.

· Bake in hot oven (400°) 25 minutes, or until done. Makes about 12 muffins.

VARIATION

Sweet Milk Muffins: Omit baking soda in recipe for Buttermilk Muffins. Increase amount of baking powder to 2½ tsp. and substitute ¾ c. sweet milk for the buttermilk.

Note: You also can use the variations we suggest for Guest-Supper Muffins (recipe follows).

GUEST-SUPPER MUFFINS

Extra-special, made by the Biscuit Method. Serve plain or fancy

2   c. sifted all-purpose flour
2½ tsp. baking powder
2   tblsp. sugar
¾   tsp. salt
½   c. shortening
1   egg, well beaten
¾   c. milk

• Sift together flour, baking powder, sugar and salt into mixing bowl. Cut in shortening until crumbs are the size of small peas. Make a hollow in center.
• Combine egg and milk; add all at once to hollow in dry ingredients. Stir only until dry ingredients are just moist (batter will be lumpy).
• Fill greased muffin-pan cups two thirds full.
• Bake in hot oven (400°) 25 minutes, or until done. Makes about 12 muffins.

VARIATIONS

Blueberry Muffins: Quickly fold 1 c. blueberries into batter for Guest-Supper Muffins, and bake as directed.

Cranberry Muffins: Chop 1 c. cranberries; sprinkle with 2 tblsp. sugar. Sprinkle into batter.

Bacon Muffins: Quickly stir ½ c. finely crushed, crisp cooked bacon into dry ingredients.

Date Muffins: Add ⅔ c. coarsely cut-up dates to dry ingredients.

Raisin Muffins: Quickly fold ½ to ¾ c. seedless raisins into batter.

Pennsylvania Dutch Muffins: Sprinkle tops of batter in muffin-pan cups with cinnamon-sugar mixture, 1 tsp. cinnamon combined with ½ c. sugar. Bake as directed.

Georgia Pecan Muffins: Quickly fold ½ c. chopped pecans into batter.

Jelly Muffins: After batter is in pans, top each muffin with 1 tsp. tart jelly and bake.

CRANBERRY-RAISIN MUFFINS

Muffins that complement chicken salad—splashes of red add brightness

1   c. whole cranberries
¼   c. raisins
¼   tsp. ground cloves
½   c. sugar
2   c. sifted all-purpose flour
4   tsp. baking powder
¾   tsp. salt
1   egg, beaten
1   c. milk
3   tblsp. melted shortening
    or salad oil

• Chop cranberries and raisins. Add cloves and sugar.
• Sift flour, baking powder and salt into mixing bowl. Add cranberry mixture.
• Combine beaten egg, milk and shortening. Add to dry ingredients; stir only until blended.
• Bake in well-greased muffin-pan cups in hot oven (425°) about 25 minutes. Makes 12 medium-size muffins.

Leftover Muffins

Split and toast plain or cereal muffins and serve with chicken à la king. Serve toasted fruit muffins for dessert with ice cream or fruit topping.

CEREAL MUFFINS

The batter for these muffins takes to almost any fruit—see variations

1 ¼ c. milk
1 ½ c. whole-bran cereal
1 ½ c. sifted all-purpose flour
⅓   c. sugar
1   tsp. salt
3   tsp. baking powder
1   egg, beaten
¼   c. melted shortening or salad oil

· Combine milk and cereal in large mixing bowl.
· Sift flour with sugar, salt and baking powder.
· Add egg and melted shortening to the milk and cereal; add the dry ingredients. Mix only until dry ingredients are moistened (batter will be lumpy, not smooth).
· Fill greased muffin-pan cups two thirds full. (If desired, sprinkle tops with sugar-coated flakes or cereal.)
· Bake in hot oven (400°) 20 to 25 minutes. Makes 12 medium-size muffins.

Note: You can use 3 c. corn flakes or 2 c. ready-to-eat oat cereal instead of the bran cereal.

VARIATIONS

To basic Cereal Muffins recipe, add ingredients as indicated for each variation; blend these in before adding the dry ingredients.

Blueberry-Cereal Muffins: Add 1 c. fresh or unthawed frozen blueberries, or 1 c. well-drained canned blueberries.

Apple Muffins: Sprinkle 2 tblsp. sugar and ½ tsp. cinnamon over ¾ c. finely diced tart apples. Toss lightly; add as directed.

Pineapple Muffins: Add ¾ c. well-drained crushed pineapple.

Bacon-Cereal Muffins: Crumble 4 strips crisp cooked bacon; add as directed.

Cranberry-Cereal Muffins: Add 1 (7 oz.) can whole cranberry sauce.

CARAWAY PUFFINS

Nice for a women's luncheon. Biscuit mix makes these easy

2   tblsp. soft butter or margarine
½   c. creamed cottage cheese
¼   c. sugar
1   tsp. grated lemon peel
¾   tsp. caraway seeds
1   egg
1 ⅔ c. prepared biscuit mix
⅓   c. milk

· Cream butter, cottage cheese and sugar. Add lemon peel, caraway seeds and egg; beat with electric mixer until very smooth.
· Stir in biscuit mix alternately with milk; do not beat. Spoon batter into greased muffin-pan cups, filling two thirds full. Bake in hot oven (400°) 20 to 25 minutes, or until lightly browned. Makes 12 puffins.

Popovers Light as Air

Never underestimate miracles that take place in ovens. The popover, the bread that puffs up in a remarkable way, is a classic example. It's a pity that all women who bake this hot bread do not have glass in their oven doors so they can watch the popovers grow tall, golden and beautiful.

Contrary to the belief of many women, popovers are exceptionally easy to bake—almost child's play. This is what happens in baking. The oven heat turns the liquid in the thin batter into steam, which is responsible for the bread's lightness. You need to have the proper balance of flour, eggs and milk in the batter and to use the correct oven temperature to enable the thin, shiny, brown popover crust to hold its shape.

Country hostesses serve popovers for all meals from breakfast to dinner, but they especially like to offer them in dinners featuring steak or roast beef. Sometimes they serve only butter with the bread, but frequently they also have marmalade or jam on the table.

Here is a recipe from a reader of FARM JOURNAL who says the popovers she makes with it are so light they almost float away.

PERFECT POPOVERS

Serve the crisp, brown pockets hot with lots of butter and jelly or jam

1   c. milk
1   c. sifted all-purpose flour
½   tsp. salt
1   tblsp. melted butter or salad
     oil
2   large eggs

• Pour milk into small bowl of electric mixer; sift in flour and salt. Beat at medium speed until batter is smooth, about 1½ minutes, scraping bowl frequently. Add butter and eggs; beat to mix thoroughly, about 1 minute. (Avoid overbeating; it reduces volume.)

• Ladle batter into well-greased custard cups, filling cups half full. Place cups on baking sheet and place on rack in center of hot oven (400°) or moderate oven (375°). (A 400° oven gives popovers a rich brown crust, slightly moist inside, while a 375° oven produces popovers that are a lighter brown and drier inside.)

• Bake in hot oven (400°) about 40 minutes (or about 50 minutes in 375° oven). Keep oven door closed until about 5 or 10 minutes before end of baking time or popovers may collapse.

• Remove popovers from oven, prick their sides with kitchen fork or metal skewer to permit steam to escape. Lay popovers on their sides in custard cups and return to oven, heat turned off and door left ajar, for 5 minutes to dry inside (or longer to keep warm for serving). Makes 7 popovers baked in 5 oz. custard cups.

Popular Pancakes— Plain and Fancy

Pancakes, FARM JOURNAL Family Test Group members tell us, are the quick bread they make most frequently. Perhaps the attitude of men has something to do with it. One rancher expresses it this way: "Take a stack of pancakes, spread liberally with butter and pour on plenty of syrup. That's my favorite winter breakfast. Hot cakes stick to the ribs when you're outdoors in bitterly cold weather doing the chores."

While pancakes for breakfast rate high, pancake suppers, glamorous dessert pancakes and main dishes (pancakes rolled around substantial fillings) also are popular. Most farm kitchen cupboards hold packages of pancake mixes, but there are occasions when women bake them "from scratch" for their families and guests. The recipes in this cookbook are this type.

POINTERS FOR PERFECT PANCAKES

• Preheat griddle over low heat.
• Beat the batter just enough to moisten the dry ingredients. It will have lumps.
• Start baking when the griddle is at the right temperature. Portable electric griddles and skillets are ideal to use because their heat is controlled. Also because you can sit down and bake the pancakes at the table. To test the temperature of the griddle, if the heat is not electrically controlled, sprinkle a few drops of water on it. If little beads of water dance around, the griddle is ready. If you use an electric griddle or electric skillet, follow manufacturer's directions. Grease the griddle or not, as the manufacturer directs.
• You may have to grease the griddle when you bake the first batch of pancakes, but rarely for later bakings, especially if the batter contains 2 tblsp. or more fat.
• Transfer the batter to the griddle with a ¼-cup measure to get pancakes of uniform size. Use a tablespoon or soup ladle for silver-dollar-size pancakes. You can pour the batter from a pitcher (a drip-cut one is best), but it's more difficult to get pancakes of uniform size.
• Turn pancakes when the rim of each cake is full of broken bubbles and the whole top has bubbles, some

of which are broken. Turn only once. Bake until underside is golden.
• If pancakes must wait, spread them out in single layers in folded towels in a low oven—just warm enough to keep pancakes from cooling.

Here are superior pancake recipes from farm and ranch kitchens collected from one end of the United States to the other.

FAVORITE BUTTERMILK PANCAKES

Variations of this recipe make fine desserts—try them

2 c. sifted all-purpose flour
1 tsp. baking soda
1 tsp. salt
2 tblsp. sugar
2 eggs, slightly beaten
2 c. buttermilk
2 tblsp. melted butter

• Sift flour, baking soda, salt and sugar into mixing bowl.
• Combine eggs, buttermilk and melted butter. Stir into flour mixture just to moisten flour. Do not overmix. The batter will have a few lumps.
• Bake on a hot, lightly greased griddle or in an electric skillet heated to 375°.
• Dip batter with a ¼-cup measure to get pancakes of uniform size. Turn cakes when bubbles appear and break over top and around the edges; turn only once. Serve hot with butter or margarine, or with Whipped Butter (recipe follows), and syrup.

VARIATIONS

Banana Pancakes: Add ⅔ c. diced bananas to batter for Favorite Buttermilk Pancakes. Bake; sift confectioners sugar over top of pancakes. Pass Whipped Butter, honey and a tart jelly to give a choice of toppings.

Blueberry Pancakes: Drain canned blueberries well. Add ⅔ c. to batter for Favorite Buttermilk Pancakes. Bake; sift confectioners sugar on top of pancakes. Serve with Whipped Butter and maple syrup. You can fold ⅔ c. frozen or fresh blueberries into the batter instead of canned blueberries. Fold additions lightly into pancake batter just before you are ready to bake the pancakes.

Whipped Butter: Put ½ c. butter (¼ lb.) in small bowl of electric mixer. Let stand at room temperature 1 hour. Start beating at low speed; when all the big pieces of butter are beaten smooth, beat at high speed until butter is fluffy. This takes about 8 minutes. Cover and refrigerate until an hour before serving. Makes 1½ cups.

CORN GRIDDLECAKES

You can bake tiny cakes and serve with maple syrup like corn fritters— good with fried chicken or ham

1 c. sifted all-purpose flour
2 tsp. baking powder
1 tsp. sugar
½ tsp. salt
2 eggs, well beaten
¾ c. milk
2 tblsp. melted butter or margarine
1 c. whole kernel corn

• Sift together flour, baking powder, sugar and salt. Beat in eggs, milk and butter until batter is smooth. Stir in corn.

• Drop from ⅓-cup measure on preheated griddle and bake until golden brown on both sides. Serve hot with butter and table syrup for breakfast. Makes 9 to 10 griddlecakes.

Note: You can double this recipe. Then you'll need 1 (1 lb.) can whole kernel corn.

SOUR CREAM BLUEBERRY PANCAKES

Light, fluffy pancakes with that interesting flavor sour cream adds

1 c. sifted all-purpose flour
3 tsp. baking powder
¼ tsp. salt
1 tblsp. sugar
1 egg
1 c. milk
¼ c. dairy sour cream
2 tblsp. melted butter
½ c. blueberries

• Sift together flour, baking powder, salt and sugar.
• Beat together egg, milk and sour cream.
• Pour milk mixture over dry ingredients and blend with rotary beater until batter is just smooth. Stir in butter. Fold in blueberries.
• Pour 2 tblsp. batter onto hot griddle for each cake. (Pour 1 tblsp. batter onto hot griddle for each cake if you want silver-dollar-size pancakes. If you have the time this is a festive way to serve them.) Brown on one side until golden. Turn and brown on the other side. If cakes brown too fast, lower heat. Serve hot with butter and maple syrup or Maine Blueberry Syrup (recipe follows). Makes

12 pancakes using 2 tblsp. batter, or 24 silver-dollar-size pancakes.

VARIATION

Sour Cream Pancakes: Prepare batter for Sour Cream Blueberry Pancakes, but omit the blueberries. If you have leftover batter, cover and store in the refrigerator. It will keep 2 or 3 days, but will thicken. When you are ready to use it, add 1 to 2 tblsp. milk in which you dissolve ½ tsp. baking powder for each cup of batter. Bake as directed in recipe for Sour Cream Blueberry Pancakes.

Maine Blueberry Syrup: Simmer together 2 c. blueberries, ½ c. sugar, ½ c. water and a thin slice of lemon to make a syrup. This takes about 10 minutes. Makes about 2½ cups.

BLUE RIDGE PANCAKES

A Southern farm breakfast special worthy of adoption across country

1 c. sifted all-purpose flour
1 tsp. salt
1 tsp. sugar
1 tsp. baking soda
1 tsp. baking powder
1 c. white cornmeal (or yellow)
3 eggs, separated
2 c. buttermilk
2 tblsp. melted butter or
    margarine

· Sift together flour, salt, sugar, baking soda and baking powder into bowl. Stir in cornmeal to mix thoroughly.
· Beat egg yolks until thick and lemon-colored. Add buttermilk and butter. Beat egg whites until stiff.

· Pour buttermilk mixture into dry ingredients and stir just to blend and moisten them. Fold in egg whites.
· Drop from ⅓-cup measure onto preheated and greased griddle; bake until golden brown on both sides. Makes 16 pancakes.

DOLLAR RICE CAKES

Marvelous way to use leftover rice

¾ c. sifted all-purpose flour
1 ½ tsp. baking powder
¼ t. salt
½ tsp. sugar
1   egg, separated
1   c. milk
2   tblsp. melted butter or
     margarine
½ tsp. vanilla
½ c. cooked rice

· Sift together flour, baking powder, salt and sugar.
· Beat egg yolk with fork; add milk, butter and vanilla. Stir in dry ingredients and beat with rotary beater until smooth.
· Fold in rice and egg white, beaten until stiff.
· Bake tablespoons of batter on hot griddle, turning once. Serve with butter and maple or cane syrup. Makes 34 small pancakes.

BLINTZES

Serve these Russian-Jewish pancakes with butter, fruit preserves or syrup

1 c. sifted all-purpose flour
1 tblsp. sugar
¾ tsp. salt
1 c. dairy sour cream

1   c. small curd creamed
      cottage cheese
4   eggs, well beaten

• Sift together flour, sugar and salt. Combine with remaining ingredients, stirring just enough to moisten the flour.
• Drop from ¼-cup measure onto hot, greased griddle and bake until golden brown on both sides. Serve hot. Makes 14 to 16 blintzes.

French Pancakes—Crêpes

You don't need to be a juggler to bake the tender, thin pancakes the French call crêpes. They are easier to make than you may think. French cooks put on quite a show when they turn crêpes—they toss them in the air. The marvel is that they always land on the unbrowned side. You'll have better luck, unless you practice flipping them, if you use your pancake turner. In France, where omelets appear often at mealtime, the omelet pan frequently is the utensil in which cooks bake crêpes, although small, heavy skillets also fill the bill. A heavy 8″ skillet is a good choice.

It takes time to bake crêpes. The home economist and homemaker who tested the Basic French Crêpes recipe said it took about 40 minutes to bake 16 pancakes. You can bake them ahead. If you plan to use them the same day, stack them and cover with a towel. You can freeze crêpes for use days later. Here's how to do it:
• Stack 6 to 8 cool crêpes, wrap tightly in foil and put in freezer. When you want to use them, place

the packages on a rack and set in a warm place for 2 to 3 hours. To thaw faster, place packages in a very slow oven (275°) 15 to 20 minutes.

You can bake crêpes and serve them flat, or you can roll them around fascinating fillings for desserts, or around substantial fillings for main dishes to serve heated or cold. Here is the recipe for Basic French Crêpes, the way American women make them, and suggestions for how to use the thin pancakes.

BASIC FRENCH CREPES

You can make wonderful dishes with these delicate, light brown pancakes

1   c. milk
3   eggs, well beaten
¾   c. sifted all-purpose flour
1   tblsp. sugar
¼   tsp. salt

• Beat milk into well-beaten eggs. Sift together flour, sugar and salt into milk mixture. Beat with rotary beater or electric mixer until batter is smooth.
• Pour about 2 tblsp. batter into a lightly buttered 8″ skillet, preheated over medium heat. Begin at once to rotate pan to spread the batter evenly over the bottom. Turn once; bake until *light* golden brown on both sides. Repeat, buttering skillet for each baking. Makes 16 crêpes.

WAYS TO SERVE DESSERT CREPES

Strawberry Stack: Serve unrolled, in stacks of 3 pancakes, with sweetened strawberries between. Cut in wedges.

Strawberry Roll-ups: Place sweetened sliced strawberries on half of each pancake. Top with 1 scant tblsp.

whipped cream. Roll up and arrange, seam side down, on serving platter or plate, allowing 2 roll-ups to a serving. Sprinkle tops with confectioners sugar.

Hot Strawberry Crêpes: Roll crêpes around sliced, sweetened strawberries. Melt 3 tblsp. butter in chafing dish or electric skillet; place crêpes, seam side down, in butter. Heat thoroughly. Serve with sweetened whipped cream.

Crêpe Stacks with Orange-Honey Sauce: Combine ½ c. honey, ½ c. butter, ⅓ c. orange juice and 1½ tsp. grated orange peel in small saucepan. Heat, stirring to blend. Arrange 3 stacks of 5 crêpes each on heatproof platter. Pour 1 tblsp. Orange-Honey Sauce on each pancake in stacks; place in slow oven (300°) to heat, 12 to 15 minutes. Cut each stack in half for a serving and pass remaining warm sauce to pour over crêpes. Makes 6 servings.

Swedish Pancakes: Bake crêpe batter in small (3″) pancakes. If you have a Swedish griddle with indentations, by all means use it. Arrange a circle of about 6 overlapping pancakes on a dessert plate. Place a spoonful of raspberry jam or lingonberries in center of each ring and top with a puff of whipped cream.

Midwest Fish-stuffed Crêpes

Most farm women keep a few cans of salmon and tuna on hand in their cupboards. But not many have discovered teaming the fish with thin pancakes to make exciting, hearty main dishes. When taste-testers voted on Midwest Fish-stuffed Crêpes, made by a recipe contributed by a Kansas rancher's wife, they described it with one word—excellent. You'll want to try this recipe. It produces a substantial fish dish that meat-and-potato farmers praise. That's a tribute to its tastiness.

MIDWEST FISH-STUFFED CREPES

Crunchy texture of celery and water chestnuts in creamy sauce pleases

1	(7¾ oz.) can salmon, drained
1	(7 oz.) can tuna, drained
1	(5 oz.) can water chestnuts, drained and chopped
¼	c. finely chopped celery
1	tblsp. finely chopped onion
5	tblsp. butter or margarine
⅓	c. flour
1	tsp. salt
⅛	tsp. pepper
2½	c. milk
6	tblsp. grated Parmesan cheese
1	tblsp. lemon juice
16	Basic French Crêpes

• Combine salmon, tuna, water chestnuts and celery in a bowl.

• Cook onion in butter until soft (do not brown). Blend in flour, salt and pepper. Slowly add milk, stirring constantly, until mixture comes to a boil. Remove from heat and stir 2 tblsp.

GOOD MORNING BREADS—Start the day with tempting warm breads. These Potato Doughnuts are delicious. Pecan Rolls are made from the centers (recipes, pages 68–69). Sugar-Top Coffee Cake (page 111) is extra-good.

cheese and lemon juice into sauce.
• Stir 1 c. sauce into salmon-tuna
mixture. Put a generous spoonful of
mixture on center of each crêpe. Roll
up; place seam side down on ovenproof platter, or in a 13×9×2″ pan.
Spread remaining sauce over crepes.
Sprinkle with remaining 4 tblsp.
cheese.
• Bake in moderate oven (350°) about
30 minutes. Serve hot. Makes 8 servings.

Company Chicken in Crêpes —Country Style

The more you experiment with
main dishes of stuffed crêpes, the
more you will appreciate why many
people, especially in Europe, are so
fond of them. Company Chicken in
Crêpes is a good example of a distinctive, delicious main dish. You can
bake the crêpes and make the chicken
filling in the morning and refrigerate
until near mealtime in the evening.
The filling may thicken too much in
the cold, but it takes only a minute
or two to reheat it.

If you plan to bake crêpes and
use them right away, it's a good idea
to roll them as you take them from
the skillet. Place them in a pan and
keep warm in a slow oven.

Turkey in Crêpes is one of the best
ways to use some of the leftover
Thanksgiving or Christmas bird.

COMPANY CHICKEN IN CREPES

*Delicate white meat and asparagus
boost this dish to the gourmet class*

3 chicken breasts
1 chicken bouillon cube, or 1
     envelope instant chicken
     broth
1 c. water
6 tblsp. butter or margarine
⅓ c. flour
1 tsp. salt
1 c. dairy half-and-half, or light
     cream
1 (8 to 10 oz.) pkg. frozen cut
     asparagus, cooked (1 ¼ c.
     cooked)
16 Basic French Crêpes
¼ c. toasted, slivered almonds

• Place chicken breasts, bouillon cube
and water in medium-size skillet.
Cover and simmer until chicken is
tender, about 40 minutes. Take chick-
en from broth and cool enough to
handle. If necessary, add water to
broth to make 1½ c.
• Remove skin from chicken and then
remove chicken from bones. Dice
chicken. (You should have 3 c.)
• Melt butter, stir in flour and salt.
Add broth and dairy half-and-half;
cook, stirring constantly, until sauce
thickens and is bubbly. Stir in chicken
and asparagus.
• Put spoonful of chicken mixture on
each crêpe; roll around filling. Place,
seam side down, in single layer on
ovenproof platter or in a 13×9×2″

FRUIT AND NUT BREADS—Serve them for dessert, as coffee bread or as
base for sandwiches. Top to bottom: Orange-Prune Coffee Bread, Pine-
apple-Date Loaf, Peachy Oatmeal Bread (recipes, pages 108, 140, 142).

pan. Spoon remaining chicken mixture over top. Sprinkle with almonds.
• Bake in moderate oven (350°) about 20 minutes, or until sauce is bubbly. Makes 8 servings of 2 crêpes each.

VARIATION

Turkey in Crêpes: Substitute 3 c. diced cooked turkey breast for chicken. Use canned chicken broth instead of water and chicken bouillon.

WILLAMETTE VALLEY PEAR CREPES

Oregon women combine pears and brown sugar in luscious dishes

1 (1 lb.) can pear halves
⅓ c. brown sugar, firmly packed
1 tsp. grated lemon peel
1 (3 oz.) pkg. cream cheese, softened
1 tblsp. milk
¾ tsp. brandy flavoring
1 tblsp. granulated sugar
8 Basic French Crêpes

• Drain pears; pour syrup from fruit into saucepan and add brown sugar and lemon peel. Heat, stirring occasionally, to boiling.
• Slice pear halves in lengthwise quarters.
• Blend together cream cheese, milk, brandy flavoring and white sugar. Spread over crêpes to about ¾" from edge. Place pear slices on about one fourth section (wedge) of each crêpe. Fold crêpe in half; fold section that is not pear-topped over again to make a triangular case. Repeat with remaining crêpes.
• Place in chafing dish. Pour heated sauce, made from pear syrup, brown sugar and lemon peel, over crêpes. Place over heat at table. Makes 8 servings.

Note: You can heat this dessert in your electric skillet instead of a chafing dish.

Waffles Are Wonder Breads

Waffle bakers never had it so easy as they do today. Just think how much easier it is to plug in your heat-controlled waffle iron than it was to hold a heavy, long-handled one over fireplace coals or to judge the correct temperature of the waffle iron heating on the range. Eliminated also, along with the guesswork of obtaining the correct cooking temperature, are the mysteries of what makes waffles exceptionally good.

You want to bake waffles that are golden-crusted with a thoroughly cooked interior. And you want them light. Old-time Southern plantation cooks, to emphasize lightness, said that they could hold the good waffle on the point of a pin. You want tender waffles with a crisp crust. After all, the main difference between waffles and pancakes is the crisp, patterned crust.

HOW TO BAKE PERFECT WAFFLES

• Preheat grids to the right temperature before you pour on the batter. If your iron has no heat indicator, sprinkle a few drops of water on it. If little beads of water dance, it's time to bake the first waffle.
• Follow the manufacturer's directions for greasing or not greasing

grids. Clean the grids after use with a dry, stiff brush; never wash them with water and detergents.

• If you separate the eggs, fold the beaten whites into the batter only until little white fluffs still show. The batter has a pebbly rather than smooth look.

• Open the grids only at the end of baking to avoid pulling waffle apart and causing it to fall.

• Stir the batter, when mixing it, just enough to moisten all dry ingredients. Overmixing makes tough waffles. If you heat butter or shortening to melt it, cool slightly before stirring into the batter.

• Hold the waffle, when you take it off the grid, on the fork for a few seconds. This encourages the formation of a crisp crust. Or leave the waffle on the grid briefly after you open it. For extra crispness, go a step farther and bake the waffle a minute longer.

Waffles are a three-meal bread. Serve them for breakfast and start everyone off feeling well fed and fit. Top them with creamed chicken, turkey, ham, dried beef and other foods for a hearty, tasty main dish for luncheon or supper. Dress them up for dessert and you have inviting refreshments for evening guests.

When you have leftover waffle batter, bake it; cool the waffles thoroughly and then wrap them individually. Store in freezer. These waffles come in handy. Just drop them into electric toaster to reheat.

Here are recipes for waffles that meet the requirements—waffles that are golden, crisp, light, delicious and easy-to-make.

SUNDAY SUPPER WAFFLES

Country women vote the waffles made with four eggs a top favorite

2 c. sifted all-purpose flour
4 tsp. baking powder
1 tsp. salt
2 c. milk
4 eggs, separated
1 c. melted butter or margarine,
   or salad oil

• Start heating waffle iron.
• Sift together flour, baking powder and salt.
• Combine milk and egg yolks. Beat egg whites until stiff.
• Add milk-egg yolk mixture to dry ingredients; beat with electric mixer at high speed, or with rotary beater, just enough to moisten dry ingredients.
• Stir in slightly cooled butter. Fold in egg whites, leaving little fluffs of them showing in batter.
• Pour batter from pitcher onto center of lower grid until it spreads to about 1″ from edges. Gently close lid at once; do not open during baking.
• Bake until steaming stops or signal light shows waffle is done.
• Loosen waffle with fork and lift it from grid. Place on warm plate. Reheat waffle iron before pouring on more batter. Makes about 8 waffles.

VARIATIONS

Buttermilk Waffles: Follow recipe for Sunday Supper Waffles, but use 3 tsp. baking powder and 1 tsp. baking soda, and substitute 2 c. buttermilk for the milk. Do not separate eggs; beat them until foamy, and combine with buttermilk.

Ranch Breakfast Waffles: Reduce butter in Sunday Supper Waffles to 6 tblsp. to ½ c., or use 6 tblsp. to ½ c. bacon fat (drippings) instead of the butter. Use 2 instead of 4 eggs; do not separate eggs, beat them and combine with the milk.

Ham Waffles: Sprinkle 2 tblsp. finely chopped cooked ham over batter as soon as you pour it on waffle grid.

Corn Waffles: Add 1 c. drained, whole kernel corn (canned) to batter. This is an excellent base for creamed ham or chicken.

Cheese Waffles: Add ½ c. grated process cheese to batter.

Nut Waffles: Sprinkle 2 tblsp. coarsely chopped pecans or walnuts over batter as soon as you pour it on the grids. You can break the nuts with fingers instead of chopping them.

Bacon Waffles: Cook 6 slices bacon until crisp; drain and crumble into the batter for Sunday Supper Waffles.

Cornmeal Waffles for Sunday Supper

If you like the way cornmeal tastes, these waffles are for you. They have a true corn flavor. The Missouri farm woman who sent the following recipe features the waffles in Sunday evening suppers, especially for drop-in guests.

"I start the meal," she writes, "with chilled pineapple juice or cranberry juice cocktail. Creamed chicken tops the first round of waffles—the main course. For dessert it's another round of waffles with butter to spread and

cane or other table syrup to pour on for the sweet taste."

SOUTHERN CORNMEAL WAFFLES

Crisp-crusted, feather-light waffles that truly are exceptionally good

1 ½ c. white cornmeal
¼ c. all-purpose flour
½ tsp. salt
½ tsp. baking soda
1 tsp. baking powder
2 tsp. sugar
2 eggs, beaten
2 c. buttermilk
½ c. melted lard or shortening

· Put cornmeal in mixing bowl. Add flour, salt, baking soda, baking powder and sugar. Stir to blend.
· Combine eggs and buttermilk; gradually add to cornmeal mixture, beating with a spoon until smooth. Add lard and beat again.
· Pour enough batter on preheated waffle grid to spread to about 1″ from edges. Close iron.
· Bake until steaming ceases and signal light indicates waffle is done (2 to 3 minutes). Waffle should be brown on outside and cooked within. Makes 8 large (7″) waffles.

Gingerbread Waffles for Company

When a friend telephones late in the afternoon that she and her husband are coming over to spend the evening, one of the first thoughts most women have is: What shall I serve for refreshments? It's a good time to remember waffles. There's something very sociable about them—sitting around the table, talking and watching the golden waffles come piping hot off the grids.

Even if supplies in the cupboard and freezer are at low ebb, almost always you have what it takes to make exciting Gingerbread Waffles. And if you have vanilla ice cream, heavy cream to whip or frozen whipped topping on hand, you have the trim to give waffles a festive, party look.

GINGERBREAD WAFFLES

Dice bananas into bowl of whipped cream and pass to spoon over waffles

¼   c. butter or margarine
½   c. brown sugar, firmly packed
½   c. light molasses
2   eggs, separated
1   c. milk
2   c. sifted all-purpose flour
1½ tsp. baking powder
1   tsp. cinnamon
1   tsp. ginger
¼   tsp. allspice
¾   tsp. salt

• Cream butter and brown sugar until light and fluffy; beat in molasses, egg yolks and milk.
• Sift together flour, baking powder, cinnamon, ginger, allspice and salt. Beat egg whites until they form soft peaks.
• Stir dry ingredients into creamed mixture just enough to moisten all ingredients. Fold in egg whites.
• Bake batter in preheated waffle iron until lightly browned. Serve at once with scoops of vanilla ice cream, or frozen whipped topping. Sweeten whipped cream slightly. Makes about 7 waffles.

Southern
Rice Buttermilk Waffles

Ask a Southern woman what to do with cooked rice, buttermilk and eggs —she may suggest you try these Rice Buttermilk Waffles. Serve them hot off the grids with fluffs of Whipped Butter (see Index) blended with peach or other fruit preserves. You'll give your family and friends unforgettable eating pleasure. To round out the menu for supper, have sausage or bacon and a mixed fruit salad.

RICE BUTTERMILK WAFFLES

Tender delicate waffles with luscious peachy spread . . . serve with bacon

3   eggs, separated
2   c. buttermilk
6   tblsp. melted shortening
2   c. sifted all-purpose flour
½   tsp. salt
1   tblsp. baking powder
1   tsp. sugar
½   tsp. baking soda
1   c. cooked rice (cooked
    in salted water)
Peach Butter

• Beat egg yolks until thick and lemon-colored. Add buttermilk and shortening.
• Sift together flour, salt, baking powder, sugar and baking soda. Add to egg yolk-buttermilk mixture. Stir until smooth. Stir in rice.
• Fold in egg whites, beaten stiff.
• Bake on hot waffle iron. Serve with Peach Butter. Makes 8 (7″) waffles.

Peach Butter: Beat ½ c. (1 stick) butter until fluffy. Beat in ½ c. peach preserves and a dash of nutmeg. Beat again; pass to spread on hot waffles. Vary the spread by substituting apricot or apricot-pineapple preserves for peach preserves. Makes 1 cup.

WHOLE WHEAT WAFFLES

When short of time to bake whole wheat bread, make these waffles

2   c. whole wheat flour
2   tsp. baking powder
¾   tsp. salt
3   eggs, separated
1 ½   c. milk
¼   c. melted shortening

• Combine flour, baking powder and salt; stir to mix. (Stir whole wheat flour before measuring.)
• Beat egg whites; set aside.
• Beat egg yolks, add milk and shortening. Add all at once to flour mixture and beat until dry ingredients are moistened.
• Fold in egg whites, leaving little fluffs of them showing in batter. Pour onto preheated waffle iron; bake until steaming stops or signal light indicates waffle is baked. Serve hot with butter or margarine and syrup, honey or apple butter. Makes 6 (7") waffles.

WHEAT GERM WAFFLES

Good-to-eat and good-for-you waffles with wheat germ the star ingredient

1 ¾   c. sifted all-purpose flour
3   tblsp. sugar
2   tsp. baking powder
¾   tsp. salt
⅔   c. wheat germ
2   c. milk

⅓   c. salad oil
2   eggs, separated

• Sift together flour, sugar, baking powder and salt. Add wheat germ and stir to mix well.
• Combine milk, salad oil and egg yolks in small bowl. Beat thoroughly.
• Beat egg whites until stiff peaks form.
• Add milk-egg yolk mixture all at once to dry ingredients. Beat to make a smooth batter.
• Fold in beaten egg whites; let small flecks of egg whites show in batter.
• Bake until golden on preheated waffle iron. Makes about 9 (7") waffles.

CHEESE-BRAN WAFFLES

These waffles are different and delicious—a good start for a busy day

2   c. sifted all-purpose flour
3   tsp. baking powder
1   tsp. salt
¾   c. bran flakes
¾   c. shredded sharp Cheddar cheese
2   eggs, separated
1 ½   c. milk
¼   c. melted shortening or salad oil

• Sift flour with baking powder and salt. Add bran flakes and cheese. Toss lightly.
• Add egg yolks, milk and shortening to flour mixture. Beat until smooth.
• Beat egg whites until stiff but not dry. Fold into batter. Let little fluffs of egg whites show.
• Bake in a hot waffle iron. Serve immediately with butter and honey or maple syrup. Makes 4 large waffles.

Note: You can use the same amount of bite-size shredded whole wheat or shredded rice biscuits (crushed with a rolling pin) instead of bran flakes.

Chocolate Waffles à la Mode

Crown warm, red-brown chocolate waffles with bright pink or green peppermint stick ice cream, or slightly sweetened whipped cream with crushed hard peppermint candy folded in, and you'll have a dessert everyone likes. Feature it as the windup for a meal or for evening refreshments for a few guests. Or suggest that the teen-agers at your house serve it when some of their friends drive by to spend the evening.

Teen-agers will think they've hit a jackpot of good eating if you set out a choice of toppings for the waffles. Provide vanilla, chocolate and other flavors of ice cream, a pitcher of chocolate sauce to pour over and a bowl of chopped nuts to sprinkle on top. And remember honey butter, for it has a big following. It's easy to whip a cup of butter or margarine until fluffy and gradually beat in ½ c. honey. Heap in a bowl.

You can serve any kind of waffles you like, even plain ones, but no kind will win greater approval than Chocolate Dessert Waffles.

CHOCOLATE DESSERT WAFFLES

Picture-pretty dessert—chocolate waffles with ice cream topping

2 c. sifted all-purpose flour
½ tsp. salt
1 tsp. baking powder
½ tsp. baking soda
¼ c. granulated sugar
½ c. butter or margarine
2 (1 oz.) squares unsweetened chocolate
3 eggs, separated
2 tblsp. brown sugar, firmly packed
1 ½ c. buttermilk
½ tsp. vanilla

• Sift together flour, salt, baking powder, baking soda and granulated sugar into mixing bowl.
• Melt butter and chocolate together over hot water.
• Beat egg whites until stiff, but still moist.
• Beat egg yolks in a second mixing bowl; add brown sugar, butter-chocolate mixture, buttermilk and vanilla. Add to dry ingredients; beat with electric mixer at high speed, or rotary beater, to make a smooth batter. Fold in egg whites, leaving little fluffs of white showing in batter.
• Pour onto greased, preheated waffle grid until batter spreads to about 1″ from edges. Close lid gently and at once.
• Bake until steaming stops or signal light shows waffle is baked. Loosen waffle with fork and lift from grid to warm plate. Reheat waffle iron before pouring on more batter. Serve waffles hot, topped with ice cream or whipped cream. Makes 6 waffles, or 12 servings.

VARIATION

Cocoa Waffles: Omit chocolate and sift ½ c. cocoa with dry ingredients. Increase buttermilk to 2 c. and add 2 tblsp. more butter.

Breads You Cook in Steam

About all that dumplings and brown bread have in common is that they cook to perfection in steam and boast of many staunch devotees. Big platters of tender chicken in gravy, wreathed by plump, feather-light dumplings, continue to appear on dinner tables across the farm belt. And Saturday night suppers along New England's countryside still feature fragrant pots of baked beans and their favorite companion, hot steamed brown bread. These food teams are as American as the Fourth of July, a rich heritage too good to abandon.

For young women who are uneasy about making these great traditional dishes, we give recipes and directions that insure success. We have modernized the old-time favorites for the ingredients and appliances of today.

HOW TO MAKE
FEATHER-LIGHT DUMPLINGS

You make dumplings about the way you make drop biscuits, but cooking them in steam gives a different look and taste. The rules for producing perfect dumplings are simple. This is all you have to do:

• Drop the soft dough from a spoon onto tender chicken or meat simmering in broth, or stock, *not into the broth.* Dumplings are delicate and need support while they cook.

• Cook slowly 10 minutes with the kettle *uncovered;* then cover and cook 10 minutes longer without lifting the cover. If you have a domed cover, use it, for it helps to prevent sogginess.

• Remove dumplings and chicken or meat to a heated platter and keep warm in the oven while you make the gravy. Spoon some of the gravy over and around the dumplings; serve the remainder of it in a bowl or gravy boat.

FLUFFY DUMPLINGS
Puffs as light as thistledown

2 c. sifted all-purpose flour
3 tsp. baking powder
1 tsp. salt
¼ c. shortening
1 c. milk

• Sift flour, baking powder and salt together into a bowl.

• Cut in shortening with pastry blender until mixture resembles coarse cornmeal or crumbs.

• Lightly mix in milk with fork to make a soft dough; stir as little as possible.

• Drop tablespoonfuls of dough on top of chicken pieces or meat and vegetables in stew. Simmer 10 minutes uncovered; then cover tightly and simmer 10 minutes longer. Makes about 12 dumplings.

VARIATIONS

Chive Dumplings: Add 3 tblsp. snipped chives to sifted dry ingredients and cook as directed for Fluffy Dumplings.

Cheese Dumplings Add ¼ c. grated sharp cheese to sifted dry ingredients. Excellent for beef-vegetable stews.

Herb Dumplings: Add ¼ tsp. dried sage or dried thyme to sifted dry ingredients.

Savory Dumplings: Add ½ tsp. celery seeds to sifted dry ingredients.

Parsley Dumplings: Add ¼ c. snipped parsley to sifted dry ingredients.

SOUTHWESTERN TOMATO DUMPLINGS

Colorful complement to beef stews

1 ½ c. sifted all-purpose flour
¾ tsp. salt
2 ¼ tsp. baking powder
1 tsp. chili powder
¾ c. tomato juice

• Sift together flour, salt, baking powder and chili powder. Stir in tomato juice.
• Drop tablespoonfuls of soft dough over meat and vegetables in beef stew. Cover and simmer 15 minutes without lifting lid. Makes 8 dumplings.

Boston Brown Bread

While recipes for steamed brown bread vary, molasses sweetens and flavors them all. They may contain cornmeal, a dark flour, such as whole wheat or rye, or frequently white all-purpose flour. Today many women steam the bread in 1-lb. baking powder cans, or No. 2 (1 lb. 4 oz.) cans. A few country kitchens in New England boast of old, slender bread molds, most of which are inherited prizes. Since the owners hold onto them with pride, you rarely see the molds at auctions.

The place of brown bread, as any Yankee will tell you, is beside a pot of baked beans, but the brown circles also make delightful sandwiches with coffee, tea or milk. Many women like to steam enough bread to have at least an extra loaf to wrap and freeze for later use.

As one Massachusetts apple grower's wife says: "I try to build up a supply of several loaves of Boston brown bread in my freezer. With baked beans also in the freezer, or in cans on the cupboard shelf, I always have the makings for a fine supper for company and the family. I also can green tomato pickles and mustard pickles to bring out from the fruit closet for bean suppers. To round out the feast, I make a salad, often coleslaw, and fix a dessert, usually with apples."

STEPS TO SUCCESS

Heed these tips and you'll steam excellent brown bread:
• Grease the cans or molds and fill them ½ to ⅔ full of batter.
• Cover cans with double thickness of plastic wrap and hold in place with rubber bands; or you can lay waxed paper or foil loosely over top of each can or mold and tie with string to hold it in place. The paper prevents steam that collects on the kettle's cover from falling onto the bread.
• Place cans on a trivet in a deep kettle with tight-fitting lid. The kettle should be large enough that you do not have to add more water during the steaming. (Or use a steamer if you have one; follow the manufacturer's directions.)
• Pour in boiling water to come halfway up the sides of the cans or molds.
• Cover kettle and simmer from 3 to 3½ hours, or the time specified in the recipe.

• Take cans or molds from kettle and remove covers. Place them in a very hot oven (450°) 5 minutes. Cut out end of can with can opener and push out loaf. Slice and serve hot.

• To reheat cooled or frozen bread, place it in a colander and cover with a clean dish towel. Steam over boiling water until hot.

Here is an updated recipe for Boston Brown Bread (if you do not want to steam the bread, see Index for Oven-Baked Brown Bread):

BOSTON BROWN BREAD

New England farm supper: baked beans, this bread, ham, green tomato pickles

    1 c. sifted all-purpose flour
    1 tsp. baking powder
    1 tsp. baking soda
    1 tsp. salt
    1 c. cornmeal
    1 c. whole wheat flour
    1 c. raisins (optional)
    ¾ c. molasses
    2 c. buttermilk or sour milk

• Sift together all-purpose flour, baking powder, baking soda and salt into mixing bowl. Stir in cornmeal, whole wheat flour and raisins.

• Combine molasses and buttermilk. Stir into dry ingredients and mix thoroughly.

• Pour into 4 well-greased No. 2 cans (these cans usually contain 1 lb. 4 oz. fruit). Fill two thirds full or slightly less. Cover cans with double thickness of plastic wrap and fasten in place with rubber bands.

• Place on rack in kettle with tight-fitting lid. Add hot water to reach about halfway up the cans. Cover kettle and steam 3 hours. Remove from kettle, uncover cans and place in very hot oven (450°) 5 minutes. Remove bread from cans (cut out the end of can with can opener and push bread out) and slice with a heavy thread drawn around the loaf, crossing ends. (Cutting hot bread with knife may make a gummy slice.) Serve hot. Makes 4 loaves.

Note: To sour milk, pour 1 tblsp. vinegar into a 1-cup measuring cup. Fill with sweet milk. Let stand a few minutes.

Breads Out of the Fry Kettle

Cake-style doughnuts, warm and sugary, and two specialties—hush puppies and sopaipillas—are excellent examples of quick breads you fry in fat. All three breads ably support the foods they accompany, such as cider or coffee with doughnuts; fried fish with hush puppies; and with sopaipillas, Spanish-American dishes seasoned with hot chili peppers or chili powder.

SUCCESS STEPS
IN FRYING BREADS

• Heat fat or salad oil 3 to 4" deep in heavy kettle to 370° on deep-fat-frying thermometer, unless recipe specifies otherwise. Or heat fat until it browns a cube of bread in 60 seconds. Or use electric deep-fat fryer or electric skillet; follow manufacturer's directions. Correct temperature is of prime importance. If it's too high, the breads brown before they are cooked inside, and if it's too low, the bread absorbs some of the fat and becomes soggy.

• Cook only as much bread at a time as will float easily on the fat. If you fry too much, the food may cause the fat to cool down; it's also difficult to turn it to brown on all sides.

• Turn bread when it rises to the top of the hot fat, using care not to pierce it or it will absorb fat. Cook until bread is brown; the total cooking time often is brief—2 to 3 minutes.

• Lift bread with slotted spoon from fat, hold over the kettle of fat for a second and then place on folded paper towels to drain.

• When you have finished frying, save the fat for reuse: Heat 3 or 4 raw potato slices to 1 qt. fat until fat bubbles. Strain fat through sieve lined with 2 or 3 layers of cheesecloth into a can or jar; cover tightly and store in a cool, dark place.

Delicious Doughnuts

Salute the home freezer for its major role in reviving a lively interest in homemade doughnuts. Now that you can fry a big quantity of hot cakes and keep them fresh in the freezer to use as you need them, farm women frequently make a production out of frying them.

A Colorado dairyman's wife, a FARM JOURNAL Family Test Group member, describes how she does it: "I mix the dough and put it in the refrigerator to chill," she says. "Soft doughs, like those for good doughnuts, roll easier when cold. I roll out the dough and my elder daughter cuts it while I begin the frying. My younger daughter shakes the warm doughnuts, drained on paper towels, in a paper bag containing sugar. When they are cold, we package them in plastic bags, 12 to a bag.

"We like doughnuts for breakfast, so I take a bag from the freezer the first thing in the morning before we go out to do the chores. They thaw in 30 to 35 minutes. By the time we return to the house, all I have to do is take them out of the bag. If we decide to eat before we start outdoor work, I remove the doughnuts from the bag, spread them on a baking sheet and run them in a hot oven (400°). They thaw and heat in 10 to 15 minutes. The heat melts the sugar coating, but you can still enjoy its sweetness. Sometimes we freeze doughnuts without sugaring and then roll them in sugar after they thaw and warm in the oven. It's difficult to tell these doughnuts from fresh-fried ones."

Here are recipes for doughnuts from farm and ranch kitchens (see Index for yeast-leavened—or raised —doughnuts).

WONDERFUL DOUGHNUTS

Subtly spiced—increase spices if you wish. Serve plain, sugared or glazed

4   eggs, beaten
⅔   c. sugar
⅓   c. milk
⅓   c. melted shortening
3 ½ c. sifted all-purpose flour
3   tsp. baking powder
¾   tsp. salt
½   tsp. cinnamon
¼   tsp. nutmeg

• Combine eggs and sugar; beat until

light. Add milk and cooled shortening.

· Sift together flour, baking powder, salt, cinnamon and nutmeg. Add to egg mixture; mix until smooth. Chill soft dough thoroughly in refrigerator.

· Roll dough out gently 1/3" thick. Cut with floured doughnut cutter; let stand 10 to 15 minutes.

· Heat fat or salad oil 3 to 4" deep in heavy kettle or deep-fat fryer to 375°.

· Transfer doughnuts to kettle of fat on broad spatula, using care not to alter shape. (If possible, place board of doughnuts near frying kettle.) Slip into hot fat. Add only enough doughnuts at a time as can float on the fat or that can be turned easily. Turn doughnuts as they rise to the surface.

· Fry 2 to 3 minutes, or just until doughnuts are a golden brown.

· Lift doughnuts from fat with kitchen fork (tines through center holes), using care not to prick them. Drain on paper towels in a warm place. Makes 30 doughnuts.

TRIMS FOR DOUGHNUTS

To Coat with Sugar: Shake warm doughnuts, one at a time, in a paper bag containing 1/2 c. granulated sugar or confectioners sugar. To increase spicy flavor, stir 1 tsp. cinnamon into sugar and mix well before adding doughnuts.

To Glaze: Add 1/3 c. boiling water to 1 c. confectioners sugar. Mix well. Dip warm doughnuts, one at a time, into the warm glaze.

To Coat with Nuts and Sugar: Dip warm doughnuts, one at a time, into warm glaze. Then dip into mixture of nuts and sugar, 1/2 c. finely chopped nuts to 1/2 c. sugar. For spicy taste, add 1 tsp. cinnamon to 1/2 c. sugar.

GINGERBREAD DOUGHNUTS

Spicy, lemon-glazed Halloween doughnuts to serve with cider or coffee

1/2   c. dark brown sugar, firmly
       packed
1   egg, beaten
1/2   c. molasses
1/2   c. dairy sour cream
1/2   tsp. baking soda
2   tsp. baking powder
3   tsp. ginger
1/2   tsp. salt
2 1/2 to 3 c. sifted all-purpose flour
Lemon Glaze

· Combine brown sugar and well-beaten egg. Stir in remaining ingredients, except flour and glaze. Work as quickly and lightly as possible, adding just enough flour to make a soft dough. (The dough should leave the sides of bowl and be as soft as you can have it for shaping.)

· Flour your hands and pull off 4 pieces of dough, each the size of a plum. Roll each piece quickly between the hands to make a strip and then form a ring, pinching ends together. Drop at once into hot fat (360°); cook 4 doughnuts at a time.

· When doughnuts rise to the surface, turn occasionally until they are browned on each side. (Doughnuts will be a dark brown.) Drain on paper towels. Repeat to use all of dough.

· While doughnuts are slightly warm, dip tops in Lemon Glaze. Place on racks for glaze to harden. Makes about 18 doughnuts.

Lemon Glaze: Combine 1 c. sifted confectioners sugar, 1 tblsp. light cream, 1 tsp. lemon juice and ½ tsp. grated lemon peel. Stir until smooth.

Quick Doughnuts

Cut centers from refrigerator biscuits and deep fry as for doughnuts.

Hush Puppies Go with Fish Suppers

Fry hush puppies the next time the fishermen in your family return home with a catch. Decide to serve this corn bread with the fish and you're well on the road to a wonderful fish supper.

Fishermen named the bread, which originated around Southern campfires. "Hush, puppies," they called, as they tossed corncakes to whining dogs to quiet them. Now hush puppies are almost as important as fish at a Southern fish fry. The liking for this deep-fat-fried corn bread traveled across country. Packaged mixes for making it are available in many areas.

You can fry the bread in your kitchen. The trick is to cook hush puppies until they are golden all over and done inside. Success depends on using the correct temperature, measured with a deep-fat-frying thermometer, and in dropping small portions of batter into the hot fat.

Here is a recipe from a Mississippi farm woman; she uses white cornmeal, but you can use either white or yellow.

HUSH PUPPIES

Hush puppies and fish coated with cornmeal and fried—what a team!

1 ½ c. white or yellow cornmeal
½ tsp. salt
¼ tsp. baking soda
¼ c. finely chopped onion (or green onions)
¼ c. buttermilk
⅓ c. water

• Combine cornmeal, salt and baking soda; stir in onion.
• Add buttermilk and water, and stir just enough to moisten dry ingredients.
• Drop by rounded teaspoonfuls into hot fat (375°) and fry until golden brown, turning once. Remove from fat with long-handled slotted spoon. Drain on paper towels. Serve at once. Makes about 35 to 40 hush puppies.

Sopaipillas with Honey

Sopaipillas look like little sofa pillows. You fry them like doughnuts, but they come from the kettle puffed up with hollow centers. If you've visited in Old Town, Albuquerque, New Mexico, the chances are excellent that you ate this fried bread. New Mexico is its original home.

You serve the bread hot from the kettle. Natives break off a corner of the puff and fill the golden cup with honey, which is delectable and soothing to eat along with Mexican-type dishes seasoned highly with chili peppers. Sometimes, if you're under a lucky star, you encounter mesquite honey, with its own sweet, delicious flavor.

Packaged sopaipilla mixes are available in New Mexico and some adjacent communities, but not on a national scale. You can fry your own sopaipillas with this recipe from a Southwestern ranch kitchen. They'll be an exciting conversation piece with Mexican dishes.

SOPAIPILLAS

Serve this bread at your next chili supper—you'll get many compliments

1 ¾ c. sifted all-purpose flour
2   tsp. baking powder
1   tsp. salt
2   tblsp. shortening
⅔   c. cold water

• Start heating salad oil or fat.
• Combine flour, baking powder and salt. Sift into mixing bowl. Cut in shortening with pastry blender. Add enough water to make a stiff dough.
• Turn dough onto lightly floured board and knead lightly until smooth. Cover with clean dish towel and let rest 10 minutes.
• Roll dough very thin (about ⅛" thick) into a rectangle about 15×-12". Cut in 3" squares.
• When oil is very hot (385 to 400° on deep-fat-frying thermometer), drop a few squares of dough into it at a time. Turn frequently so that sopaipillas will puff up evenly. Remove with a slotted spoon; drain on paper towels. Serve hot with honey. Makes 18 to 20 sopaipillas.

All-American Corn Breads

Indians taught our early European colonists how to use cornmeal that they ground between stones. Corn breads appealed to people from the start and they continue to have an important place in country meals.

Cornmeal comes in three colors— white, yellow and blue. You'll rarely find blue meal, made from calico or Indian corn, in supermarkets outside the Southwest. Some people, especially those in the South and in Rhode Island, prefer white meal, but both yellow and white meal enjoy wide acceptance.

Our grandfathers often took corn they grew to gristmills to have it ground into meal. Most of the meal today is the granulated kind made from kiln-dried corn with the germ removed. It keeps much better than water-ground meal, but many country people say that it lacks the rich flavor of the water-ground type. Some neighborhood mills still sell water-ground cornmeal. Farm women, when they can get it, package it tightly and store it in the freezer, where it keeps satisfactorily.

Southerners like little or no sugar in corn breads, which usually are on the thin, crusty side, while northerners prefer sweeter and thicker breads. You use the Muffin Method to make most of these breads—you combine the meal and leavening, add the egg and liquid and stir enough to moisten the dry ingredients.

There are exceptions to the rule. Spoon bread is one of them. You bake this Southern delicacy in a deep casserole; it comes out light, fluffy and so soft that you serve it with a spoon instead of cutting it with a knife. Spoon bread, seasoned with chopped chili peppers, is one of the great dishes of the Southwest, which includes the southern third of Colorado, New Mexico, Arizona and part of Texas.

You'll find recipes for many kinds of corn breads in this cookbook. (See Index for Anadama Batter Bread, Hush Puppies and Sopaipillas.) You can use white or yellow meal in most of them, but if a woman sharing her recipe specifies white or yellow meal, we give her preference.

MEXICAN CORN BREAD

As truly Southwestern as turquoise and silver jewelry

1 (8 oz.) can cream-style corn
1 c. yellow cornmeal
2 eggs, slightly beaten
1 tsp. salt
½ tsp. baking soda
¾ c. milk
⅓ c. melted lard or butter
1 (4 oz.) can green chilies, chopped
¾ c. grated sharp Cheddar cheese
2 tblsp. butter

• Combine corn, cornmeal, eggs, salt, baking soda, milk, lard, chilies and half the cheese.

• Meanwhile, melt 2 tblsp. butter in a 1½-qt. casserole or a 9″ skillet. Place in oven until butter is hot, but do not let brown (if skillet has a wood handle, protect it by wrapping well in aluminum foil).

• Pour the batter into the warm casserole and sprinkle top with the remaining cheese.

• Bake in hot oven (400°) 40 minutes. Serve hot with spoon. Makes 6 servings.

Note: A FARM JOURNAL Family Test Group member from Arizona pours half the batter into the casserole without adding the chilies or cheese. She sprinkles on half the chilies and cheese, then adds the remainder of the batter and sprinkles on the second half of the chilies and cheese. You can omit the chilies, but the bread would not be acceptable in the Southwest. The flavor the chilies provide makes this an unusually good corn bread.

Three Corn Bread Favorites

There are about as many favorite corn bread recipes as there are kitchens. Here are three regional specialties . . . take your pick. The chances are good that where you live will determine your selection.

If you want to bake corn sticks, grease corn stick pans very well (use about ¼ c. shortening). Heat in oven while mixing batter. Spoon batter into heated pans to fill them about three fourths full. Bake in hot oven (425°) 12 to 15 minutes. Use any of the three following recipes. You will have enough batter to make 12 to 14 corn sticks.

SOUTHERN CORN BREAD

It upholds fame of Southern cooking

2 eggs
2 c. buttermilk
1 tsp. baking soda
2 c. white cornmeal
1 tsp. salt

• Start oven heating to 450°. Gener-

ously grease a 9×9×2" pan; heat in oven while mixing batter.
• Beat eggs; add buttermilk.
• In bowl stir together baking soda, cornmeal and salt. Add egg-buttermilk mixture all at one time; beat with rotary beater or electric mixer until smooth. Pour into heated pan.
• Bake in very hot oven (450°) 20 to 25 minutes, or just until set. Serve hot, cut in squares, with butter. Makes 9 servings.

Note: Some Southern women add 1 tsp. sugar to the other dry ingredients.

GOLDEN CORN BREAD

This is Yankee-style corn bread

1   c. sifted all-purpose flour
¼   c. sugar
4   tsp. baking powder
¾   tsp. salt
1   c. yellow cornmeal
2   eggs
1   c. milk
¼   c. soft shortening

• Sift together into bowl flour, sugar, baking powder and salt. Stir in cornmeal.
• In a small bowl beat eggs with fork; add milk and shortening. Add all at one time to cornmeal mixture. Stir with fork until flour is just moistened. Even if batter is lumpy, do not stir any more.
• Pour into well-greased 9×9×2" pan. Bake in hot oven (425°) 20 to 25 minutes, or until done. Cut in squares and serve hot with butter. Makes 9 servings.

VARIATION

Bacon Corn Bread: Add ⅓ c. crumbled, crisp cooked bacon to batter for Golden Corn Bread just before pouring into greased baking pan.

NORTH-SOUTH CORN BREAD

A bread with many champions on both sides of the Mason-Dixon line

¼   c. sifted all-purpose flour
1¼   c. white or yellow cornmeal
2   tblsp. sugar
3   tsp. baking powder
1   tsp. salt
1   egg
1   c. plus 2 tblsp. milk
3   tblsp. soft shortening or bacon drippings

• Start oven heating to 425°. Generously grease a 9×9×2" pan; place in oven to heat while mixing batter.
• Stir together flour, cornmeal, sugar, baking powder and salt.
• Beat egg; combine with milk; add with shortening to dry ingredients all at one time and beat with rotary beater just until smooth. Pour into heated pan.
• Bake in hot oven (425°) 20 to 25 minutes, or just until set. Serve hot, cut in squares, with butter. Makes 9 servings.

Timesaving Corn Bread Mix

Some farm women mix the dry ingredients and lard for corn breads when they have free time. This Corn Bread Mix is an example of how they "store time" to use on busy days. The mix produces tender, light breads on the sweet side in contrast to the crisp-crusted, less sweet Southern corn breads. It's at its best in coffee breads and other breakfast specialties. Try the recipes that follow and see if you don't agree.

CORN BREAD MIX

A big help when you're rushing to get a good breakfast ready on time

4 ¼ c. flour
2 ½ c. cornmeal
1 ½ c. nonfat dry milk
¼ c. baking powder
1 tblsp. salt
1 ½ c. lard or shortening

• Sift together flour, cornmeal, dry milk, baking powder and salt into a large bowl. Repeat two times.
• Cut in lard with a pastry blender to blend thoroughly.
• Place in jar or canister, cover and store in a cool place. Use mix within a month. Makes about 10 cups.

PINEAPPLE COFFEE CAKE

This will put cheer on the breakfast table, and it's quick to make

¼ c. butter
¼ c. honey
1 (8 ½ oz.) can crushed pineapple
¼ c. shredded coconut
2 c. Corn Bread Mix
½ c. sugar
1 egg, beaten

• Melt butter in 8×8×2″ pan. Add honey and blend. Drain pineapple and reserve juice. Spread drained pineapple and coconut in pan, distributing mixture evenly.
• Combine mix and sugar in bowl.

Add water to pineapple juice to make ½ c. Combine egg and juice; add to dry mixture and stir just to blend and moisten. Pour batter evenly into prepared pan.
• Bake in hot oven (400°) about 25 minutes. Remove from oven and cool in pan 5 minutes. Invert over plate; let stand 1 minute. Remove pan and cut in rectangles or squares. Serve warm. Makes 6 or 9 servings.

CORNMEAL GRIDDLECAKES

Old-fashioned recipe, up-to-date style

2 c. Corn Bread Mix
2 eggs, beaten
½ c. water
1 tblsp. molasses

• Place mix in bowl.
• Combine eggs, water and molasses. Add to mix and stir just until moistened.
• Spoon batter on preheated griddle and bake until browned on both sides. Turn only once. If the batter thickens during the baking, thin with a little cold water.
• Serve on warm plates with butter and syrup or honey. Makes 8 large or 16 small griddlecakes.

SUGARED MUFFINS

Great with ham and eggs

1 egg, beaten
½ c. water
2 c. Corn Bread Mix
¼ c. melted butter
¼ c. sugar
½ tsp. cinnamon

• Combine egg and water; add to

Corn Bread Mix; stir just to moisten.
• Fill greased muffin-pan cups two thirds full.
• Bake in hot oven (425°) 15 to 20 minutes. Remove from pan.
• Dip tops of muffins in melted butter and then in sugar and cinnamon, mixed. Serve at once. Makes 6 muffins.

FAST-FIX CORN BREAD

Cheerful for supper on a rainy day

4 ½ c. Corn Bread Mix
1 ⅓ c. water
2   eggs, beaten

• Place mix in bowl.
• Combine water and eggs. Stir into mix just to moisten mix. Batter will not be smooth. Pour into a greased 9×9×2″ pan.
• Bake in hot oven (425°) about 25 minutes. Makes 6 servings.

FRESH CORN SPOON BREAD

Best partner fried chicken ever had

3   ears fresh corn (about)
⅓ c. cornmeal
2   c. hot milk
¼ c. butter (½ stick)
2   tsp. sugar
1 ½ tsp. salt
⅛ tsp. pepper
1   tblsp. minced green onion
2   eggs, separated

• Split each row of corn kernels vertically with a sharp knife. Cut off about one third of the kernels around each ear. Repeat until all are removed. Scrape the cob with a tablespoon to get the remaining pulp and juices. Measure. You should have 1½ c.

• Mix the corn with cornmeal and stir in the hot milk. Cook, stirring over medium heat, until thickened, about 5 minutes. Remove from heat and stir in butter, sugar, salt, pepper and onion.
• Beat egg yolks. Add a little of the hot corn mixture to yolks, then add yolks to hot corn mixture in saucepan.
• Beat egg whites until stiff and fold into corn mixture.
• Grease bottom of 1½-qt. casserole, but not the sides. Turn corn mixture into casserole. Set in pan of hot water.
• Bake in slow oven (325°) about 1 hour, or until knife inserted in center comes out clean. Serve at once. Makes 6 to 8 servings.

Country Kitchen Nut Breads

Fruited nut breads are giving fruitcakes a run for popularity. When FARM JOURNAL women editors visit farm homes, their hostesses frequently tell about their families' preference for loaves of these quick breads over the richer, more tedious-to-bake and more costly fruitcakes.

The moist, sweet nut breads freeze beautifully. You can make them weeks ahead for the Christmas holidays, parties and to serve on short notice when friends stop by unexpectedly. If you package a few thin slices together, they thaw much faster than a loaf—almost while you fix tea or coffee.

Nut breads make excellent sandwiches. Spread with butter or cream cheese, with or without marmalade or jelly, they are marvelous companions for tea, coffee or salads.

Nut breads are the exception to the rule that you serve quick breads hot. Cool the loaf after baking, wrap it in foil or plastic wrap, place in a cool place, such as the refrigerator, and let stand at least overnight before you slice it. Then, if you use a sharp knife, you can cut even, thin slices. You can keep the breads many days, or weeks if you put them in the freezer. Their flavors mingle and ripen and improve during storage.

"Fruited nut breads," says a Minnesota FARM JOURNAL Family Test Group member, "are something a junior cook can bake for her grandparents, aunts and uncles. Our 12-year-old daughter runs up the road to her grandparents' house on Christmas morning with a basket holding a couple of loaves of nut bread she baked, wrapped and tied with red ribbons. It's becoming a family tradition. Grandmother says she listens for her grandchild stamping snow off her boots—she's at the door in a hurry with her Christmas greeting.

"Grandmother likes the gift on several counts. She has lots of company during the holidays and nut bread comes in handy. And she especially appreciates presents her grandchildren make. Grandfather also is proud that his granddaughter gathered the nuts for the loaf in the October woods on the farm. He believes children should learn how to use the foods that are free to people who live on the land."

Take your pick of the fruit-nut bread recipes in this cookbook. And if any of the loaves have deep cracks on top, remember these are not blemishes, but the trademarks of many of the best loaves.

Honeyed Date Bread
—Extra Special

A California ranch woman mailed the recipe for this superlative date bread to her sister, who lives on an Iowa farm. When the sister made the bread, she gave it a Midwestern touch. She used ¾ c. chopped pecans, all she had in the kitchen, and ¼ c. chopped black walnuts that she gathered on the farm. The results were so pleasing to family and friends who sampled the bread that we give her version of the recipe, which also is superior when made with the kind of walnuts that grow in California and Oregon groves.

HONEYED DATE BREAD

*This loaf is guaranteed to please . . .
it's dark, moist and delicious*

2 c. pitted fresh dates
2 tblsp. shortening
⅔ c. brown sugar, firmly packed
½ c. honey
¾ tsp. vanilla
¾ tsp. grated orange peel
¾ c. hot water
¼ c. orange juice
1 egg, beaten
2 c. sifted all-purpose flour
1 tsp. baking soda
1 tsp. salt
¾ c. coarsely chopped pecans
¼ c. chopped black walnuts

• Cut the dates in small pieces with scissors. Put dates, shortening, brown sugar, honey, vanilla, orange peel, hot water and orange juice into a mixing bowl. Stir to mix; set aside for 15 minutes.

• Add egg and mix well. Sift in flour, baking soda and salt; stir just enough to moisten dry ingredients. Fold in nuts. Turn into a greased 9×5×3″ loaf pan.

• Bake in slow oven (325°) 1 hour, or until bread tests done with cake tester inserted in center of loaf. Let stand in pan 10 minutes; turn onto wire rack to cool. Wrap in foil or plastic wrap and store in cool place, or freeze, overnight or longer before slicing. Makes 1 loaf.

PINEAPPLE-DATE LOAF

Tastes like a mellow fruitcake—improves after standing overnight

¼ c. soft butter or margarine
½ c. sugar
1 egg
¼ tsp. lemon extract
1 (8½ oz.) can crushed
    pineapple
¼ c. chopped nuts
2½ c. sifted all-purpose flour
2½ tsp. baking powder
¼ tsp. baking soda
1 tsp. salt
½ c. finely chopped, pitted
    dates
¼ c. water
¼ c. chopped maraschino
    cherries, well drained

• Cream butter and sugar; add egg and lemon extract. Drain pineapple, reserving liquid. Add crushed pineapple and nuts to creamed mixture.

• Sift dry ingredients together. Add dates and mix well, separating date pieces with your fingers. Stir dry ingredients into creamed mixture alternately with reserved pineapple juice plus ¼ c. water. Fold in the chopped maraschino cherries.

• Pour into a greased 9×5×3″ loaf pan. Bake in moderate oven (375°) about 55 minutes. Cool in pan 10 minutes. Remove from pan; cool completely. Makes 1 loaf.

CRANBERRY BREAD

A Merry Christmas loaf dotted with berries—makes elegant sandwiches

1½ c. chopped raw cranberries
4 tsp. grated orange peel
3 tblsp. sugar
3 c. sifted all-purpose flour
3 tsp. baking powder
½ tsp. baking soda
¾ tsp. salt
¾ tsp. nutmeg
1¼ c. sugar
2 eggs, beaten
¾ c. orange juice
¾ c. water
½ c. melted shortening
1 c. chopped walnuts

• Combine cranberries, orange peel and 3 tblsp. sugar. Stir to mix and set aside.

• Sift together flour, baking powder, baking soda, salt, nutmeg and 1¼ c. sugar.

• Add eggs to orange juice and water; mix well. Add with cranberry mixture and shortening to dry ingredients. Stir just enough to blend and moisten all dry ingredients. Fold in nuts.

• Turn into a greased 9×5×3″ loaf pan.

• Bake in moderate oven (350°) 1½ hours, or until cake tester or wooden pick inserted in center comes out clean. Set pan on wire rack; cool 20 minutes. Turn bread out on wire rack and cool completely. Wrap in aluminum foil or plastic wrap; store in refrigerator or other cool place, or freeze. Do not cut for 24 hours. Makes 1 loaf.

MIDGET RAISIN LOAVES

Christmas gift for neighbors—a loaf for every member of the family

⅓ c. shortening
¾ c. sugar
1 tblsp. grated orange peel
1 egg
3 c. sifted all-purpose flour
3½ tsp. baking powder
1½ tsp. salt
1 c. milk
⅓ c. orange juice
1 c. chopped pecans
½ c. snipped raisins
Orange Topping

• Cream shortening, sugar, orange peel and egg together until mixture is light and fluffy.
• Sift together flour, baking powder and salt. Add to the creamed mixture alternately with milk and orange juice. Fold in pecans and raisins, snipped into pieces with scissors.
• Turn into 7 greased 4½ × 2¾ × 2¼″ loaf pans. (These midget loaf pans can be found in the housewares section of many stores.)
• Bake in moderate oven (350°) about 40 minutes, or until cake tester inserted in center of loaf comes out clean. Let stand in pan 10 minutes.

• Turn onto wire rack to cool. While slightly warm, spread with Orange Topping. Makes 7 individual loaves.

Note: You can bake the batter in a 9×5×3″ greased loaf pan. Bake in moderate oven (350°) about 1 hour and 15 minutes, or until bread tests done. Makes 1 loaf.

Orange Topping: Combine 1 c. sifted confectioners sugar, 1½ tblsp. orange juice and ½ tsp. grated orange peel. Stir until smooth.

ORANGE-FIG NUT BREAD

Just the bread to serve to afternoon callers with a cup of tea or coffee

¾ c. boiling water
1 c. finely chopped figs
2 tblsp. butter or margarine
1½ c. sifted all-purpose flour
½ c. sugar
1 tsp. salt
3 tsp. baking powder
1 tsp. vanilla
1 egg, beaten
4 tsp. grated orange peel
⅓ c. orange juice
¾ c. whole-bran cereal
½ c. chopped walnuts

• Pour boiling water over figs and butter; let stand for 10 minutes.
• Sift together flour, sugar, salt and baking powder.
• Add vanilla, egg, orange peel and juice to figs. Beat well.
• Add sifted dry ingredients and cereal to fig mixture. Beat well. Fold in chopped nuts.
• Pour into a greased 8½ × 4½ × 2½″ loaf pan; push batter into corners.
• Bake in moderate oven (350°) 45 to 50 minutes, or until a cake tester

or wooden pick inserted in center comes out clean. (For ovenproof glass loaf pan reduce oven temperature to 325°.)
· Let stand in pan 10 minutes. Loosen sides of loaf with knife; turn onto wire rack to cool. Wrap in foil or plastic wrap and store in a cool place, or freeze. Let stand overnight before slicing. Makes 1 loaf.

BANANA BREAD

One of the most popular nut breads —chop nuts fine for easy slicing

3 ½ c. sifted all-purpose flour
3   tsp. baking powder
1   tsp. salt
1   tsp. baking soda
2   c. mashed, ripe bananas
      (4 to 6)
2   tblsp. lemon juice
¾   c. shortening
1 ½   c. sugar
3   eggs
¾   c. milk
½   c. chopped pecans or walnuts

· Sift together flour, baking powder, salt and baking soda.
· Mash bananas with rotary beater or fork. Add lemon juice and mix.
· Cream shortening and sugar with electric mixer at medium speed, or with spoon. Add eggs and beat thoroughly until very light and fluffy (4 minutes' beating in all). Add sifted dry ingredients alternately with milk; fold in bananas and nuts. Beat after each addition.
· Pour into 2 greased 8½ ×4½ ×2½ ″ loaf pans.
· Bake in moderate oven (350°) 1 hour, or until cake tester or wooden

pick inserted in center of loaf comes out clean. Cool in pans 10 minutes. Remove from pans and cool on wire rack. Wrap in foil or plastic wrap and let stand in cool place overnight before slicing, or freeze. Makes 2 loaves.

PEACHY OATMEAL BREAD

You'll enjoy this as a dessert or a coffee cake. Eat it with a fork

1 ¾ c. sifted all-purpose flour
¾   c. granulated sugar
4 ½   tsp. baking powder
¾   tsp. salt
1 ½   tsp. cinnamon
¾   tsp. nutmeg
¼   tsp. cloves
1 ½   c. quick-cooking rolled oats, uncooked
½   c. chopped nuts
⅔   c. milk
1   egg, slightly beaten
½   c. melted butter or margarine
1   (1 lb. 14 oz.) can cling peaches, well drained
⅓   c. brown sugar, firmly packed
3   tblsp. melted butter or margarine

· Sift together flour, granulated sugar, baking powder, salt and spices. Stir in oats and nuts.
· Combine milk, egg and ½ c. melted butter. Stir into dry ingredients until moistened. Do not beat.
· Pour batter into a greased 8×8×-2″ baking pan. Bake in moderate oven (375°) 40 to 45 minutes. Cool in pan.
· Chop or slice peaches. Arrange on cooled bread. Sprinkle with brown sugar and dribble 3 tblsp. melted but-

ter on top. Broil 4" from broiler unit until topping bubbles and tops of peaches begin to brown. Makes about 9 servings.

Note: You can freeze this bread if you wish. Defrost and add topping just before serving.

To Cut Nut Breads

Cool the bread several hours or overnight before slicing. If in a hurry, partly freeze bread; it will slice without crumbling.

GLAZED LEMON BREAD

So good we reprint it from Freezing & Canning Cookbook—*make butter sandwiches to serve with fruit salads*

⅓   c. melted butter
1¼ c. sugar
2   eggs
¼   tsp. almond extract
1½ c. sifted all-purpose flour
1   tsp. baking powder
1   tsp. salt
½   c. milk
1   tblsp. grated lemon peel
½   c. chopped nuts
3   tblsp. fresh lemon juice

• Blend well the butter and 1 c. sugar; beat in eggs, one at a time. Add almond extract.
• Sift together dry ingredients; add to egg mixture alternately with milk. Blend just to mix. Fold in peel and nuts.
• Turn into a greased 8½ × 4½ × 2¾" ovenproof glass loaf pan. Bake in slow oven (325°) about 70 minutes, or until loaf tests done in center.

• Mix lemon juice and ¼ c. sugar; immediately spoon over hot loaf. Cool 10 minutes. Remove from pan; cool on rack. Do not cut for 24 hours (it will slice easily). Makes 1 loaf.

Note: If you bake this bread in a metal 8½ × 4½ × 2½" loaf pan, use a moderate oven (350°).

SWEET POTATO NUT BREAD

Sweet and moist, extra light. This big recipe makes loaves and muffins

½   c. soft butter or margarine
½   c. shortening
2⅔ c. sugar
4   eggs
2   c. cold, mashed sweet potatoes
3½ c. sifted all-purpose flour
1   tsp. salt
1   tsp. cinnamon
1½ tsp. nutmeg
2   tsp. baking soda
1   c. chopped walnuts
⅔   c. cold, strong black coffee

• Cream butter, shortening and sugar. Add eggs, one at a time, mixing well after each addition. Blend in sweet potatoes.
• Sift together dry ingredients; add nuts. Stir into creamed mixture alternately with cold coffee.
• Pour batter into 2 greased 9×5×3" loaf pans and 8 greased muffin-pan cups. Bake in moderate oven (375°) 1 hour for loaves and 25 minutes for muffins, or until they test done in center.
• Cool 10 minutes; remove from pans and cool completely. Makes 2 loaves plus 8 muffins.

CARROT SANDWICH BREAD

Sliced thin, this nut bread makes marvelous sandwiches. Do try it

1   c. finely grated raw carrots
1   c. brown sugar
1   tsp. baking soda
1   tblsp. melted shortening
1   c. boiling water
2   eggs
2½ tsp. baking powder
1   tsp. salt
1½ c. sifted all-purpose flour
1   c. whole wheat flour
1   c. chopped walnuts

• Combine carrots, sugar, baking soda and shortening in a large bowl. Pour on boiling water and stir just to mix. Set aside until cool.

• Beat eggs with a fork and add to cooled carrot mixture. Sift in the baking powder, salt and all-purpose flour. Stir in whole wheat flour. Fold in walnuts.

• Pour into a greased 8½ × 4½ × 2½″ loaf pan. Let stand 5 minutes.

• Bake in moderate oven (350°) 1 hour. Remove from pan and cool on wire rack. Bread slices better if allowed to stand, wrapped in aluminum foil or plastic wrap, in a cold place overnight. Makes 1 loaf.

OVEN-BAKED BROWN BREAD

Molasses-flavored nut bread for sandwiches—fine escort for baked beans

1½ c. sifted all-purpose flour
1½ c. rye flour
1   c. yellow cornmeal
1   tsp. baking soda
1   tsp. salt
½   c. seedless raisins
⅔   c. chopped walnuts
2   c. buttermilk
½   c. dark molasses
Butter

• Stir together flour, rye flour, cornmeal, baking soda and salt to mix thoroughly. Stir in raisins and nuts.

• Slowly add buttermilk and molasses alternately to dry ingredients; beat after each addition.

• Pour batter into a greased 9×5×-3″ loaf pan.

• Bake in moderate oven (375°) 50 minutes, or until cake tester or wooden pick inserted in center of loaf comes out clean.

• Remove from oven and let stand in pan 5 minutes; loosen sides with knife and turn out on wire rack. While still warm, brush top with butter. Serve warm with baked beans. (Make bread and butter sandwiches with cool loaf.) Makes 1 loaf.

Index